To Ne[...]

& f[...],

Best wishes,

—Rowland

28. 6. 2000.

DREAMS OF SUCCESS

Rowland C Stratford

MINERVA PRESS
ATLANTA LONDON SYDNEY

DREAMS OF SUCCESS
Copyright © Rowland C Stratford 1998

All Rights Reserved

No part of this book may be reproduced in any form
by photocopying or by any electronic or mechanical means,
including information storage or retrieval systems,
without permission in writing from both the copyright
owner and the publisher of this book.

ISBN 0 75410 561 X

First Published 1998 by
MINERVA PRESS
315–317 Regent Street
London W1R 7YB

2nd Impression 2000

Printed in Great Britain for Minerva Press

DREAMS OF SUCCESS

Names of people and places in this book are fictitious but real events have been used as a basis for the narrative.

This book is dedicated to my late mother

About the Author

Born in London and educated in Middlesex, Rowland C Stratford became an articled clerk on leaving school and qualified as a Chartered Accountant in 1963 (Fellow, 1974).

He now has a flourishing Personal Tax Accountancy practice in East Anglia, where he lives with his family.

Anyone who is interested in persistence as a means of achieving success should read this book. However, great emphasis is also placed on thoroughness, consideration and interpersonal skills, all cornerstones of Rowland C Stratford's own successful career.

Part One

WHEN I STARTED my articles to become a Chartered Accountant, I had no idea how difficult the work would prove to be or how much dedication was required.

I was sitting at my office desk, which was covered in books, vouchers and working papers. For the last hour, I had been endeavouring to balance a set of accounts relating to a local butcher's business. There was a difference of two pounds and I still hadn't found it. Adding machines were not allowed and pocket calculators were not then in use. The year was 1959.

On commencing my articles, I could not have envisaged the utter mess some people's records would be in when they were brought to an accountant's office. Often clients would bring in perhaps one book and a heap of receipts, invoices, and so on, and I would be told to prepare a set of accounts.

I looked out of my office window and thought back to when I had decided to become a Chartered Accountant. My careers master had suggested in 1955 that as mathematics and English were my best subjects – I had obtained a considerable number of O levels – accountancy would probably be suitable for me. He hadn't mentioned the considerable time required for studying or the headaches involved in trying to prepare a set of accounts from very incomplete records. In fact, he had painted a rosy picture which persuaded me to join a small firm of accountants as an articled clerk.

I was twenty years of age and had just passed the intermediate exam, halfway to qualifying as a Chartered Accountant. Out of approximately 1,600 articled clerks who had sat the exam, I had been placed in the first few hundred of successful candidates, so I had been well satisfied.

The office where I worked was situated over a bank in a busy high street in Hayford, Middlesex. My desk was butted up to a window which overlooked the high street, and I was sometimes tempted to let my thoughts stray, particularly when the office work got tedious or dull.

It was my coffee break and when drinking my coffee and eating my cheese roll, I began to think about what I had achieved so far and what I intended to do in the future. I was not an introverted young man, but I liked to keep my thoughts to myself. On looking back, it seemed to me that I had always been somewhat quiet, but I told myself that this was perhaps not a bad quality.

At five years of age, 1944, during World War II, I had attended a primary school which was situated not far from the office where I was working. It was a frightening time: buzz-bombs were falling; but children still had to be educated, and they were well looked after with milk and vitamins.

The first V-1 flying bombs – jet-propelled and pilotless – carried a ton of explosives and flew at speeds of up to 370 miles per hour. Many women and children were evacuated in 1944. In September 1944 the first V-2 rockets, which were remote controlled and launched from Germany, travelled faster than the speed of sound; they were directed at London. The children at my school had to quickly get to large, specially built air-raid shelters as soon as the siren sounded and had to remain there until the all-clear signal was given.

My schoolteacher for the last two years at my secondary school took an interest in those pupils who he could see were trying their best; he often used to work overtime to encourage them and I attributed my success in passing my GCE O levels partly to him. Some teachers are extremely conscientious and dedicated, and those pupils who were educated to a high standard were fortunate indeed to benefit from this dedication.

On my passing my O levels the headmaster asked my parents to call and see him. He was extremely pleased with the very high marks. This gave me tremendous satisfaction at the time and I commenced my professional career with great expectations.

Although my parents were not required to pay a premium to the sole practitioner, the Chartered Accountant running the small firm of accountants where I was working, my salary was fixed at two pounds per week for five years.

As my father was a precision engineer – he helped to build the Fairey Gannet and Swordfish aeroplanes during World War II – and my mother with a part-time job at a local chocolate factory, shortage of money was to prove to be a problem during my articles. My parents never complained, however, as they were anxious to ensure that I became a Chartered Accountant and to them the hardship was worthwhile.

I looked up from my desk, turning towards the remainder of the general office. The floor was devoid of carpets; there were only bare wooden floorboards. There were two old green metal cupboards in which clients' records were stored and four scratched and worn filing cabinets holding clients' files. Seven desks and chairs were provided. There were no fluorescent lights – only ordinary lights, with 60-

watt bulbs: a dismal scene, was my impression. The desks and chairs were occupied by various accounts clerks.

There was Mr Andrews, a thin, elderly man, rather stooped, who chain-smoked. He was a heavy whisky drinker and this was reflected in his purplish-coloured nose. He was an educated man, who I gathered because of his incessant drinking had found himself working as a lowly accounts clerk. I often had a chat with him. He used to tell me about the time he was a manager at a large commercial firm.

The desk next to him was occupied by Mrs Teaming, a plump, elderly widow, also an accounts clerk. She was smartly dressed but had rather a temper. Regrettably, she often complained about how cold she was. As the heating in the general office was inadequate, I suppose she had a point.

Further down the room was Mary, a middle-aged Irish lady, single, and charming in her own way, but lacking ability. However, no matter how many mistakes she made, the managing clerk did not reprimand her. I understood they socialised together and this probably explained the position.

There were two articled clerks other than myself – Ben and David. Both were older than me and had sat their final exams and failed in one or two subjects. Ben was a short young man with freckles and tousled hair and David was tall, heavily built, and played rugger in his spare time. Both young men were quite friendly with me and we often went on outside audits together.

At the end of the room sat Mr Johnson, the managing clerk. He was a very large man who had been a sergeant major in the army. No matter how hot the weather became, he always wore his heavy three-piece dark grey suit. He was a swarthy, pugnacious man in his middle fifties. His large bulbous nose was covered in warts and there were large calluses on his knuckles; he had dark, bushy eyebrows. Most of the staff were frightened of him; he ruled them with a rod of iron.

There were three other offices, one occupied by two lady typists called Jane and Beryl. Jane was a pale, petite married lady in her early thirties. She was extremely bright but was often away from work because of an anaemic condition. Beryl was a short, dumpy lady, full of life and always joking.

Then, in quite a small office, was Mr Davis, the principal (Chartered Accountant), whose name appeared on the nameplate and the letter-headings. Mr Davis was a short man with a florid complexion. He drank heavily, and whenever I saw him was most irritable.

I later found out that he suffered from high blood pressure and his skin very easily cut, if caught on, say, a paper clip or staple. Apart from special times such as pay increases or someone's birthday, he was rarely seen by the staff.

The accounts clerks and articled clerks were generally required to work quietly, particularly as figure work needed much concentration.

As I was looking around the general office, a loud, gruff voice reverberated around the room. It was Mr Johnson and he called my name, beckoning me towards his huge oak desk. I trembled slightly. Although I was twenty years of age, I was slim and weighed about ten stone compared to Mr Johnson's sixteen. The tone of his voice reflected annoyance. I rose from my desk reluctantly and walked over to his desk. Mr Johnson's face looked stern and he was puffing away at one of his cheroots.

He peered at me through a cloud of smoke and said, 'You are one penny out in your additions – I don't think much of that for someone who has just passed his intermediate exam!' He pointed towards the accounts I had prepared. 'Add those figures up.' I added them up and yes, he was quite right. There was a difference of one penny.

I nervously picked up my working papers.

'The difference must be found,' said Mr Johnson, in a voice loud enough for the whole staff to hear.

David, one of the other articled clerks, laughed as I crept back to my desk. I grimaced at him. I could not help thinking what an unfair world it was at times. Passing my intermediate exam had meant I was halfway to becoming a Chartered Accountant and yet I was treated like an inexperienced junior. I vowed that when I became fully qualified and had my own business I would never treat my staff in such a humiliating way.

After about an hour, I located the one penny difference, and took my working papers back to Mr Johnson. He merely looked up at me, making no other comment except, 'Found it, then?'

I walked back to my desk and looked at the large, dark brown office clock showing a few minutes to 1 p.m. I started to tidy my desk and soon afterwards joined the rest of the staff leaving the office for lunch.

Ben and I would often go to a local workmen's café which provided substantial meals for a modest price. The café was owned by a man named Ron. Ben and I walked up the crowded high street. Hayford was a busy town and there were many people about. Ben was a cheerful young man and was always gossiping. I preferred, on the whole, to listen.

'Did you know a new young lady is commencing work here on Monday?' asked Ben, as he kicked a tin can off the pavement into the gutter. I hadn't heard about the young lady and asked Ben if he knew what she was like. 'I only know she is seventeen years of age and this would be her first job straight from school,' Ben told me.

We soon reached Ron's Café which was nearly full. 'Two of the usual, Ron, please,' I said, squeezing through the crowd of workmen. We eventually found two vacant seats and sat down to wait for our main course. Usually we had steak and kidney pie, followed by ice cream, on a Friday.

It was not long before the waitress, a bubbly young lady, came along with our meals. 'There you are, you toffs,' she joked.

We were the only customers sitting there with office suits and we often had to take rude comments from the waitress and sometimes from the workmen. None of it was malicious and as long as we had a substantial meal at a modest price, we could not have cared less. In fact, it was a welcome change from the monastic atmosphere which often pervaded the general office where we worked.

The meals were good, but with one exception. The cook always swamped the meat and potatoes with gravy. Being young men and hungry, we nearly always cleared out plates but suffered sometimes, later in the afternoons, with our stomachs gurgling away.

I looked around the café, which was brim-full. Very rarely did you see a female customer, as the workmen were a bit rough-and-ready and at times used colourful language.

Ben and I paid for our meals. 'Cheerio, Ron. See you on Monday.' Ron looked up from the cash register and waved. I don't think he heard what I said above the hullabaloo of the customers.

We meandered back to the office, calling at a confectioner's on the way. The confectionery shop was owned by a Mr Kent. 'I'll be calling to see you, Mr Read, on Wednesday,' he said.

It was always the same whenever Mr Kent spoke; he spoke very loudly. He had a hearing aid which obviously did not, at times, work. His loud voice never failed to make me jump. He was a client of Davis & Co. and several times during the year called to see me for the preparation of his accounts. 'I'll be pleased to see you as arranged,' I said, collecting my bar of chocolate. We wandered back to the office.

As we approached the building, an old tramp called to us. He was filthy, dressed in clothes which were torn and stained. 'Can you two young gentlemen spare a bob for a war veteran?' he asked, rolling one of his trouser legs up to disclose a nasty wound. He was limping and I was sorry for him. I felt in my pocket but all I had was a threepenny bit and two pennies. These I offered to him. He snatched them from me. 'Mean young buggers,' he said and limped away.

Little did he know but that was all the spare money I had until Saturday afternoon, when my father usually gave me a few pounds spending money. I was to remember this incident vividly for many years. I suppose the tramp's comments reflected his poor condition and bleak outlook.

Ben and I reached the outside office door, which was open, climbed the stairs to the main inner door of the general office and stood waiting with some of the other staff for Mr Johnson to open up with his key. There were only two keys available. One was held by Mr Johnson and the other by Mr Davis.

Right on 2 p.m. Mr Johnson arrived. He usually went to an expensive restaurant where I gather he paid for his meals at cost prices. He knew the proprietors who were clients of Davis & Co. In the early 1960s certain managing clerks would not dream of fraternising with the staff at work. They felt they had to keep their distance.

Mr Johnson, smoking his usual cheroot, spoke through the cloud of smoke. He was panting a bit after his climb up the stairs. No doubt he had put on some weight since his army days. 'Champing at the bit – anxious to get down to work!' were his facetious comments. One or two of the staff laughed but inwardly probably thought as I did, Silly old fool. At last it was five thirty and I cycled home.

The following Monday morning, I put my cycle in an old shed which was situated in an overgrown, weedy garden surrounded by a high wall, just behind the bank building, locked the door, safely put the key in my pocket and climbed the stairs to once again wait for the general office door to be opened by Mr Johnson.

This was the morning I was to interview Mr James, the grocery shop owner.

Articled clerks who had passed their intermediate exams were allowed to interview clients, usually those whom either Mr Davis or Mr Johnson had decided were suitable.

As I was queuing with other members of staff, a young lady I had not seen before appeared at the top of the stairs. She walked confidently towards us and said, 'I'm Rose Turner, the new junior accounts clerk.' I looked at her closely.

As I was looking, Mr Johnson appeared with his key. 'Come in and I'll introduce you all to Miss Turner,' he said.

We all trooped into the office and grouped together. Eventually I was introduced to Rose, and as our eyes met, there was, I felt, an instant mutual attraction. I had never experienced this feeling before and I knew something very special had occurred.

Rose was a well-built young lady, smartly dressed. She wore a light blue dress with a small flowered pattern; her brown shoes were highly polished. But it was her face I was looking at mainly. Her skin was flawless and she had just a touch of make-up. She wore small pearl earrings and had a lovely scent on, which I later discovered was Chanel No. 5. It was her sparkling blue eyes and smile that I noticed particularly.

'I am pleased to meet you, Tom,' she said and shook me by the hand. I felt an exciting, strange tingling sensation. This was the beginning of a relationship which was to affect me for years. I had never experienced this feeling before with other young ladies I had met; I knew at once Rose was special.

At the time, I wondered what was happening; of course I saw clearly later that this was the great affection called love. Rose had a lovely face. I could see at once she was intelligent by the way she looked around the office when she was being introduced to the various staff. Rose was shown her desk, which was near mine. As I went to sit down, I looked over my shoulder and Rose was looking directly at me. She smiled and turned to talk to Mary, the middle-aged accounts clerk.

At ten twenty I walked round to Mr James, the grocer shop owner. His shop was only a few minutes' walk from the office and I arrived at the front door at precisely ten thirty. Mr James's small shop was squeezed between a clothier's and a stationer's. The window dressing was very neat and tidy, with samples of his wares set out in neat rows. There was only one display window and a small door to the right of it, as you faced the shop from the busy pavement. The shop had an air of grace about it, and Mr James's tidy, neat appearance was reflected by the smartly painted shiny white window frames and door.

Mr James, a dumpy man with a cheerful round face, was just outside his shop, assisting a customer with some groceries into her car. He looked up as I approached and said, 'I'll be with you in a few minutes, Mr Read.' The customer, a small, elderly lady, looked thankful that Mr James was helping her.

I waited patiently and was gazing into the shop window, when Mrs James opened the door. 'Come through, Mr Read. Mr James will be with you shortly,' she said. As I followed Mrs James I glanced back and saw Mr James chatting away merrily. He enjoyed every minute of his life and customers were always pleased with the personal attention given to them.

I followed Mrs James, who had on a spotlessly clean apron, through the shop to a small lounge at the rear. The room looked on to a modestly sized garden, full of colourful flowers and shrubs. Sparrows were greedily drinking from the granite bird bath. 'Would you like a coffee, Mr Read?' Mrs James asked as she left the room.

'Thanks very much, Mrs James. Milk and sugar, please,' I replied.

Mrs James was a short, slim lady with jet-black hair drawn back in a bun. She had that friendly, warm approach which put me completely at my ease.

I took my working papers out of my briefcase and set them out on a small table, close to a window through which the garden could be seen. After a few minutes, Mr James appeared, saying briskly, 'Sorry I've kept you waiting.' He sat down opposite me and patiently waited for my questions.

As I shuffled my working papers, the inner door of the lounge opened slightly and a small dog peeped round. 'Come in and sit down, Toby,' said Mr James. The little dog obediently made his way to a basket which was in the corner of the room. He did not bark but curled up contentedly.

I had prepared Mr James's annual accounts from his records, which were generally neatly kept, but I always ended up with an unexplained cash difference, that is, the cash received always exceeded the cash expenditure.

'Can you explain what this cash has been spent on, Mr James?' I knew from experience of interviewing him that there was no intention to defraud, only that the cash must have been spent on items not recorded.

Although Mr James was meticulous in his personal clothing, he had this out-of-character habit of spending cash on small items and forgetting to record them.

'If you can't prove that the cash was incurred on business items, I shall have to put the unexplained difference down to private drawings,' I continued, looking directly at him. He looked back at me with his face beaming.

'Quite correct, Mr Read. You do what is right.'

I soon finished asking the remaining questions, drank the last of my coffee and got up to go back to the office.

'Why on earth do you stay at Davis & Co., Mr Read?' Mr James asked me. 'You could easily commence your own accountancy practice.'

I shook hands with him. 'I am due to take my finals in a few years' time, but at the moment I am still under articles with Mr Davis,' I replied. The confidence in my abilities demonstrated by Mr James was like a breath of fresh air. He was one of those people who always made others feel as if they were most important and I thought what a wonderful quality that was to possess.

'Goodbye, Mr James. I'll get your accounts finished and send a typed copy for your approval before they are sent to the Inland Revenue,' I said, and I moved towards the door of the lounge.

I had already calculated the provisional income tax liability based on the draft accounts and imparted the details to Mr James, as he was expecting a higher liability.

Walking back to the office, I could not help comparing the happy atmosphere in the grocery shop run by Mr and Mrs James, and the dull, routine grind of work at my office. Then I thought about Rose and my whole attitude shifted. She was lively and had quickly changed me. I no longer dreaded going back to my desk in the general office but looked forward to seeing her. I could not properly explain my feelings but my whole outlook on life was different.

The following lunchtime, I had left Ben to do some shopping for his parents, and I wandered back to the office fifteen minutes early.

I found Rose waiting outside the inner office door. She looked up as I approached. Her auburn hair was glistening and she looked radiant. She had been reading a magazine but quickly put this into her bag as I spoke to her. 'All on your own, Rose?' I asked.

This was the first time we had been together without the rest of the staff around us. There was a fleeting moment when the atmosphere was tense, and then our eyes met. I felt this strange feeling and I moved towards Rose.

As I moved towards her, she moved towards me. Her fresh, fragrant scent enveloped me. Suddenly our lips met, and this was the first of many kisses.

I had never experienced a sensation like this. It must have lasted a few seconds only. We could both hear footsteps at the end of the long corridor. We sprang apart.

Ben appeared at the top of the stairs. He did not say anything, but merely whistled cheekily. His eyes were raised towards the ceiling.

I looked at Rose and her cheeks were red. I felt hot and I am sure my cheeks were like beetroot. One of my accountancy books was in my hands and I pretended to read it.

Eventually, one or two members of staff appeared with Mr Johnson. The door was opened and we all went into the office, sat at our desks and commenced work.

I tried my best to concentrate but soon found it to be impossible. To avoid making arithmetical mistakes, I commenced drafting the skeleton of some accounts.

As I turned in my chair to put some discarded papers in a nearby bin, I met the intent gaze of Rose. She pursed her lips and her eyes again sparkled. I knew at that moment she was very interested in me, and her feelings were reciprocated.

For the rest of the afternoon, I could not put that kiss with Rose out of my mind. At five thirty I got up and moved towards the office door. Rose had already left, as she had to hurry each afternoon to catch her bus.

I got my cycle out of the shed and sped off. My mind was in a turmoil.

The following day, I saw Rose at the office and she was working at her desk. She smiled, made some comment about the weather and that was that. I was disappointed but on reflection I could understand that, surrounded by other members of staff, of course she could not say anything of a personal nature.

Lunchtime arrived and I was walking towards Ron's Café. I was on my own, as Ben was away for the day on an outside audit. Suddenly I heard footsteps close by and Rose spoke to me. 'Would you like to go for a walk with me after your lunch?' she asked.

I thought, That should be me saying that to her and without hesitation I replied, 'I would be pleased to, Rose.'

I met her outside Ron's Café. This was the start of a romance that was to last several years.

The following week, I had to go and see a new client, Mr Dome. He was an artist and worked from a large, old converted shed, not far from the office.

Mr Johnson had given me a few brief details about the prospective client, including his name and telephone number. I telephoned him for an appointment and made arrangements to see him during the afternoon.

On arriving at Mr Dome's converted shed, which was at the rear of a shop in the high street, I looked around in amazement. The shed was about eighteen feet by twelve and looked derelict. It had an ordinary tarpaulin-covered roof but there were signs of extensive wear. Rubbish was everywhere – bits of discarded wood, nails, etc. – and there was a general feeling of neglect.

I knocked on the shed door and I was greeted by a small man. He was poorly dressed and his soiled clothes and shoes were spattered with paint. His face was covered by a straggly beard and already there were flecks of grey approaching.

'Come in,' he said. 'I assume you are Mr Read. I'm Fred Dome.'

I entered the shed, which was littered with pieces of wood and canvases. There were some framed paintings and others, unframed, leaning against a bench.

'Sit down, Mr Read,' said Mr Dome, dragging two battered old chairs from a heap of junk in the corner of the shed. The only thing that was new was the shiny red telephone. We sat down and I got a notepad out of my briefcase.

'I've been operating here for six months,' said the artist, drawing from his pocket some loose tobacco and some papers; he proceeded to roll a cigarette, a skill I had never seen performed before. In a matter of seconds he was puffing away. He did not offer to roll one for me and I was grateful.

'Could I see your records, Mr Dome, please?' I asked. He pointed towards a scruffy looking exercise book and a pile of invoices and receipts.

'When a customer pays me, I record the amount received in that book,' he said.

'What about expenses?'

He nodded at the invoices and receipts.

I quickly added up his income and the total came to a pittance. 'Have you recorded everything, Mr Dome?'

'I might receive the occasional amount of cash and not record it. Doesn't happen very often,' he replied, glancing sideways.

Hopeless, I thought. Anyway, I decided to discuss a simple system of bookkeeping with him. Mr Dome was quite cheerful. It was obvious that he enjoyed his painting. The only problem was that he wasn't at the moment making any money out of his venture.

Apparently he had lost his job as a packer at a local factory and thought that he would try to make a living out of a hobby – painting pictures, mainly of scenes of boats.

Some paintings I thought were very good, although the framing, which was perhaps done by him, spoiled the overall effect. As I was speaking to Mr Dome, a noticeable smell of onions became stronger. When I first entered the shed, I thought that he had cooked himself a meal, but when I looked around, there were no cooking utensils to be seen. Then it dawned on me. It was Mr Dome himself, who had probably not washed for weeks.

Eventually, after setting out the new bookkeeping system, I shook hands and quickly moved towards the door. I needed to get some fresh air as quickly as possible.

As I was about to open the door, I tripped over one of Mr Dome's legs. In fact I kicked him rather hard by mistake, and apologised profusely.

'No need to worry on that score,' he said, and tapped his leg, the one I had inadvertently kicked. 'You won't harm this – it's metal.' I hadn't realised it but he had a false leg!

He told me that he had experienced a horrific accident many years ago and one leg had to be amputated.

I quickly said goodbye and left.

As I looked back, Mr Dome was standing at the shed door, apparently completely oblivious of his poor financial position. I felt sorry for him.

I found out some months later that he had unfortunately closed his business down and left the area, owing the owner of the shed many months' rent.

ALTHOUGH I WAS having to study two or three hours most evenings and sometimes on Sundays, most of my weekends were free for leisure.

Rose and I started going out together on a regular basis; she fully understood that I had to spend many hours working towards my final exams and I appreciated her consideration for my predicament.

We tried to meet at lunchtimes or immediately after five thirty, when the office closed. I could see that she was very interested in me; she had made this abundantly clear on several occasions.

The more I saw of Rose, I knew that she was the only girl I was really interested in. Several other young ladies made it plain that they wanted to go out with me, but as Rose was on my mind I always ended up politely saying no.

I could not put my deep thoughts into words when talking to Rose; I just felt that her feelings were the same as mine and there was no need to express myself verbally. Later it was apparent I should have expressed my thoughts clearly by saying directly to Rose that I loved her.

I just had this deep feeling inside that the attraction between us was right. I had heard that there was sometimes instant attraction between a man and a woman and then I knew exactly what that meant.

Rose had repeatedly told me that she liked me considerably and was keen for me to meet her parents. For some reason, I kept putting this matter to one side.

One day at the office, Rose edged towards me. She asked me coyly, 'Have you noticed anything different about me?' I looked at her closely. To me she looked her usual bright self. I couldn't see any difference, only that she had changed her earrings.

She laughed and said to Jane, one of the typists, 'I told you he wouldn't notice!'

Rose was slightly taller than me and weighed about half a stone more. 'I came in with my low-heel shoes to make my height less so I would not appear taller than you, and you haven't even noticed,' she teased.

I smiled; if she was prepared to go to these lengths, she must think a lot of me. I left her and the other lady clerks and typists chatting away; as I left there was further laughter. They were not laughing at me, but merely enjoying the moment.

I could not help thinking what a difference Rose had made to my life at the office and also to my private life; I rejoiced at the thought of our first meeting.

The next day, I was due to interview a client, a dentist called Mr Palmer.

As one came out of the inner office door and along the corridor, there was a vacant room which was used to store old records and files and also to interview clients who wished to call at the office to see the articled clerks. A number of clients were interviewed by the principal, Mr Davis, and also the managing clerk, Mr Johnson, but those interviews were usually conducted in Mr Davis's office.

Mr Palmer was due to call at three thirty, and at three fifteen I picked up my briefcase containing my pens, pencils, and so on, and took out his file from one of the filing cabinets in the general office.

On reaching the interview room, I sat down at the table and looked around. It was a sunlit room, not touched by the office cleaner very often. There were three old, green metal cupboards and four shabby wooden chairs. The sunshine made apparent the dust everywhere. No carpets were to be seen – only bare floorboards. I could not help thinking what a poor impression was made on clients being interviewed there.

I spread out my working papers and waited for Mr Palmer to arrive.

A few minutes after three thirty there was a knock at the door. 'Come in, please,' I said. I looked up, and Mr Palmer, smiling, came towards me with his hand outstretched.

I had interviewed him for the first time the previous year when he had commenced his practice, and I was anxious to ascertain his income and expenditure results.

As he sat down, I noticed again his faultless appearance. He was a slim man of about forty years of age, with shiny black hair. His suit was light blue with a touch of grey to it; his shirt was brilliant white and he wore a multicoloured silk tie. The scent of an expensive cologne wafted towards me. I had never seen a man dressed so immaculately.

Mr Palmer was meticulous and I would have been surprised if he had not succeeded in his dental surgeon's business.

'How have you got on in your first year?' I asked.

He looked at me keenly with his bright blue eyes. 'There's my records. I'll leave you to tell me,' he replied.

I picked up his accounts book and vouchers; I could see directly that his bookkeeper had apparently done her job well. Everything appeared, on the surface, neat and tidy. I quickly looked at the total income figure. Dentists were well known to receive high incomes, but of course they deserved it, being highly qualified. Some of the work they had to undertake was very dangerous and carried a great risk. Their training was rigorous.

Mr Palmer had indeed, subject to the overhead expenditure, done extremely well in his first year of practice.

'I'll prepare your accounts and then report back to you. On the surface you appear to have done very well,' I told him.

Mr Palmer smiled and commented, 'Keep the tax down as much as possible, won't you.'

I made the usual evasive remarks, shook hands with him and saw him to the door.

He was a dignified man, and it was a pleasure to interview him. If only all clients were like him, I thought, with some of their characteristics in my mind.

As the weeks went by, Rose and I became close, walking in the local park, or looking at the local shops at lunchtime during the week.

We often discussed my progress concerning my studying and I knew she was looking forward to the time when I passed my final exams and became a Chartered Accountant. I was quite confident that it was only a matter of time and I would have my certificate and be able to use the letters ACA after my name. This was not being overconfident but based upon my progress with the correspondence course.

One of my favourite pastimes was visiting the swimming pool on a Saturday morning. I was a keen swimmer, my father having taught me the breaststroke at an early age. Later, going with a group of friends, I soon taught myself the front crawl.

As I was sitting in an office most weekdays, I needed the exercise, and swimming provided the answer.

I saw Rose and asked her if she would like to come with me, one Saturday. 'I can't swim,' was her quick reply. She did not appear to be enthusiastic, but was prepared to have a try. 'I could teach you to swim,' I said. I had previously been successful in teaching some youngsters to swim a few years before and I was fairly confident that I could at least impart the rudiments of swimming to her.

I arranged to meet her outside the swimming pool.

My cycle was my main mode of travelling; public transport was at times erratic.

When I arrived at the pool, Rose was at the gates waiting for me. After I locked up my cycle in the shed provided, we joined the queue of people, which mainly comprised young teenagers, with a sprinkling of middle-aged and elderly people.

After about twenty minutes we bought our tickets and walked towards the changing rooms. Separate changing rooms were provided for males and females.

'See you in the pool,' I said. I could not help wondering what Rose would look like in a bathing costume.

After changing, I locked the cubicle door and went straight through to the pool. Rose was nowhere to be seen, so I dived in at the deep end and decided to swim a few widths.

As I pulled myself up to the edge of the pool, I looked towards the females' exit from the changing rooms and noticed Rose climbing down the steps at the shallow end. She looked somewhat apprehensive and I quickly walked towards her.

When we were queuing outside the pool, she had mentioned that she had never been to a swimming pool before.

'You won't let me sink, will you, Tom?' she said apprehensively.

'I'll try not to,' I said. I tried to concentrate on helping Rose but as I looked at her, I thought how lovely she appeared in her colourful swimming costume. Later I ascertained she had bought it especially for the occasion.

I commenced giving her a few elementary lessons, about floating in water. Most females usually float much more easily than males and this gives them the confidence they need.

Our hands met and I endeavoured to support her in the water. She started to sink and grabbed me for support. Her lovely scent was immediately apparent. She was comely, well-built, but I thought she looked beautiful.

I was slightly built and wiry. I did my best to support her and to prevent her from sinking, but gradually she did so, spluttering and unfortunately swallowing some water.

I considered that she was very brave, as she again tried to float. At no time did she blame me, even when she repeatedly sunk under the water. The shallow end was only 3' 6", and there was little chance of her coming to harm.

After a while, she began to float and she hugged me with delight. I was pleased with her efforts and particularly impressed by her persistence when trying to float.

Eventually she seemed to be floating quite well, and I decided to swim a few lengths and then return to give her a few lessons in the breaststroke.

When I returned to the shallow end, she was standing at the edge of the pool talking to a young man; I could not help but feel a pang of jealousy. Surely Rose was not a flirt; I began to have my doubts. As I spoke to her, the young man quickly moved away. Rose spoke, 'I'm going to get changed, Tom. I feel a bit cold.' I nodded. The noise in the pool had increased with groups of youngsters shouting to each other.

When I reached my changing cubicle I quickly dried myself and put on my clothes. As I emerged from the changing room I saw Rose and suggested that we had hot drinks and biscuits in the swimming pool café.

'I really enjoyed that,' she said. As I was a keen swimmer, I hadn't enjoyed the time spent in the pool, apart from the contact with Rose; but I did not want to spoil her day.

'That's good,' I said, thinking if this was going to continue on a regular basis it was going to be hard work for me; I felt exhausted.

We had our hot drinks and biscuits, and wandered outside.

I went to get my cycle and Rose walked with me. We reached the gates leading to the pool. 'See you on Monday,' she said and kissed me on the lips.

I mounted my cycle after seeing her on the bus, and pedalled away towards my home. It was a splendid feeling, knowing that a young lady with the qualities of Rose liked me so much.

'TOM, MR GRANGE for you.'

The receptionist put me through to him and I heard his quiet but distinct voice. 'How are you keeping, Mr Read? It's some time since we saw each other.' Mr Grange was always friendly and respectful towards me and I was pleased to handle his accountancy and taxation affairs. He played the piano professionally and was the leader of a local group, comprising himself as the pianist, a drummer and a violinist.

His wife was a professional model and worked mainly in London. She was a beautiful lady and often had her photographs displayed in a number of magazines. Mr and Mrs Grange had been married for about six years and had been clients of Davis & Co. for two years.

I had prepared their accounts and tax returns since they came to Davis & Co. and usually went to see them, to collect their business records and have a general chat with them, at their home, which was situated opposite a church not far from the high street.

Continuing our telephone conversation, I noted that Mr Grange wished to see me the following morning if that was convenient and looking at my diary, I confirmed that it was; an appointment was made for ten thirty. 'We'll see you then,' said Mr Grange. I put the telephone down and resumed my work.

The following morning I walked along the busy high street and I was in a cheerful, reflective mood. My studies were progressing well and I was optimistic about my future. The ability to get on well with clients and indeed people generally is a great asset. If one is polite and courteous to people, this is generally reciprocated; although of course, there are exceptions.

I soon reached the turning leading towards the church, and the flat occupied by Mr and Mrs Grange. There were eight flats altogether, four facing the church and churchyard. The flat occupied by Mr and Mrs Grange was at the top of a flight of stairs. I ran up the stairs, two at a time and on reaching the top was pleased that I was not out of breath; the swimming had obviously been beneficial.

A knock at the white painted door soon resulted in footsteps approaching. Mr Grange appeared and shook me warmly by the hand.

'Come in, Mr Read, and make yourself at home,' he said.

He ushered me along the narrow hall into the lounge, which was sumptuously furnished. He peered up at me as I towered over him. I was five feet eight inches but he was only three feet ten inches – a dwarf.

Some people considered that it was odd that he had married a lovely looking lady but it did not surprise me at all. What he lacked in height, he more than made up for by kindness and his personality. He had the gift of making people about him feel good and this quality was really appreciated by the people who went to listen to his band or indeed, dance to the music.

Mrs Grange appeared from the small kitchenette. 'Hello, Mr Read. I am just making coffee. I'll be with you in a few minutes.'

She smiled as she spoke. Her attire comprised a smart, light blue, close-fitting dress, pearl necklace and white shoes. Long blonde hair cascaded down her shoulders and she had just a touch of lipstick on.

Mr Grange was wearing a specially made grey suit, with a light blue shirt and multicoloured tie. His round face was beaming.

As soon as he began talking to me, I forgot about the fact that he was a dwarf, except when he motioned to me to sit at a table by the window overlooking the churchyard and he had to pull himself up to sit on a specially made high chair.

The various business records were spread over the table and as I reached for my briefcase, Mrs Grange appeared, carrying a tray on which the cups of coffee and biscuits were placed. She sat down, handed Mr Grange and myself cups, pushing the milk and sugar nearer. She glanced at her husband as she did so and I could see that they were happy. What did it matter if they looked odd when walking along together? The most important point was they clearly enjoyed each other's company.

'If I may look at your records first, Mrs Grange?' I asked. She again smiled sweetly and handed me her accounts book and other papers.

Quickly looking at her total income for the last financial year I could see that it had increased dramatically compared to the previous year. 'You appear to have earned much more than last year,' I said, showing her the accounts book.

'I've had a very lucrative contract with a mail order company which sells dresses,' she said. 'This is a sample.' She pointed to the dress she was wearing.

No wonder the company was willing to pay her such large sums, I thought. I turned towards Mr Grange who pushed his records towards me.

'I wish I could make the money my wife makes,' he commented with a twinkle in his eye.

Looking at his accounts book, I could see that the gross income was good but unfortunately his overheads were high. He had to pay the other two musicians, travelling expenses and other incidental expenses. As a result, his net income was usually quite modest.

However, he was happy, and I could quite understand why. He enjoyed playing the piano for a living; he had a beautiful wife who was kind to him and they were both in good health.

With their joint incomes they could easily have bought a detached house or a bungalow but they were quite content with their cosy flat; as they both travelled so much they had no need for a large dwelling place.

I made a few notes, placed my working papers in my briefcase and settled in my chair to listen to their comments. They were both chatting freely and I felt content in the happy atmosphere which pervaded the flat.

Looking at my watch, I saw that I had been in their company for an hour and a half; the time had flown. I rose from my seat, said my farewells and quickly made my way to the front door.

Mr and Mrs Grange stood at the top of the staircase. It was clear to me that they thought the world of each other. The fact that they looked odd as a couple did not matter one iota!

I WAS SITTING at a desk with Ben. We were at a carpenter's business premises, about a mile from our office. The name of the carpenter was Mr Stanton and he'd called us out to carry out the three-monthly check on his records. He maintained a full set of double entry books, including sales and purchase ledgers, and was always anxious to have them perfectly balanced. A number of men were employed by Mr Stanton, who had run his thriving carpentry business for some ten years.

I had never visited his premises before and I gazed around his office. A part-time bookkeeper was employed. She came into work two days a week but was not working when Ben and I were there. The office was smartly furnished with clean, modern cabinets and shelves, together with two well-designed wooden desks and chairs – no doubt made by Mr Stanton or his employees.

Ben and I had been working since nine thirty that particular morning and we had our coffee and rolls about ten thirty.

I rose from my seat. 'I'm just going to the toilet, Ben. Do you know where it is?'

'Through there.' Ben pointed to a door. He had been to check Mr Stanton's records a number of occasions before, so he knew his way around.

As I walked towards the office, I glanced at Ben. He had a cheeky grin but didn't comment further. I quickly walked along the narrow hall and reached the second door on the left as Ben indicated. I opened the door and walked in. I was surrounded by coffins, some with their lids open. Quickly I backed out. I knew then why Ben had been grinning. He hadn't told me that part of Mr Stanton's lucrative business involved the making of coffins for the local undertaker!

I returned to the office. Ben looked up, still grinning, and asked, 'Found the toilet then?' He burst out laughing at the look on my face. A few minutes later, we were both joking about the matter. I vowed I would get my own back on Ben... when he was least expecting it!

As we left Mr Stanton's office, he pulled up in a van, got out and walked towards us. I had never seen him before, but instantly liked him. He was a small, thickset man of about forty with freckles and ginger hair. 'Before you go, I have something for you,' he said.

We waited outside, near his van, and he soon reappeared, carrying parcels. 'Thanks for checking my books,' he said, and handed the parcels to us, which we soon opened. Inside were two splendid wooden bowls. 'That's my hobby – turning on a lathe.' He pointed to the fine grain in the wood. The bowls were indeed works of art.

'Thanks very much,' Ben and I chorused, as we said our farewells to Mr Stanton, who was standing with his arms folded, smiling.

He didn't tell us, but I was pretty certain I knew where the wood for the bowls came from. Some of the best coffins are made from quality timber and there must have been numerous surplus pieces and offcuts. Every time I look at my wooden bowl, I cannot help but think of the time that Ben played a joke on me!

THE FOLLOWING TUESDAY, I had an appointment to go and see a painter and decorator in a town a few miles away. He was self-employed and it was the first time I had visited his premises. He had asked specifically for me to call and see him, as he had recently fallen in his garden and sprained his ankle and was unable to visit the office.

I arrived at the appointed time and was greeted by Mr Calder at his front door.

His hobby was growing chrysanthemums, as I could see from the splendid display in his front garden.

He lived in a detached house with his wife and son, who worked with him in his business. Everything about his house looked substantial, from the massive oak door with its brass letter box and door knocker to the large peg tiles covering the huge roof. Mr Calder was a man who liked things to last.

'Come in, Mr Read,' he said by way of greeting. Limping, he led me along a wide passage.

We turned right into an enormous kitchen, stopping briefly to speak to Mrs Calder, a small, quietly spoken, refined-looking lady with an apron; she was baking some scones. 'I'll bring some for you when I make your tea, Mr Read,' she said amiably.

I did enjoy the pleasantries and good manners of some of the clients I visited.

A door leading to the kitchen took us into a conservatory which looked out on to the rear garden. Masses of chrysanthemums were displayed; there were also some splendid rose bushes and two mature apple trees.

A large golden retriever appeared, wagging his tail. Appealing eyes looked up at Mr Calder. 'You're after a sweet, you softy,' Mr Calder said, reaching for a tin placed high on a shelf. 'There you are.'

The dog crunched away and licked his master's hand. He crept under the table and lay down happily, in an old cardboard box.

'He's ten years of age,' said Mr Calder. 'Never been any trouble.'

I looked at Mr Calder. He was heavily built, with receding grey hair and stubble on his chin. He was a coarse looking man of some sixty years of age and appeared to have had a rough life. He was respectful towards me and very well principled. He called a spade a spade and could not abide anybody who was dishonest. This was reflected in his records which were kept immaculately.

'You've prepared my accounts for two years, Mr Read, and I would like you to tell me if I can improve my bookkeeping system,' he told me.

I knew that his accounts book was always balanced to the penny but there were one or two improvements which I could have suggested to eliminate duplication and, as a result, save time.

'Well, Mr Calder, your records are kept well, but I could make a few suggestions to save you time.'

His eyes lit up; his time was very important to him.

I quickly explained the improvements and made a few notes to assist him. He was pleased and as I was again examining his accounts book, Mrs Calder appeared with a tray.

'There's your scones and tea. The scones are hot and the butter is in the dish.' A warm feeling welled up inside me. Kindness and consideration are two of the best qualities and I never cease to be appreciative when people display them.

Mr Calder smiled at me and said, 'After we've had our tea, I'll show you my chrysanthemums – if you are interested.' Gardening was never one of my favourite occupations, mainly because I never seemed to have the time, but I did appreciate flowers.

We walked through the conservatory into the rear garden. I listened patiently whilst Mr Calder explained the problems associated with growing the plants. He went to shows and had won many prizes so he knew what he was talking about.

I looked at my watch; the time had flown. 'I must make a move, Mr Calder. I have another appointment in thirty minutes,' I said. I moved towards the hall and made my way to the front door. 'If you have any problems with the new bookkeeping system, give me a ring.' I said my farewells to Mr and Mrs Calder and quickly walked towards the bus stop. I looked back and they waved cheerfully.

I WAS CONCENTRATING on my studies but also endeavouring to learn as much as I could about the practical side of accountancy. Although much of my time was spent in the office, often I had to go to clients' premises to check their records.

One day, Mr Johnson, the managing clerk, informed me that I was to spend some weeks away from the office on an outside audit. David, one of the other articled clerks, was to be in charge and it was suggested that I learnt as much as possible.

Neither David nor myself had a car or motorcycle at that time and had to rely on public transport.

'Have you got all your pens, pencils, and so on?' asked David. I assured him that I had. These were kept in my briefcase as a matter of course.

We commenced our journey from the office and travelled some miles by bus. On arriving at the office supply company, we looked around.

The limited company operated from a unit on an industrial estate and supplied wholesale office equipment and stationery to various retailers in the area. The unit, which was fronted by a large loading bay and parking area, comprised a warehouse, containing the various office equipment, stationery, etc., and an office with two rooms.

We were met by an old gentleman with a grey beard; he was scruffy in appearance and he asked us to follow him.

We went through one room, where a typist was working, and into another containing a large desk and the usual filing cabinets and chairs.

'Here are the records. I'll leave them to you,' said the old gentleman and left, after stating that he would be away all day but if we wished to see him the following day, he would be working in the typist's room.

David and I soon settled down to work, laboriously ticking entries in large leather-bound ledgers.

For several years, David had conducted the audit on his own and knew the records well. If I had any questions, he quickly answered them.

After a few hours, David got up from the desk and stretched. 'Time for lunch,' he said, moving towards the coat-hangers.

David was much taller that me, thickset, and interested in most sports. He was full of confidence and I liked him. I understood from him that he was going to get married the following year to a dental nurse; I had never seen her, but according to some of the office staff she was a very pleasant, lively young lady.

We set off to a local restaurant. David had told me that it was small but spotlessly clean; he had visited it regularly in previous years, and knew the food was good.

On arriving there, we easily found a vacant table and sat down.

A middle-aged waitress approached us. 'I remember you,' she said, looking at David. 'You came here for several weeks last year.'

We looked at the menu and chose roast beef and apple pie and ice cream. I thought if this was typical of the perks of audit work away from the office I would seek to go out more often!

The principal, Mr Davis, reimbursed his clerks for travelling expenses and for meals purchased whilst articled clerks were away on audits.

David and I soon finished our meal and, after a brief walk, returned to the wholesale office equipment unit.

After half an hour, David looked up and told me, 'I shall be going out for a few hours. I'm going to see a rugger match.' I had no idea if this had been agreed with Mr Davis but I had no authority over David's actions so I just got on with my work.

At about four thirty David returned; he said nothing at all about the rugger match. 'Time to go home,' was all he said. I collected my bits and pieces, put them in my briefcase and we commenced our journey back to Hayford.

I later discovered that David had skived off. No one in authority found him out.

After the outside audit I settled down to the usual work at the office in Hayford.

I CONTINUED TO have to cycle from my home to the office in Hayford. During the spring and summer months, the travelling was quite pleasurable but during the winter months, when the thick smog was about, I often arrived at work covered in black filthy grime; I wore appropriate clothes to protect my office suit but at times had to wear a smog mask. The air around the London area, especially during the winter, was very bad during the early 1960s.

One day I was halfway to work and came across a crowd of people surrounding a young man who was lying at a strange angle on the pavement. Blood was streaming from his head; apparently he had fallen off his motorcycle, which was on its side nearby; one of his legs appeared to be broken.

I stared at the young man; there was no movement at all. He looked like a wax dummy.

'It seems to me as if he is dead,' said a tall, middle-aged man with glasses who was standing by my side. 'Going too fast – skidded and fell off his motorcycle, on to his head.'

This was the first time I had seen someone who was possibly dead and it upset me greatly.

An ambulance appeared on the scene, its siren blaring noisily. Two ambulance men quickly lifted the young man on to a stretcher, into the ambulance and sped away.

'No point in hurrying,' said the bespectacled man. 'He is definitely dead.'

He was quite right, of course, as I ascertained later from a report of the accident in the local paper. I continued to the office, locked my cycle away and mounted the staircase.

Rose was standing with a group of other staff. I spoke to her and said, 'I've just seen a young chap who has fallen off his motorcycle. I'm fairly certain he is dead.'

She spoke a few words of comfort to me, as she could see I was trembling slightly. I thought at the time how considerate she was and her kindness reinforced my strong feelings towards her. She was young but very sensible for her age. It was never one of my strong attributes to openly express my private thoughts, but I knew inwardly that Rose was the only girl for me. Although Rose and I worked in the same office, the opportunities for us to be alone were few and far between. We both had our own office duties, Rose typing sometimes, as well as doing clerical work. When we spoke in the office it was mainly about office matters but at times we managed to whisper privately to each other.

At lunchtime, I caught her up as she was walking along the high street. Sometimes we had a meal together but mainly she had her lunch with the other office ladies.

Suddenly one day, she looked directly at me and said, 'I'm going ice-skating on Saturday. Would you like to come with me?' I had no other definite plans for Saturday so I readily agreed.

MR JOHNSON CALLED me over. He was sitting ramrod straight at his desk, opening a pack of his favourite cheroots. Taking a cheroot out, he lit it with his old army lighter. The smoke drifted towards me and I coughed slightly.

I had tried smoking on one or two occasions but I'd felt sick each time, so I decided to be a non-smoker.

Not much was known about the effects of smoking – and indeed passive smoking – in the 1960s. It was thought to be 'with it' to smoke and young people were often influenced by older people to indulge in the habit. So much more is known now about the dangers of smoking.

'I want you to go and see Mr Raven of Raven & Co. Ltd., a weaving company,' said Mr Johnson. 'He has some problems with balancing the main accounts book.'

Mr Johnson did not look at me as he spoke, but pushed a piece of paper towards me. I picked it up and noticed it had the name and address and telephone number of Raven & Co. Ltd. on it.

'Please telephone Mr Raven for an appointment,' he said, and began sorting through some papers on his desk, dragging the smoke from his cheroot deeply into his lungs. That was his way of dismissing me from his presence.

Miserable old man, I thought, ponderously walking back to my desk. As I was picking up my telephone receiver, I wondered what Mr Raven would be like.

A young-sounding telephonist answered my call. 'Hold on please; I'll get him for you.'

After a few minutes, there was a click and I heard a man's voice. 'Mr Raven speaking. How can I help you?' He sounded pleasant and spoke in a low but clear tone.

'I'm Tom Read of Davis & Co., Mr Raven, and I've been asked by Mr Johnson to arrange an appointment to call and see you,' I told him.

I heard a loud laugh from Mr Raven. 'I seemed to have made a bit of a botch of my accounts book this month. I can't get it to balance.'

Apparently he maintained the book, as it contained confidential information which he did not require his bookkeeper to see.

'Would two thirty this afternoon be all right for me to call to see you?' I asked. He confirmed that this would be ideal and I made a note in my diary accordingly.

After lunch at Ron's Café, I picked up my briefcase from the office, left a message with Beryl, the typist, saying that I would probably be about two hours, and proceeded to walk to Raven & Co.

The company's premises were situated off the high street, only five minutes' walk from the office. It was raining slightly but I always kept a light mac in my briefcase; slipping the mac over my suit I walked along the busy pavement, through the bustling crowds.

I soon stood outside the small factory; the premises did not look impressive. In fact, they looked somewhat scruffy. At the front of the building was a small forecourt on which six cars were parked. There were three motorcycles, and a number of pedal cycles leaning against the fence. I could clearly see two young ladies in the office, at the front of the building. One was typing and the other looking at a book. They looked up as I opened the door. The younger of the two ladies came over towards me. 'Can I help you?' she asked. She was slim with fair hair and an attractive smile.

'I'm Mr Read, I have an appointment with Mr Raven for two thirty.' It was a few minutes before that time.

'I'll go and tell Mr Raven you are here,' said the young lady, and disappeared through the side door.

The other young lady, a brunette, looked up from the book she was writing in. 'Please sit down,' she said, pointing towards a bench-type seat to the side of the front door.

As I sat down, I could hear a muffled thumping noise. After a few minutes, the first young lady appeared, followed by a man in his middle thirties. He was dressed smartly in a dark grey suit, white shirt and a light blue silk tie. A matching silk handkerchief spilled over his jacket pocket. His face was thin, even to the extent of being bony, and his small dark brown moustache was clipped neatly. His hair was thick and parted down the middle. He strode confidently towards me, smiled and shook hands with me warmly.

'I'm pleased to meet you, Mr Read.' He really meant it!

Sometimes one takes an instant liking to a person and this happened with Mr Raven. I just sensed that he was genuine.

'If you follow me, Mr Read, I'll show you where my office is,' he told me.

He led me down a narrow passage and as we walked along, the thumping noise noticeably increased.

He noticed my sideways glance and commented, 'The noise from the looms is rather disturbing at first. One gets used to it. I'll show you the factory, after you have looked at my accounts book.'

We turned left into a room that was comfortably furnished with padded armchairs and a large mahogany desk.

In the middle of the room was a huge table surrounded by eight good quality wooden chairs. 'That's for directors' board and shareholders' meetings,' he said, pointing at the large table.

We sat down, Mr Raven in his padded armchair and myself in a similar one opposite him.

'Coffee or tea, Mr Read?' he enquired, picking up his internal telephone receiver.

'Coffee would be fine, thanks,' I replied. My caffeine intake did not seem to harm me, as I usually drank weak coffee or tea.

He produced his accounts book, from a drawer in his desk.

'Usually I don't have much trouble balancing the book, but this week I've spent a couple of hours looking for a difference of two hundred pounds, without success,' he said.

I knew the feeling and sympathised with him.

Adding up figures continuously, after a while, one gets a knack for locating errors and as I looked at the accounts book, I spotted a figure three which could have been taken for a five. There it was. I had found the difference in a matter of a few minutes.

Some would have said by luck, but I put it down to experience.

'That's great,' was Mr Raven's jubilant reaction. He quickly thrust the book back into the drawer.

'Let's have our coffee and I'll show you the factory,' he said. I could tell by his enthusiasm that this was where his real interest lay – the factory floor.

A tray containing two cups of coffee had been placed on his desk. 'Milk and sugar, Mr Read? Please help yourself.'

I sat back, relaxed and well satisfied with my visit. Munching some chocolate biscuits, I was soon chatting to

Mr Raven as though I had known him for years. We were on the same wavelength.

Having finished our coffee and biscuits, he suddenly sprang up from his chair. His eyes were bright but friendly. 'If you would like to follow me, I'll show you the factory,' he said eagerly. His enthusiasm was infectious and I followed him with anticipation. As we continued along the narrow passageway, the noise increased. Soon he opened another door which led to the factory area.

'We'll have to shout to each other to make ourselves heard,' he said loudly.

I just about heard him. There were eight huge, ancient looms in operation and they were causing all the noise. Mr Raven explained to me about warps and wefts and the different yarns needed for different operations.

The workers were concentrating on their various jobs; although one or two men glanced towards us, it was only fleetingly. The work looked to me to be highly dangerous and I could understand them not wishing to be disturbed. At the far end of the factory area were two large rooms, one for the raw materials and the other for the rolls of cloth. Mr Raven knew his pet subject inside out and was proud of his workers and the finished products. I could tell that by the way his face lit up when explaining matters to me. A small door led us to the narrow passage and looking along it, I realised it was the same one we had entered at the other end of the factory. I followed him back to the office and we sat down.

My head was throbbing, as a result of the noise. I later found out that some workers had gone deaf there over a period of time. The noise had affected their eardrums. One male worker had fractured a wrist when it got caught in a loom and the danger was very apparent to me.

'What do you think of our factory, Mr Read?' asked Mr Raven.

My reply concentrated on the positive attributes and I deliberately omitted mentioning the negative points, such as the inherent danger of working there and the terrible noise.

We shook hands, and I left him waving to me at his office door.

'Goodbye,' I said to the two office ladies, and made my way out to the comparative quiet of the street.

When I reached the office at Davis & Co., I reported to Mr Johnson that I had located Mr Raven's difference.

'Took you all of two and a half hours,' Mr Johnson grunted. His upper lip curled contemptuously.

I walked towards my desk, feeling that I would have liked to have wrung his oversized neck. Why waste time explaining that it had in fact taken me only a few minutes, to locate the difference in the accounts book?

Experience and optimism were beginning to affect my attitude towards life and inwardly I was smiling.

Although I had never been ice-skating, I could roller skate. I had become quite good at the latter, roller skating on the pavement near my parents' house when I was a youngster.

'You'll soon get the hang of ice-skating,' said Rose, smiling.

The ice-skating rink was not far from Rose's home and I arranged to leave my cycle with her parents.

Saturday morning came, and it did not take me long to reach her home. I was met at the door by her mother who, although slighter in build than Rose, had similar features. She was prim, clean, and very tidy looking. She obviously paid attention to her appearance. I could see instantly where Rose got her fastidious ways from.

'I'm pleased to meet you, Tom,' said Rose's mother. I could feel her intent gaze. She was obviously having a close look at the young man who was taking her daughter out. 'Please come in and wait a few minutes,' she said, and quickly turned away.

I followed Mrs Turner along the narrow hallway of the semi-detached house and turned right into the lounge. I looked around. Everything looked so clean and immaculate. She was very house-proud. The furnishings reflected the personalities of Rose and her mother exactly.

'Mr Turner is away for a few days,' said Mrs Turner, asking me to sit on the settee. We chatted for a few minutes and then Rose appeared. She was dressed in smart casual clothes, including well-fitting slacks.

'You look nice,' I commented.

Her eyes shone. She smiled at me encouragingly and said, 'If you don't mind, Tom, we'll call at Keith's house before catching the bus to the ice rink.

Keith was a young accounts clerk who had recently joined the office; he had no intention of taking any exams. After leaving school with one O level he had decided to try accountancy to see if he liked it or not. He was on a probationary period of six months and it remained to be seen if he liked the work, or indeed if Mr Davis was happy with him.

He lived a few streets away from Rose's home. I indicated to Rose that I would like to see Keith, who was away from the office with a virus – I was anxious to see if he was recovering.

Rose and I said goodbye to Mrs Turner and we started walking towards Keith's home. After a short walk we soon arrived and Rose knocked on the door.

I looked around. It was a small terraced house, built in rather dismal surroundings, completely different to the area where Rose's home was situated. The paintwork on the dark green door and window ledges was peeling badly. In fact, the whole property looked dilapidated and in need of considerable renovation.

A small man, dressed in oil-covered overalls, opened the door.

'We have come to see how Keith is,' said Rose. She towered over Keith's father.

He looked up at her pensively from his lowly height of about five feet two inches. 'Come in and I'll show you to his bedroom,' he said.

We followed him up a narrow staircase; the walls were devoid of wallpaper. They had been painted a sickly yellow colour.

Keith's father pointed to a door at the top of the stairs. 'He's in there. I've got to get back to my car. I'm changing a wheel.' Suddenly he was gone and we were left there.

Rose knocked on the door and I followed her in.

Keith, who had known Rose for several years, was sitting up in bed reading. He looked up and said, 'Thanks for calling to see me.' I thought he looked pale but alert.

We enquired about his health and he told us that he felt a lot better than a few days ago. Rose produced a paper bag and gave it to Keith, who opened it.

'Just what I wanted,' he said. He emptied the black grapes into a bowl placed on a small bedside cupboard.

He looked at us and smiled; I rather liked him, even though he was at times a bit cheeky.

'I understand that you are an item,' he joked.

Rose and I looked at each other in surprise. We had never mentioned our mutual liking but from our actions it was, I suppose, obvious to all the office staff.

I spluttered somewhat and mumbled a few words. I quickly changed the subject, asking him how he kept himself occupied during his illness.

'Mainly by reading books on aviation,' he replied.

After a while the conversation virtually dried up and Rose and I started to get fidgety. Rose suggested to me that we had better be on the move if we were to get to the ice rink on time.

Slowly we edged towards the bedroom door, wishing Keith all the best and a quick recovery from his illness. He was very pleased that we had called to see him; he winked at us as we left him. 'See you back at the office in about a week's time,' he said.

We descended the staircase, saying goodbye to Keith's father, who popped his head round the kitchen door as we walked along the hallway. Thankfully, we were soon out in the fresh air.

The sky was azure and the sun was shining. I thought, Thank goodness I am not stuck indoors like Keith. The bus stop was only a few yards from Keith's house and we had been waiting about ten minutes when a double-decker came along. The journey did not take long.

I was quite talkative, which was very unusual for me, as I was often quiet, especially on public transport where other people could so easily overhear one's conversation. I felt confident and on top of the world; this I put down to being with Rose, who exuded confidence. She was not an extrovert but she was completely self-assured. Although academically I was far ahead of her, she clearly had the dominant personality.

Rose was extremely intelligent; the fact that she had passed two O levels did not matter to me, as I knew passing exams was sometimes a matter of luck.

We made our way towards the ice rink; I must admit at first I was rather apprehensive. The place was a well-known venue for young people to socialise; on entering the building, however, I felt completely at ease.

We paid for our tickets and moved towards the lady who was hiring the skates out. 'What sizes do you want?' she asked. We both found skates to fit us and slowly approached the ice.

As soon as we reached the edge of the rink, Rose commenced skating and I could see she was excellent, with no fear of falling at all. It was quite apparent that she had ice-skated many times before and looked very confident. I stepped warily on to the ice.

As soon as I commenced skating, I found the experience vastly different from roller skating. I immediately overbalanced and fell over. Numerous skaters rushed past me, some giggling and others looking down at me sympathetically.

Rose came over and helped me up. 'You will soon get the hang of it,' she said.

'I hope so,' I replied, feeling a bit uneasy.

Eventually I did end up skating reasonably well without falling, but I didn't like at all the weak feeling in my ankles, which had become swollen. After a while, I told Rose I'd had enough and would wait for her at the edge of the rink.

She continued to skate for a few minutes but noticing me sitting there waiting for her, she came over. 'Let's go home, Tom,' she said.

I thought how considerate she was to notice that I really wasn't enjoying myself. We took our skates back to the hirer. On the way out, I saw a kiosk and bought some sweets. I handed a packet to Rose and we began our journey back to her home.

'You didn't really enjoy yourself, did you?' she asked.

'I must admit I prefer roller skating,' I replied. People cannot always like the same pastimes and I thought it was best to be honest with her.

We boarded the bus and were soon at her home.

'See you on Monday, Rose,' I said, and she looked at me as I was closing the garden gate.

She waved, but again I saw that same look I had noticed before. She was smiling, but I sensed something was not quite right. Were there doubts creeping into her mind?

On Monday morning I didn't have a chance to speak to Rose, only to say briefly that I appreciated her company on Saturday. I was due to see a client, a car salesman called Mr Peal, at two thirty that afternoon. He operated from his parents' home which was not far from the office.

At lunchtime, I was walking on my own towards the office having been to Ron's Café, and I saw Rose crossing the road towards the outside door of the main office. I called to her and she looked round. I hurried across the road, avoiding the oncoming traffic, and caught up with her.

I hoped she would not raise the subject of the ice-skating again. She did not mention Saturday's outing but was chatting away about a dress she had just bought.

'When I left you on Saturday, Rose, you looked at me as if to say something but you seemed to change your mind,' I said.

She looked at me and said, 'I don't remember that at all.' She kissed me on the cheek and smiled.

Perhaps she had decided to shelve the matter, but I knew that something had concerned her. Not wishing to upset her, I refrained from delving further.

I N THE AFTERNOON, I located Mr Peal's address. His parents' house was detached – a large, rambling building, standing in about half an acre of land. I opened the gate, which although made of wood with hardly any paint remaining, had its hinges oiled thoroughly.

There were hardly any flowers or shrubs; but seven or eight cars, mostly appearing to be in good condition, were parked in the front garden.

I approached the front door, which was painted grey, and I used the large brass door knocker. On glancing at the window to the right of the door, I noticed someone moving the curtains and looking out.

As soon as I knocked at the door, there was the sound of barking. A young man of about twenty-five years of age opened the door and an Alsatian leapt towards me, snarling, its jaws slobbering.

'Down boy!' said the young man, and the dog immediately slunk away.

'You are Mr Read. I've seen you at the office once or twice.'

'Yes, that's quite right. I interviewed you when you were first starting up on your own,' I commented.

Mr Peal was wiry, with keen eyes and a thin, long face. He was attempting to grow a moustache, without much success. His face was unshaven and he was wearing jeans, a shirt and a dark blue pullover.

My first reaction was that he looked shifty. This is no reflection on car salesmen, as I have met a number I liked instantly.

Mr Peal gave me a furtive glance and asked me to follow him.

'My mother and father are out at work,' he informed me. 'We had better deal with the accounts book through here.' He was walking quickly down a dimly lit hall when suddenly he turned left into a large room which I understood to be the dining room.

Sitting down at the table, he motioned me to do likewise.

As I sat down, I noticed the Alsatian under the table. His upper lip curled back to disclose yellow jagged teeth and he growled menacingly.

'Quiet,' said the young man. The dog lay down with his head resting on the floor; saliva dribbled on to the dirty, worn carpet.

The room was full of pictures; some to me looked valuable and there were fine ornaments on the window sills and mantelpiece. Although the room was obviously used for having meals, there was a large settee against one of the walls. The double bay window looked out on to a large garden full of overgrown trees and shrubs.

I produced my working papers from my briefcase. Mr Peal looked nervous as I put the draft accounts and my query sheet on the table. His eyes darted from side to side.

'Your second year's accounts disclose a very small profit, insufficient in my opinion for you to live on,' I said.

He immediately became greatly agitated. He shouted, 'Who are you to say that to me?' I was a bit taken aback, being generally used to respect from the clients I visited.

I knew that the accounts were unlikely to be accepted in their present form by the Inland Revenue and so I persisted. 'You cannot live on the profit disclosed by these accounts.'

'Yes I can,' he retorted. 'My parents often give me cash to pay for many of my clothes. I don't pay them for my meals.' He looked at me aggressively. His dog looked up, again baring his teeth.

Clearly I was not going to get anywhere with Mr Peal so I quickly cleared a few routine points and decided I would report back to Mr Johnson at the office.

Mr Peal had not shaken my hand when I met him at the door and neither did he do so as I was leaving. My last impression of him was him slamming the door and the sound of his dog barking loudly.

On returning to the office, I told Mr Johnson what had occurred.

'Leave it with me, Tom. Put the file on my desk,' he told me.

I had done my best and it was now up to Mr Johnson or Mr Davis to interview Mr Peal.

A few weeks later, I ascertained that Mr Peal had been seen by Mr Johnson and it was decided that Davis & Co. would cease to act for him. It was quite apparent that Mr Peal was on the fiddle and he was told in no uncertain terms to leave the office. I never saw him again, and indeed had no wish to.

Over the years, I have learnt to trust my instinct when meeting people. There have of course been exceptions to this rule, but not many.

Outside work, it often seemed to me that it was Rose who usually suggested the social activities, so I made up my mind to ask her at the earliest opportunity whether she would like to go to the cinema on the following Saturday. There were several local ones.

On asking her, I was very surprised at her reaction. 'I'm afraid I can't go this Saturday,' she said. 'I've arranged to go out with some girlfriends.'

I thought, Surely she could change her arrangements? She continued to chatter on about shopping and subjects I thought were completely unimportant. I was not listening attentively. All I wanted was for her to agree to go to the cinema with me. I suppose my face must have shown my disappointment because she suddenly looked at me quite seriously and said, 'I can go with you Saturday week.' My feelings changed from gloom to brightness in seconds and my thoughts raced ahead.

L ATER IN THE week, there was great consternation among the staff. Jane, one of the typists, had been taken ill at home and her husband had telephoned to let us know that unfortunately she was in hospital.

For some time, most of the staff had known that she had suffered from anaemia; she was always cheerful but often looked very pale and soon became tired.

Beryl, the other typist, and Mrs Teaming, an accounts clerk, arranged to go and see Jane at the local hospital. A 'get well' card, signed by all the staff, was given to Beryl and Mrs Teaming to take with them. A collection was made and some fruit was purchased for her.

Jane was well liked by all the staff. I was horrified to learn that some days later her condition had quickly deteriorated and she had died.

For many years, she had been having treatment for anaemia and none of the staff had known. She was fiercely independent and I suppose she did not want sympathy from the staff. She wanted to be treated the same as them – on equal terms.

I felt sad as I liked Jane and often had a friendly chat with her. Many people who are very ill have this inner strength which is passed on to others.

I had seen her husband on one or two occasions, and I thought how well they were suited. It was later ascertained that Jane had, in fact, died from leukaemia, a condition about which little was known in the early 1960s. Jane's life was not in vain, however. People still talk about her great courage and other lives have been that much better as a result.

M R JOHNSON CALLED across the office, 'Tom – telephone call! It's Mr Baines.'

I picked up the telephone and Mr Baines spoke. 'Mr Read, I'd like you to call to see me please. I've got problems with my bookkeeping.' He sounded concerned. I made arrangements to go to see him later in the week.

His house and builder's yard was about half a mile from the office, so I decided to walk there. It was a pleasant day. The sun was shining and the air was fresh.

I had met Mr Baines on several occasions before, and I liked him. He was what one called a rough diamond; however, he was completely open and honest. His wife was a small, cheerful lady, and they had one young daughter of about two years of age.

I arrived at Mr Baines's house, which was situated down a cul-de-sac. There were large iron gates which squeaked as I pushed them open. To the left of the house as I approached the massive front door, there was a rough piece of grassland, on which various planks, bricks, sand and other building materials lay scattered.

I rang the bell and Mrs Baines opened the door. She had a worried look on her face. 'Come through, Mr Read,' she said. 'I'm afraid Mr Baines has had an accident.'

I followed her along a wide, well-decorated hall, which suddenly opened up to a spacious lounge, where I saw Mr

Baines lying on a couch. He looked wan and his right arm was in plaster.

'I've just got back from hospital,' he explained. 'I fell off the roof of a shed I was repairing for a customer. The first time I've fallen and injured myself in twenty-five years. I only fell six feet but I fell backwards and put my hand out to stop myself falling and fractured my wrist. Luckily it's a clean break, but I shall be off work for about six weeks.'

The last time I had seen him he had looked a picture of health. I was in a 'do-it-yourself' store buying some paint and there he was, as happy as a sandboy – just a few days ago. Then all of a sudden he was injured and unable to work.

I looked at him; he was a heavily built man of about sixteen stone, nearly fifty years of age. His face was round and he had a thick, black moustache; he was nearly bald.

Resting on a cushion, he went on, 'I leaned over, put my weight on the edge of the shed and suddenly it gave way. At the hospital I had some injections and I still feel a bit groggy. I just don't feel up to going through the books with you today, Mr Read.'

I quite understood, and after having a short chat with him and his wife, I was soon outside and walking back to the office in a reflective mood.

Life is so fragile. I could not help thinking, That fall could easily have killed him!

Later in the afternoon, I was interviewing Mr Lanes, a double glazing salesman. He had been recommended to our firm by a local businessman, an established client.

Mr Lanes was a young man of my age. He was about six feet two inches tall, broad, and he carried himself well. He wore a smart, light-grey suit; his shoes were polished and he looked extremely confident.

These were his first few months as a double glazing salesman; he had given up his previous job of a part-time barman and decided to endeavour to increase his earnings substantially.

He had deposited on the table in the interview room a cardboard box. I emptied the contents on to the blotting pad. There were various receipts and invoices, in no order whatsoever, and included were many items of a private nature which had nothing to do with his business.

'Do you have an accounts book?' I asked.

He produced his bank statements from his jacket pocket. 'When I receive commission from the double glazing company, I pay the cheques in,' he told me.

Apparently his records were virtually non-existent.

'I won't be long, Mr Lanes. I'll get you an accounts book,' I said. We kept some spare accounts books in stock and I quickly got one from the general office and returned to the interview room.

'Can't I claim the cost of my clothes?' he asked. I assured him that he could only claim expenses incurred in earning commission. He looked puzzled. 'I have to buy expensive suits and shirts to go and see my customers.'

To explain to a young man, new to self-employment, the taxation legislation applicable to business expenses was not easy within a short time. I did my best, but I think he left the office wondering about the unfairness of being self-employed. He accepted that what I was saying was correct and when he eventually required his annual accounts completing, it was gratifying that he asked specifically for me to prepare them.

I WAS STILL studying hard for my final exams; the correspondence course was excellent, but to assimilate so much information required considerable time and dedication.

My progress was good, as it was my nature to be methodical, and I endeavoured to study a few hours every evening and sometimes on Sunday mornings.

Many of my friends who had jobs not requiring studying, were earning considerably more than me and had many hours of leisure time. I could not help but feel envious periodically but I kept telling myself that once I became a Chartered Accountant it would all be worthwhile!

Rose was considerate, although sometimes I felt that she would have liked to have socialised more; after all, she was young and had plenty of energy.

When I was studying, I felt in a world of my own and it was quite easy to shut my bedroom door (my bedroom was also used as a study) and get immersed in the accountancy papers.

Now I looked forward to going to the cinema with Rose and I am afraid my thoughts began to stray once again. This would be the first time I had taken her to the cinema and I was determined that I would try to make the evening as pleasant as possible.

On the Friday, the day before we were going to the cinema, the office was closing and I had just got my cycle out of the shed.

Rose appeared as I was putting my cycle clips on. 'I'm looking forward to tomorrow, Tom,' she said.

'I'll see you at your home at 7 p.m., Rose,' I said. I began my journey home and noticed Rose at the bus stop. She waved and smiled.

ON SATURDAY, I had finished my usual chores – shopping for my parents and cleaning my cycle and so on.

I put on my best suit, a smart grey pinstripe, and a light blue shirt with a red tie, and made my way to the bus stop near my home. I was rather apprehensive but decided to try and remain calm.

Alighting from the bus I called at a confectionery shop and bought a pound of chocolates. That was most of my spare cash gone for a week, but I thought it was worth every penny.

I rang the bell when I reached Rose's front door. Her mother appeared and asked me in.

I followed Mrs Turner, and as I was turning into the lounge, Mr Turner spoke to me. I had never seen him before. He was a small, wiry man – only five feet tall – much shorter than Rose. His very bright eyes looked at me intently; I knew then where Rose got her sparkling eyes from.

He was dressed in casual clothes and had yellow rubber gloves on. 'I'm pleased to meet you, Tom.' Taking off the gloves, he shook hands with me vigorously. He was genuinely pleased to see me and seemed very affable. 'Just finished washing up,' he explained, obviously quite domesticated and unconcerned about his appearance.

Mrs Turner called from the kitchen, 'Rose won't be long.'

I sat down in the lounge with Mr Turner and we were soon talking quite freely. My first reaction was that I liked him; he seemed a pleasant man – confident, but not too much so.

There were footsteps and Rose came through the door; she had on a floral patterned dress with white shoes, and her auburn hair was tied back with a yellow ribbon. Small ruby earrings completed the picture. I thought how attractive she looked.

'I'll get my coat and we'll be off,' she said, smiling at me.

Saying goodbye to her parents, we shut the front door and walked towards the bus stop; in the early 1960s journeys by bus were common, as many people still did not possess cars.

'I like your father, Rose,' I said, and she seemed pleased; she did not comment but pressed my hand appreciatively.

The bus was packed full and we recognised a few people, obviously intent on going to the cinema too.

As we alighted from the bus, we looked around. There was a slight drizzle, but Rose soon produced a fold-up umbrella from her bag. The distance from the bus stop to the cinema was only a matter of a few hundred yards and we soon joined the queue.

Rose was holding my hand. She was extremely cheerful and talkative.

A popular film was being shown, *Around the World in 80 Days*, starring David Niven. We were both looking forward to seeing it. Cinemas were much more popular then compared to later years when television became available to the public generally.

We were getting to the front of the queue, when suddenly there was a shout from behind us. A young lady, smartly dressed and part of a group of young ladies about Rose's age, called to her. 'Who's this gent with you?'

Obviously the young lady had noticed us holding hands.

'Watch your step, Rose,' she said.

The whole group of them starting teasing Rose, in a friendly way, but she took it in good part and gave as good as she got.

'What's his name?' she asked. The cheeky red-headed girl with freckles continued the banter until we got to the ticket office.

I paid for the tickets. A plump, round-faced lady with a snub nose took the money. 'Have a nice evening,' she said, as I collected my change.

The foyer just outside the main inner doors of the cinema was very plush with thick carpets and comfortable looking settees. There were elegant light fittings on the walls, as well as the ceiling.

The last feature from the previous programme was just finishing, so Rose and I made ourselves comfortable on one of the settees. She sat close to me and I thought there was little to beat the sensation of a warm, pleasantly scented woman next to you in such circumstances.

Eventually people streamed out from the previous sitting, and we went through the large entrance doors.

I had paid for the best seats, in the upper circle. An usherette, seeing a young couple, shone her torch towards the rear rows of seats.

The cinema was very smoky, but at that time the inherent dangers of smoking were not generally realised.

We settled down and Rose produced the box of chocolates I had given to her previously. In due course, the main feature commenced.

I must admit, my mind was not on watching the film. It seemed natural to put my arm around Rose and she did not object at all; in fact she snuggled up to me. I turned my face towards Rose and at the same time, she turned towards me; we embraced.

At that stage, I could not have cared less about the film. We kissed for some time. In the dark cinema, it was very tempting to go further.

'What are you thinking, Tom?' Rose whispered.

After a few feeble fumblings, I quickly sat back in my seat.

'What's wrong, Tom?'

'Nothing,' I replied, endeavouring to look at the film.

The girl with the chocolate ices came round and I bought two, giving one to Rose, who was quiet. I had the feeling that the evening might be spoilt. I hoped not.

Looking round the smoke laden cinema during the interval, I noticed many couples necking. They were not bothered about the lights being fully on.

The lights dimmed and I put my arm around Rose. She was still quiet, unnaturally so, and I asked her if she was all right. 'Of course I am,' was her petulant reply.

The film ended, the national anthem was played and we walked towards the exit. I looked at Rose's face and knew instantly she was upset. We hardly spoke in the bus and when we reached her home she faced me. 'You do like me, don't you?' she asked.

I was uncertain what she meant. It takes two to tango, I thought.

At the garden gate, Rose kissed me on the cheek. 'I'll see you on Monday,' she said, turning towards the front door. For some reason my plans for a lovely evening had been foiled.

In the street light, I could see that she had a strained look. I had done my best to make the evening happy but she was unhappy. My mind was in a turmoil.

It was late, as I walked towards the bus stop. Eventually a bus came chugging along, and I sat there thinking about the evening. I had so many expectations, but I was soon to learn that life does not run smoothly.

Lying in bed, I was still unsettled and could not get to sleep. I decided to have a chat with Rose on Monday. It is always the lady's prerogative to draw the line and as far as I was aware, I had not crossed it. Perhaps Rose wanted somebody who was more forward than me.

Monday arrived, and when I saw Rose she appeared to be her usual cheerful self, as if nothing untoward had happened on Saturday. In fact, she thanked me for the nice evening and for the chocolates. I decided to put the matter to one side.

She continued to chat away and I was pleased to hear that she was very quickly learning typing and progressing well with her accounts work.

I HAD AN appointment to see the Jones Brothers – Bert and Len – both in their early twenties. They were carpenters and had worked in partnership for over four years.

I had prepared their accounts for the last two years and had prepared another set in draft for a third year. The purpose of my visit was to clear the queries, to enable the accounts to be finalised and typed.

The two brothers were as different as chalk and cheese. Bert was tidy, and was responsible for the bookkeeping; while Len was generally untidy and useless at figure work.

They often had arguments over their business and these bad feelings sometimes spilled over into their private lives. It was a pity really; as individuals they were quite likeable. When they got together over financial matters however, there were usually fireworks.

I could see them dissolving the partnership, as the last time I met them they had indicated to me that the arguments were becoming worse.

Their workshop, adjacent to Bert's house, was about two miles from the office and I decided to walk there. It was a pleasant day, no rain was forecast and the air was fresh.

It took me about half an hour to walk to the workshop which was situated down a cul-de-sac.

Bert's detached house was in a good part of town and was surrounded by about half an acre of land. I had been to the workshop before and walked alongside the house past piles of rough sawn timber.

Within the workshop was a small office which had a telephone connected. As I approached, the door opened and Bert and Len greeted me.

Bert was thin, about six feet tall, and wore rimless spectacles. His unshaven face was bony and his clothes hung on him. He always looked to me as if he needed a substantial meal.

Len was shorter, about my height, thickset, with a round face and dark curly hair. He was strongly built with a broad chest.

They both shook hands with me and I followed them into the workshop.

Four large wooden benches were in the centre of the workshop which measured about thirty feet by twenty. An electric saw was fitted to one of the benches and there were various tools scattered all over the place; the floor was covered in sawdust.

'Come in, Tom,' said Bert, ushering me into the small office at one end of the workshop.

Bert and Len were two of the few clients who called me by my forename. I had known them for years socially.

I drew up a chair and sat down at a small table, opposite the two brothers. Taking my working papers out of my briefcase, I wondered what reaction I would get. The accounts disclosed a much reduced net profit and I had a feeling that this would cause another argument.

I quickly cleared the routine queries and produced the draft accounts. 'Your net profit has reduced considerably,' I said, looking at Bert and Len closely.

'I know the reason for that,' remonstrated Bert. 'That's down to lazybones here.' He pointed at Len, whose face was getting more red by the minute. They glared at each other as I tried to placate them. Finally Bert said, 'Well, enough is enough. I've worked my guts out trying to make a go of this business and much of my time is spent going round to customers, clearing up jobs you should have done properly in the first place.' He again glared at Len.

'I try my best,' said Len, but I knew that wasn't true. I had known him at school and he was just a likeable scoundrel. I could well imagine him not working properly and leaving his brother to clear up afterwards.

'I've made my decision to dissolve the partnership in three months' time.' Bert grimaced at his brother as he spoke, and I thought at one moment they would come to blows.

'If that's what you want, I couldn't care less!' Len blurted out. His face was scarlet as he shouted at his brother.

By this time, I was feeling agitated. Being a quiet person, disliking arguments immensely, I decided to call the meeting to a close, making an excuse that I had an appointment in half an hour.

'I'll finalise these accounts,' I told them, 'but I won't submit them to the Inland Revenue until I hear from you. If you are definitely dissolving the partnership, let me have the records and I'll incorporate the results with the accounts I have already prepared. It will work out cheaper, fee-wise, that way.'

I collected my papers together, put them in my briefcase, drank the remains of my coffee and stood up to go.

The atmosphere was very tense as the brothers said goodbye to me.

They both looked downcast but I could not help thinking, as I walked slowly back to the office, that they would be happier working on their own. They were so different. I was surprised that they had worked together for as long as four years.

A few days later, I received a letter at the office from Bert Jones. They would be dissolving the partnership and would be trading independently. Some months later I prepared the final partnership accounts and I was pleased to hear that the brothers were much happier.

Each brother had his own sole trader's records and in fact Len's work improved so much that Bert worked with him on a number of jobs.

Bert did not have the worry of clearing up after Len, and Len, on finding that he was his own boss, realised that was exactly what he wanted. Not being able to lean on his brother, he had to 'sink or swim'.

I interviewed the brothers after they had been sole traders for six months and they appeared completely different. Both were relaxed and happy. Some brothers can work in partnership amicably, and some cannot.

The Jones brothers were happy working and having their own separate businesses, and on reflection I could understand that attitude.

Success is all the sweeter if one knows it is the result of one's own efforts!

'TOM – PHONE CALL!' shouted Mr Johnson; he sounded irate so I quickly picked up the receiver.

'Mr Bernard from the local Tax Office, Mr Read,' said a voice. 'I would like to see Mr Wayne, the smallholder, with yourself, at the earliest opportunity.'

My heart was thumping. This was the first time I had been called to the local Tax Office.

Normally my tax computations applicable to clients' accounts were agreed by correspondence directly with the Inland Revenue, without any queries whatsoever.

Mr Bernard, with whom I had corresponded on several occasions quite amicably, probably sensed my nervous reaction to his call. 'There is nothing for you to worry about, Mr Read,' he said.

An appointment was made, subject to agreement by Mr Wayne and I put the receiver down, wondering what it was all about. I had prepared Mr Wayne's accounts properly, from information and explanations supplied; however, I was still concerned.

Mr Wayne was waiting for me outside the Tax Office. He was a thickset man, with a ruddy complexion. His spectacles, mended at one corner with a piece of black tape, were slightly askew.

As he limped towards me, I looked at his old trousers, stained with soil, and his worn green pullover.

'What's this all about, Mr Read?' he enquired.

Though I had spoken to Mr Wayne on the telephone, I could not glean any information from him to assist matters. 'I have no idea what the Inspector's on about,' I replied.

We entered the Tax Office; this was a sombre, unfriendly building and as I mounted the staircase with Mr Wayne limping behind me – he had arthritis in one leg – I could not help feeling what a soulless place it was to have to work in. It was even worse than our office.

The lady at the counter, who was middle-aged and grim-faced, motioned us towards a door. 'Up those stairs, turn right and Mr Bernard's office is two doors along.'

I knocked on the door. 'Come in, please,' said Mr Bernard. He was sitting at a large, grey metal desk and rose to greet us.

I looked around. Apart from his desk and chair, there were two further chairs and a grey metal cupboard, and that was all: a bleak picture indeed.

We all shook hands and sat down; Mr Wayne looked decidedly miserable.

Mr Bernard was a small man with rimless spectacles, behind which beady eyes peered at us. He was smartly dressed, in a dark suit; his hair was receding slightly.

Tapping his pen repeatedly on his blotting pad, he spoke to Mr Wayne. 'I have reason to believe that your takings for your last financial year are not fully recorded. At this stage do you have any comments to make?'

Mr Bernard had asked me to supply him with Mr Wayne's business records some days prior to the interview, and various books and papers were spread across the desk. A copy of the typed accounts which I had prepared was also visible.

I glanced at Mr Wayne; he was beginning to perspire and his top lip was beginning to twitch uncontrollably. Looking at the floor and not Mr Bernard, he mumbled a few incoherent words.

Mr Bernard looked up from his desk and peered directly at Mr Wayne who was beginning to tremble. 'I did not hear what you said, Mr Wayne,' the Tax Inspector said. He repeated his question and again waited for an answer.

'I sometimes receive cash and don't record it,' was the eventual quiet reply.

'I suggest to you, Mr Wayne, that you have, over a considerable period, omitted cash takings from your records.' The Inspector looked grim.

He then proceeded to set out very clearly – he was obviously used to these interviews – the evidence which proved that Mr Wayne had definitely omitted cash takings from his accounts book.

Mr Wayne had in fact been selling potatoes to a local grocer whose accounts had also been reviewed by the Inland Revenue. The grocer had correctly shown the payments made to Mr Wayne but an examination of Mr Wayne's business records disclosed no sign of the money received.

I thought at one stage that Mr Wayne was going to faint; his face had gone a deathly pale colour and he looked decidedly ill.

'Could I have a glass of water, please?' he asked.

The Tax Inspector picked up his internal telephone receiver and soon a young lady brought a glass and Mr Wayne drank quickly.

After a few minutes, he appeared to recover his composure somewhat and listened to Mr Bernard.

'You have defrauded the Inland Revenue and you have let your accountant down,' said the Inspector.

I was listening to the conversation but I was there mainly as an observer. Accounts had been prepared from records and information supplied, so I had nothing to worry about in a professional capacity. I was, however, concerned that Mr Wayne had deceived me.

'You will have additional tax, penalties and interest to pay,' Mr Bernard droned on.

The interview came to an end and I shook hands with Mr Bernard; I knew he had done his job efficiently and I accepted the conclusion.

'I'll be writing to you, Mr Read, setting out the Revenue's proposals and I will await your reply.'

By the time I got downstairs and out into the fresh air, Mr Wayne was nowhere to be seen. On looking around, I located him; he was leaning against a wall, to the right of the Tax Office.

'I'm sorry about this, Mr Read,' he said dolefully.

I knew he was a rogue and had defrauded the Revenue, but I could not help feeling sorry for him at that time. Being young, I had not yet been hardened by experience.

'As soon as I hear from the Inspector, I'll contact you,' I said.

Mr Wayne looked at me; his eyes were bloodshot and watery and there was still a quaver in his voice. He mumbled something incoherent. I didn't hear what he said and he limped away. His head was bowed and he looked a picture of misery.

I walked back to the office feeling upset by the situation. I had trusted Mr Wayne and he had indeed let me down.

Accountancy to some people may seem boring but I see it differently; it is full of life because, of course, it's not just figures that accountants deal with. It's people as well.

I reported back to Mr Johnson, filed my notes of the interview and awaited Mr Bernard's letter.

After a few days the letter appeared. The tax, penalties and interest amounted to a large sum of money. Mr Wayne was forced to sell his house and he moved into rented accommodation, to settle his liabilities.

However, the Inland Revenue decided not to prosecute. It was determined by Mr Davis that Davis & Co. would cease to act for Mr Wayne. I later discovered he had moved out of the area. He had been taught a lesson which I am sure he always vividly remembered.

AT TIMES, MR Davis was, regrettably, very unpleasant to his staff; some years later I was informed of the main reason for his attitude. He was often quite unwell. The repercussions of his illness were felt by his employees. His office was located away from the main office and was visited by the staff infrequently.

I had experienced one or two of his violent rages. At one time he threatened to throw a typewriter at me and all I had done was misspell a word. I was relieved however to learn that I was not singled out for this treatment.

The articled clerks were required to call Mr Davis 'sir' at all times. If this requirement was not adhered to, they were severely reprimanded.

He drank heavily, had a florid complexion and high blood pressure. His skin cut very easily. All the staff were instructed not to use staples, in case he caught his fingers; at one time a young lady clerk took no notice of this requirement and was called into his office. She suffered violent verbal abuse. Apparently he was shaking like a leaf and quite out of control.

Such office conditions would not be tolerated now, but in the early 1960s, principals of small offices were often treated specially. They had absolute control of their staff, whose only real remedy if unhappy with working conditions was to cease employment.

THE WEEKEND ARRIVED. I had passed my driving test when I was seventeen years of age and although I was in my early twenties, I had never owned a car of my own.

My father had taught me to drive in his car, but I was only allowed to drive it occasionally; he was rather protective but I understood his attitude. There were many local car crashes involving young people.

However, the time had come when, although my earnings were still extremely low, I felt that I wanted a car of my own.

One Friday evening, I had scanned the local newspaper and noticed an advert for a 1934 B.S.A. four-wheeler sports car. I emphasise four-wheeler, as B.S.A. cars usually had only three wheels.

I decided to go with my father, the following morning, to examine the car.

We were greeted by the proprietor of the small garage. He was a very large man in a brown three-piece suit. His stomach was protruding over his trousers and a smouldering cigarette was stuck to his bottom lip.

'Any particular car in mind?' he enquired nonchalantly.

I looked across at the half-dozen vehicles parked. There was the B.S.A. sports car and I quickly walked over towards it. The proprietor lumbered after me, endeavouring to keep up with me.

As soon as I saw the car, I knew I had to have it. It had the name *Daisy Belle* emblazoned on one side. It had wire wheels and though there were one or two marks on the bodywork, there was, as far as my father and myself could see, no serious damage. Apart from the rather tatty black hood which could be replaced, the vehicle seemed in very good condition for its age.

'Have a drive,' said the proprietor, his eyes twinkling; he handed me the keys.

The price of the car was only sixty pounds; I had already made up my mind.

Neither my father or myself had ever seen a four-wheeler B.S.A. sports car, and later we found out that it was a rare model.

I sat in the driver's seat; the frame was made of wood. I started the engine. It fired first time and ran smoothly.

Obviously it had been maintained by an enthusiast. This view was supported by the various servicing invoices, receipts and notes made by the previous owner. To me, the car seemed a bargain.

I drove it round the block a few miles and returned, grinning at my father; he was chatting to the proprietor who, on seeing me drive towards him, asked, 'What do you think of it?'

Of course, he knew the answer before I replied. I paid the sixty pounds, obtained the logbook and receipt for the cash and drove on to the main road. My father and I did not have far to travel, but as I drove along I felt on top of the world. It's a very special feeling, owning a car for the first time.

There were many glances at the sports car, which was painted a brilliant red.

When we arrived home I drove directly on to the driveway; my father's car was in the garage.

My mother was standing at the front doorway and asked, 'What on earth have you bought?' She showed her dismay.

'Don't you like it?' I asked, proudly pointing to the sleek lines of the bodywork.

'I can't understanding you letting Tom buy a car like that,' she said, staring intently at my father.

He quickly got his pipe out and filled it with tobacco from a tin. 'Tom's old enough to make his up own mind,' said my father, concentrating on lighting his pipe.

Personally, looking at the sports car, I couldn't understand what all the fuss was about. 'I've bought it for the enjoyment of owning such a car,' I said.

My mother made it quite plain that she did not consider the vehicle to be very practicable – and she was eventually proved to be quite right!

My knowledge of cars was virtually nil; I hadn't even looked at the engine. A belated examination of it, however, proved to be encouraging; it looked spotlessly clean and well cared for.

IT WAS MONDAY morning and I told Rose about my purchase of the sports car. She seemed very interested. 'When are you going to take me out in it, Tom?' she asked me.

I had already made up my mind to ask her if she would like to go to the East Coast – a place called Dunstone-by-the-Sea. I had an aunt who lived there.

'Would you like to come with me to the coast next Sunday?' I asked. Rose was thrilled. 'We could drive down early Sunday morning, call briefly at my aunt's and spend a few hours on the beach,' I suggested.

Rose readily agreed and I could see, looking at her face, that she was excited about the venture. A sports car, no matter how old, seemed attractive to the younger generation.

Sitting at my desk, once again surrounded by a client's mass of invoices, his receipts and his scruffy, poorly maintained accounts book, I was beginning to dream of better things. Some clients' records were atrocious and it appeared to me that many of them considered the production of paperwork to an accountant completely farcical and in the nature of a game.

In the 1960s, accountants were often presented with boxes of very incomplete records and it was expected that accounts would be prepared for lodgement with the Inland Revenue.

I was beginning to get exasperated with this particular person's records, when the telephone rang. 'Mr Keene for you, Tom,' said the receptionist.

On picking up the receiver, I instantly recognised Mr Keene's voice, which was agitated. He spoke quickly and sounded worried. 'I'm hoping you can assist me, Mr Read. I'll explain the problem when I see you.'

Having made an appointment to meet him in the afternoon at our office, I replaced the receiver, wondering what he wanted to see me about. I continued with my work and decided to put the matter to the back of my mind until after lunch.

At two thirty I was sitting in the interview room. Mr Keene knocked at the door and, hearing my voice, entered.

He was a retailer of men's attire and his shop was in the high street. I looked at him as he accepted my offer to sit down. He was about fifty years of age, smartly dressed in a dark grey suit, light blue shirt, red tie and matching pocket handkerchief, with a gold tiepin and cuff links. He looked like a prosperous businessman, which I knew was the case. Mr Keene was about six feet three inches tall, heavily built, and erect, with a large, flushed face. He had a small pencil moustache, the same dark colour as his thick curly hair.

'I've got a serious financial problem, Mr Read, and I hope you can solve it for me,' he announced.

His eyes were bulging when he spoke and I could see that he was perspiring. Beads of sweat showed distinctly on his brow.

'As you know, I've traded in the high street for twenty years and I've made a good living. My accounts show this. During the last three months my bank balance has decreased drastically and I know something is wrong. The shop seems as busy as ever but my takings have fallen,' he continued. His face, usually creased with a wide smile, was a picture of misery.

'Have you brought your accounts book with you as requested, Mr Keene?' I queried.

He opened his briefcase and handed me the book. I examined the entries of bankings which had indeed reduced considerably during the last three months.

'Have there been any changes made in your shop during the last three months?' I looked closely at Mr Keene as I spoke.

Continuing to look downcast, he confirmed that there had been no changes in staff or the usual business procedures.

I knew that a Mrs Malting took the daily takings to the bank and indeed had done so for the last six of the ten years she had been employed by Mr Keene. All takings were banked gross, that is no cash expenses were deducted. If cash was required for expenses, this was drawn from the bank and correctly accounted for.

'Are you positive that your trade has not declined during the last three months?' I asked. I was not surprised at Mr Keene's quick reply.

'With no disrespect intended, Mr Read, I know from experience if the shop is not doing well, by the number of customers.'

Apart from Mrs Malting, he employed only Mrs Keene, who worked on a part-time basis.

Examining the accounts book, I could see nothing which was obviously wrong with the entries and asked, 'Who enters the bankings in the book?'

'I complete the accounts book myself and ensure that it balances each day,' Mr Keene said apprehensively. 'Why do you ask?'

I was not one to make hasty decisions and was therefore somewhat evasive in my reply. 'I will help you to the best of my ability, Mr Keene. Have you got your bank paying-in books with you?'

He opened his briefcase and handed them to me. 'There you are. I always keep them with the accounts book, except when I give them to Mrs Malting when she goes to the bank.'

'Can you leave your accounts book and paying-in books with me until tomorrow morning and drop in your week's till rolls, and I'll see what has gone wrong,' I suggested.

Mr Keene rose ponderously from his seat, saying, 'I hope you find the answer. I can't sleep properly and I've lost weight worrying about the matter.'

He did indeed look thinner and his haggard face clearly showed his despondency.

'It will take a load off my shoulders if you are able to find out what has gone wrong,' he said. He shook hands with me and walked laboriously towards the interview room door.

'I'll give you a ring late tomorrow morning,' I told him. I hoped that I would be able to assist him.

I picked up the accounts book, the paying-in books and my working papers and trundled back to my office desk. I had to finish off part of some work I was doing for a client on whose records I was working when I was interrupted, and I decided to deal with Mr Keene's problem first thing the following morning.

As soon as I sat down at my desk early the next day, I began to examine Mr Keene's records in depth. I considered the matter properly and perused the accounts book recording the bankings.

There was a definite downward spiral of takings during the last three months.

I picked up the bank paying-in book containing the counterfoils relating to the last six months' bankings and began comparing each daily banking disclosed with the accounts book. All entries agreed, but suddenly I noticed a slight change in the ink used on one of the bank paying-in book counterfoils. The till slips did not agree with the bank paying-in books. In my opinion, the entry showing the total cash banked had been amended. It appeared that this could be the answer to the problem. If cash had been received on a particular day and then the total altered compared to the till slip, the difference could have easily been pocketed.

The culprit seemed to be Mrs Malting, but I decided to discuss the matter with Mr Keene. I picked up the telephone receiver and was soon speaking to him. 'Could you call round to see me?' I asked. 'I may have the solution to the problem.'

'I'll be round in ten minutes,' Mr Keene replied. Obviously he was anxious to know the result of my checking.

I made my way to the interview room. There was no doubt in my mind what had happened. Spreading my working papers out, I pondered. Mr Keene trusted Mrs Malting and I wondered how he would react.

There was a knock at the door and Mr Keene appeared.

'Please sit down,' I said.

'Have you got the answer, Mr Read?' He looked at me anxiously.

I showed him the paying-in book entries and he was flabbergasted. 'I know Mrs Malting's husband has been unemployed for over a year but I trusted her implicitly,' he said. Mr Keene's eyes were beginning to redden and I saw a suggestion of tears. He was conscientious and a trusting individual and he was experiencing difficulty in accepting the facts.

'I'll have to see Mrs Malting, when I get back to my shop,' he said. His head was bowed as he turned away.

'Please let me know how you get on, Mr Keene.' I felt sympathy for him, realising that this was a great blow to him.

About half an hour later he telephoned me; he spoke quickly and I could tell he was flustered. He had seen Mrs Malting and she had directly confessed to taking cash before the daily banking; she had become very distressed and had been instantly dismissed by Mr Keene.

He and his wife discussed the matter and decided not to prosecute Mrs Malting, who I ascertained some months later had, with her husband, left the area.

Mr Keene soon obtained a replacement employee but he never again let anyone other than his wife deal with any of the business records. He had been taught a bitter lesson about human behaviour, where the temptation to steal was concerned.

When a person was trusted and that trust was betrayed, it was devastating, especially for someone like Mr Keene.

ANOTHER TELEPHONE CALL. My head was buried in a mass of paperwork. I seemed to spend a considerable amount of time balancing accounts from extremely incomplete records.

I picked up the receiver and I asked who wanted to speak to me.

'My name is Mr Lamb, said the caller. 'I'm a carpet fitter and I've been given your name by a friend of mine who has been satisfied with your work.'

I made an appointment to see Mr Lamb the following morning. It was always pleasing when new clients were sent to the firm, especially when my name was mentioned. It usually created considerable goodwill.

Sitting at my desk in the sunlit interview room, waiting for Mr Lamb to arrive, my thoughts were again straying. I would be pleased when Sunday morning arrived and Rose and I would be off to the coast.

My fanciful thoughts were interrupted by a loud knock on the door. As I rose from my desk, a small, stunted man with fierce, beady little eyes came through the door. He had on a heavy dark brown overcoat, the lapels of which were turned up.

Very rarely did I take an instant dislike to people when I first saw them but it happened then. My instinct seemed to tell me that the man could not be trusted and that was before he had even spoken to me at length.

'My name's Lamb. I spoke to you on the phone,' he murmured. He did not look directly at me when speaking but placed two brim-full boxes on to the desk.

'I started on my own as a self-employed carpet fitter two and a half years ago and now the tax man is chasing me for some accounts,' he explained.

I looked at the boxes in disbelief: the records were a complete mess. 'Sit down, please, and I'll take a few notes,' I said.

It was not long before I had obtained the details I required. All the time I was asking questions, Mr Lamb was fidgeting nervously, and he was soon out of the door when he realised the interview was over.

He looked back at me as he left and said over his shoulder, 'Keep the tax down as much as you can.' His lips twitched as he spoke.

I promised to contact him when I had prepared the accounts and had some provisional tax calculations.

About a month later, I again interviewed him, finalised his accounts and sent him a note of the firm's charges. As a result of the agreement of his accounts with the local Tax Office, his tax liability was considerably reduced.

Some weeks later Mr Davis called me into his office. 'That new client, Mr Lamb, has not paid our fees and has left the area without leaving a forwarding address,' he told me.

Despite the use of solicitors to endeavour to obtain settlement of our fees, no money was ever received from him. My instinct had been right!

I WAS IMMERSED once again in a considerable volume of paperwork, preparing the schedules required for a client's accounts, when the telephone in the office rang.

'Mr Jack Potter for you, Tom.' There was the usual clicking sound and I heard Mr Potter's gravelly voice.

'That you, Mr Read?' He sounded worried and I wondered what was concerning him. 'Received a tax bill for two thousand pounds! What's this all about?' he asked.

'I'll fetch your file and see if I can tell you.' I walked briskly to the filing cabinet and took out Mr Potter's file. Scanning through the correspondence, I could see that the two thousand pounds was based upon an estimated income tax assessment, as he had not yet brought his records in to enable accounts to be prepared and the actual assessment to be calculated correctly.

'Mr Potter, I wrote to you for your records three months ago and I still haven't received them. As soon as I do, I can prepare your accounts and get the assessment amended.'

'I've been too busy. Can you call to collect my records, Mr Read?'

By now he had quietened down somewhat, although I could tell he was still agitated. 'Would two thirty this afternoon be all right, Mr Potter?' I asked. He confirmed it would and after lunch I walked round to his home – about half a mile from the office.

He was a self-employed plasterer and he also erected false ceilings inside offices, private residences and garages. The work was hard but his accounts always reflected a healthy profit – the result of many hours of labour. In the past, he had worked with his brother who had given up the plastering trade. Mr Jack Potter now worked completely on his own, which sometimes was a handicap. I wondered at times why he always wore a thick woollen hat. When he did some work at the office erecting a false ceiling in the interview room, I saw why. He had to balance long sheets of plasterboard on his head, to prevent them from slipping when he was nailing them to the joists!

Mr Potter's house was mainly given over to private accommodation but one room facing the back garden was used as his office. I opened the garden gate and approached the front door, walking along a narrow path constructed of eighteen-inch paving stones. The garden was neglected and full of weeds. Obviously he had no time for gardening; I knew he often worked at his trade on Saturdays and Sundays.

I rang the bell, looking at the paint peeling on the door. Mr Potter lived on his own. He had been divorced about three years previously but he had two Alsatians, which were usually kept chained in the back garden; each dog had a kennel. I could hear them barking when Mr Potter opened the door.

His face looked strained. His voice did not match his appearance. Dishevelled, holed trousers and a ripped shirt covered his thin frame. I felt sorry for him as I looked at his long, bony, gaunt face. His bright eyes stared at me as he asked me in. He still had his woollen hat on.

One of his social activities was marathon running and he had won several prestigious events. This strenuous sport no doubt contributed towards his skinny appearance.

I followed him along a wide hall, turning right into a room which contained a divan, a table and some chairs. On the table Mr Potter's records were spread out haphazardly.

He asked me to sit down, and commented, 'Before you take the records, I would like to explain one or two points.'

I noted down the matters accordingly, picked up the records and put them in my briefcase.

'Are you interested in running?' he asked. He saw me gazing admiringly at the numerous trophies set out neatly on two shelves.

'I did run for my school in the one hundred yards and won a few races, but I've never taken it seriously,' I replied. 'Long-distance running always seemed too strenuous. I preferred short distances.'

Mr Potter had done well at long-distance running and I was always interested to listen to people talking about their successes. As he spoke, his mood seemed to change. He ceased to be the quiet, withdrawn plasterer. He was the runner, breasting the tape at the end of a race.

The strained look on his face disappeared and he relaxed. As he shook hands with me at the front door, he was beaming.

IT WAS EARLY Sunday morning; I had arranged to meet Rose, at her home, at about eight thirty.

My mother had made some sandwiches and put them, together with cakes and fruit, into a hamper. A large flask had been filled with coffee and I put this, together with the hamper, into my sports car, which I had cleaned and polished thoroughly.

On my arriving at Rose's, she greeted me at the front door. She was wearing well-fitting light brown slacks and a cream top; I thought how attractive she looked.

'All ready, I see,' I said. She nodded, kissed me and handed me a bag. 'I've made a few sandwiches and put in some oranges and grapes,' she said.

'We should have plenty then,' I said, pointing to the hamper at the rear of the car. This was the first time Rose had seen my new car; as she sat in the passenger's seat, she didn't say much.

I had the hood down, as it was a fine day. The sun was shining and the air was fresh. This is the life, I thought. I owned a sports car and had a good-looking girl by my side. I engaged first gear and drove slowly off.

We waved to Mr and Mrs Turner, who were peeking through the front room window.

There was not much traffic on the road and we had soon covered twenty miles. Suddenly I noticed what I thought was smoke coming from the engine. A lay-by appeared and I quickly pulled in.

'What's the matter, Tom?' asked Rose, anxiously looking at the 'smoke' which was increasing rather alarmingly.

Knowing nothing about the workings of a car, I had to confess my ignorance. On opening the bonnet, I noticed steam, not smoke, which I had originally envisaged, coming from the radiator; on touching it briefly, I found it to be very hot.

We had passed a garage about a mile back, and I decided the best course of action was to walk there and ask for assistance.

'I won't be long, Rose,' I said. She now seemed quite unruffled. Having accepted the situation, she seemed calm. That was one of the qualities I liked about her.

I reached the garage, and a young mechanic looked up from a car where he was apparently changing a wheel.

'Can you have a look at my car?' I pleaded. 'It's only about a mile up the road – steam is coming from the radiator.' I hoped he would help me.

He was very obliging and instantly asked me to get into a Ford car which was parked outside the garage. The pleasant young mechanic began talking about the weather being good, but all I could think of was Rose being left stranded in the lay-by.

We soon arrived at the stranded car. Rose was calmly reading a magazine. The steam had by this time subsided with only a wisp coming from the engine.

The bonnet was still up and the mechanic looked at the engine. 'This is an old car. I've never seen one like it. The radiator is boiling, as there's hardly any water left,' he told me.

'I filled the radiator up before our journey,' I commented.

'Unfortunately, some old cars don't have fans,' was the mechanic's reply. 'They were never designed to have one! The only thing you can do is to fill up the radiator every time it starts to steam.' As he spoke, he was filling the radiator from a bottle he'd produced from the Ford.

What have I bought? I thought. I hoped that it was not 'a pig in a poke'.

'How much do I owe you?' I asked, turning towards the mechanic. He looked slowly at Rose and then back at me.

'Nothing at all! On the house – enjoy your day,' he replied. Whistling, he smiled, waved and drove off.

When Rose and I reached Dunstone-by-the-Sea, it was about noon. We easily found my aunt's house, which was a few yards from the beach.

My aunt Grace was a widow of about sixty years of age. She was short, only five feet tall, with long grey hair. Her round face, showing some wrinkles, was smiling broadly as she greeted us at the garden gate.

'Come in. You can leave your car quite safely there,' she told me. I had parked directly outside her small terraced house.

We spent an hour with aunt Grace and then made our way to the shingle beach.

The cloudless sky was azure and the salty, breezy air was bracing; the sun shone warmly.

In a few minutes we had found a good spot, right near the edge of the sea, and spread our picnic fare out on a rug.

I had obtained two hired deckchairs from an attendant nearby.

I was a keen swimmer and we had both brought our swimming costumes, which we had changed into at aunt Grace's.

'Do you fancy a dip, Rose?' I asked.

'You have a swim and I'll watch you. I might have a paddle later,' she replied.

Stripping off my trousers and shirt, I soon plunged into the sea. It was cold, but swimming a fast breaststroke soon warmed me up. I swam about two hundred yards out to sea and looked towards Rose. She waved to me, smiling. She could have easily got annoyed about the trouble with my car but she didn't; I liked considerate people, and consideration was one of the qualities she exuded.

I swam back towards her, reaching the beach, and had difficulty keeping my feet on the shingle because of the swell. I clambered over towards her and she handed me a towel; I briskly rubbed myself down and she was quick to offer to dry my back.

Sitting on the deckchair, I looked at Rose, who had by now taken off her ordinary clothes; she had on a multicoloured one-piece swimming costume; she looked a picture and, I must admit, she set my pulse racing.

We ate our sandwiches and fruit and sat drinking our coffee, and I wished the day would never end.

Rose had her paddle but I could see that she didn't really like the sea water; she never complained, however, and seemed pleased that I had enjoyed my swim.

We asked a middle-aged couple who were sitting near us if they would mind looking after our hamper and swimming costumes. We had by now dressed. They were pleased to do so and we decided to visit the pier.

Crunching along the shingle, we soon reached the promenade. Rose put her arm through mine as we walked along; I felt ten feet tall.

At the entrance to the pier, there were a number of stalls, including one which sold ice cream. We were soon munching away at two ice creams with chocolate stuck in the top. We passed through the amusement arcade. We didn't have much time to stay there, and walked towards the end of the pier. A number of men, of all ages, were fishing and as we reached them, one of them caught a small fish. He seemed pleased, looked at it, took it off the hook and threw it back into the sea.

When we got back to aunt Grace's house we spent half an hour chatting to her and then made our goodbyes and said, 'Thanks for making us so welcome.' She looked pleased, and waved as we drove off.

Keeping my fingers crossed, I hoped the journey home would be uneventful.

As we sped down the main road leading away from Dunstone-by-the-Sea, everything seemed to be going smoothly. The air was sweeping through Rose's auburn hair and her cheeks were rosy; she had caught the sun.

I was concentrating on my driving, as far as possible; we had covered about fifty miles, when I noticed that when I took my foot off the accelerator, the engine continued to rev. Not again, I thought, stopping the car at the edge of the road.

I opened the bonnet. Although I had turned off the ignition, the engine was still moving.

Knowing little about cars generally, with much trepidation I climbed back nervously into the driver's seat.

'Do you think we'll be able to get home, Tom?' Rose enquired.

I tried to console her. It seemed I did not have any option but to continue to drive the car. It was going like a bomb but the only trouble was that when I took my foot off the accelerator, it made no difference at all!

Rose saw the funny side of it and kept giggling.

However, I was quite worried and intent on getting home safely. Eventually, I was relieved to be at last turning into the road leading to Rose's home.

'Thanks for a lovely day, Tom,' she said. She kissed me fully on the lips and stood at the garden gate. I could see she was happy and she waved to me as I drove away.

I reached home about 8 p.m., parked the car in the driveway and switched off the ignition. Miraculously, the engine stopped. What a day, I thought, patting my car.

I eventually discovered that a screw had fallen out of the carburettor and this was the reason for the trouble with the accelerator.

L ATER IN THE week, my dreams were shattered. Having parked my car outside my home, I was in my bedroom studying, when suddenly I heard a tremendously loud noise.

My bedroom was upstairs and faced the road; I quickly looked out of the window. My lovely red sports car was a mangled wreck. A large lorry had smashed straight into it.

I raced downstairs and confronted the lorry driver, who was getting shakily out of his vehicle. 'I'm sorry. I just didn't see your car,' he said. He leaned against our garden wall, perspiring profusely. I thought he was going to faint.

My sports car was crumpled up like an old tin can and had been pushed against the garden fence.

My parents came out, and the lorry driver, who was unhurt, accepted full liability; documents were exchanged and I went to telephone a garage to ask someone to take what remained of my car away.

Several weeks later, I received a cheque from the insurance company. I quickly deposited the money in my bank. It was some time before I was able to have my own transport again.

I telephoned Rose and told her about the crash; she was very supportive, which I appreciated, and I liked her all the more for it.

O F ALL THE businesses in Hayford, Mr Rawling's butcher's shop was one of the quaintest.

Periodically I had to call to see if his business records were being kept correctly; he'd got into a mess over the years, with poorly kept books, and had called at our offices to see if we could help him.

Unfortunately his tax affairs were well in arrears, but I had brought them up to date for him. He clearly admired anybody who could deal with figure work properly, and was always appreciative of my calls.

His shop was tiny and situated down a side street off the high street in Hayford. It was within easy walking distance of the office. I was often given jobs to do close to the office, because of my lack of transport.

The front door of Mr Rawling's shop closed behind me and I saw him peering at me over the counter. He was an untidy man – tall, with unruly greasy black hair.

His shop should have been clean; it wasn't, and neither was he. Glancing at him, I noticed his blood-spattered apron and grubby, unshaven face. How on earth the shop was not closed by the Health Office, I could not fathom out; I did know that he was on the committee of the local council and perhaps that had something to do with it.

The floor of the shop was covered in sawdust and it looked as if it had not been swept for weeks. Flies buzzed around some chickens and turkeys which were hanging on hooks in the shop window. I looked up at the walls. Cobwebs draped themselves over several rabbits.

Mr Rawling was serving a customer. 'I won't keep you long, Mr Read. Go through to the back,' he told me. His family, comprising his wife and two young children, lived at the back and over the shop. There were three tiny bedrooms upstairs.

As he spoke to me, he cut up a piece of beef for the customer, picking it up and placing it on the scales. His hands were dirty and his fingernails were black but the customer, an elderly man, seemed totally unconcerned.

An old, fat tabby cat jumped from the counter and sidled up to me, mewing. I looked down at the hairs clinging to the turn-ups of my trousers.

There was a nauseating smell in the shop, but obviously Mr Rawling was quite used to it.

I walked along a dingy passage, passing a room where I saw a rough wooden bench and various large pieces of meat. Mr Rawling had showed me this room when I had called previously. On one side of the room were rows of very large jars and I had asked him what they were for. 'Well, they're for pickling the pieces of meat that are left over, at the end of the week,' he said. On looking closer I could see these horrible lumps of meat, floating in what was probably vinegar. Rather than throw away the bits of meat left over, he preserved them for consumption, by himself and his family. No doubt money was saved. The butcher lived quite frugally.

At the end of the passage, I came across a room which served as a lounge and diner.

Mrs Rawling greeted me. She was a short lady, very fat, and she tended to waddle as she walked. I liked her, as she was always cheerful and seemed totally oblivious of her bleak surroundings. Her round face creased into a smile as she spoke to me. 'Sit down, Mr Read. I'll make you a coffee.'

I really did not want a drink, knowing the unhygienic origins, but rather than upset her, I thanked her. A few minutes later she appeared with a steaming mug and some biscuits.

The table where I sat was covered in crockery and cutlery remaining after a recent meal. I pushed them to one side and got Mr Rawling's file from my briefcase.

After a few minutes, he appeared. He had with him a small accounts book and some vouchers. 'Time for the inspection,' he said, as he drew up a chair and sat down.

I gazed at him. He was absolutely filthy but seemed very happy. After all, he had a small business; true, it was not doing particularly well, but he was his own boss and had a jovial wife and two fine children.

Looking at the blood-spattered accounts book and vouchers, I quickly made an arithmetical check and found, apart from a few minor errors, that the records were in order.

'Your records certainly have improved since you first came to Davis & Co. for advice, Mr Rawling,' I said.

He beamed. I had made his day. 'I do appreciate your assistance, Mr Read.'

Gathering my papers together, I listened to his absorbing chat about the day's events.

I rose from my chair. 'Well, I must be going, Mr Rawling,' I said, following him to the shop. As I was opening the shop door to leave, he placed a package in my hands.

'That's for helping me so well. You will find some sausages and a couple of chops.'

I felt a bit queasy at the thought of the preparation of the meat but thanked him and left him standing at the door, with a wide grin on his face; he was content with his life.

B ACK AT THE office, Rose had listened to the detailed story about the accident to my car. She consoled me but changed the subject to my forthcoming twenty-first birthday.

Apart from a celebration at my home with my parents, the office staff had arranged a party at a local restaurant. I knew all about the arrangements and was indeed looking forward to the occasion.

On the day of my twenty-first, I arrived at the office and congratulations were showered upon me. There was one huge birthday card which had been signed by all the staff.

Morning coffee break was about eleven and I saw Rose sitting on the edge of a desk. 'I have something for you,' she said. She walked towards the typists' office and I followed her, expectantly.

On entering the typists' office the inner door was suddenly shut. There were shouts and I looked across the room. All the female clerks and typists were lined up in a row.

'I'm first,' said Rose and kissed me on the lips. The other ladies followed suit.

One particular young lady, June, a divorcee about twenty-five years of age, who had made it plain on several occasions she was interested in me, kissed me quite passionately. Rose pretended that she was unaware of the event, but I glanced at her and I could see she didn't like it.

June had bought me a tiepin some months previously and when I asked her why, she replied, 'Because I like you.'

I endeavoured to keep myself smart. I was quite slim at the time and I was always spending any spare cash on quality clothes; I found quite a few females attracted to me. However, Rose was firmly in my mind and I was not bothered with serious relationships with other ladies.

I was becoming somewhat overwhelmed. I've never been shy where the ladies were concerned but to have a row of them lined up, each kissing me, was a bit overpowering.

I looked up, and there was Rose. She was pouting a little, at June. 'This is for you, Tom,' she said.

She handed me a small packet, gift-wrapped. On opening it, I found a velvet-covered box. Inside there was a set of gold cuff links with my initials engraved on them.

This gave me such pleasure; it was not just the receiving of the gift but it was clear to me what Rose thought about me. 'Thanks, Rose,' I said, and pressed her hand appreciatively.

It was soon time to walk to the local restaurant which was quite near the office. A large room had been kept free specially for the occasion. We all made our way there and were greeted by the proprietor, an Italian. A number of chairs and tables had been provided and the proprietor, Mr Carlini, ushered us in. He was extremely polite and we were soon sitting down, waiting for the meal to commence.

Mr Davis and Mr Johnson called in for a few minutes.

'Please be back at the office at 3 p.m.,' said Mr Davis, wishing me all the best. This was one of the few occasions he had spoken kindly to me and I returned his handshake warmly. Perhaps the tide was turning. I hoped so.

Even Mr Johnson wished me well. My dire thoughts about him momentarily evaporated.

Drinks were provided. Numerous bottles were set out on the tables. Rose was sitting next to me and we were all, soon after a general toast, drinking the table wine like water.

Everybody was chatting away and I looked around the large room. One or two of the male staff were used to drinking alcohol, but I hardly drank at all.

Mr Andrews liked his whisky and sometimes drank rum. 'Try some rum and Coke,' he said. Why not, I thought, and I soon swallowed the contents of two small glasses.

The meal, which was cooked well, was soon over and I was thinking of going back to the office. Many of the staff, as it was nearing 3 p.m., were already grouping together.

I got up from the table and as I gazed at Rose I began to feel dizzy. The room appeared to revolve as I rushed to the gents, where I was as sick as a dog.

On coming out of the gents, I found one or two of the staff, including Rose, were waiting for me. 'I shall have to go home,' I said. 'I feel so unwell and can't do figure work feeling like this.' I staggered towards the front door.

Mr Andrews said he would explain the position to Mr Davis. A taxi was called for and I was taken home.

My mother, surprised to see me home so early, was concerned, particularly as I was still very groggy and staggering. 'What on earth have you been doing?' she asked.

'Had a few drinks,' was my incoherent reply. 'Birthday celebration,' I muttered and slumped to the floor.

Somehow I climbed the stairs to my bedroom and lay down on my bed. The room seemed to be spinning and I had a terrible nauseous feeling. Never again, I thought.

The next day I was still feeling unwell and the local doctor was called. He looked at me in disgust. 'Alcoholic poisoning,' was his only comment to me. Looking at my mother, he told her I would have to be away from work for some days to allow my system to get back to normal.

I later found out that my drinks had been spiked. I never did ascertain who the culprit was.

On starting work the following week, I was told by Mr Johnson to report to Mr Davis.

'Don't think much of your performance at the restaurant,' Mr Davis said, looking at me with annoyance and repeatedly tapping his pen on his desk.

This was the reaction of a man who could drink all day like a fish without being affected at all!

No sympathy, when I endeavoured to explain that my drinks had been spiked. No enquiries about my welfare – only a reprimand. He was obviously thinking about the three and a half day's loss of work!

A NEW CLIENT, Mr Thompson, an upholsterer, had telephoned to ask me to call to see him. He had been recommended to Davis & Co. by one of the local banks.

His tiny shop was in the high street, within easy walking distance of the office.

The door of his shop was open and as I walked in, two small dogs rushed up to me, barking and with their tails wagging.

'Come here!' shouted Mr Thompson and the dogs quickly quietened down and moved to the corner of the room.

The shop was a lock-up one. Mr Thompson lived a few miles away. It consisted of one room for serving customers and also for him to work.

He had no employees. Indeed, he could not afford to pay for any. He had been employed by a large firm of upholsterers and had decided to try and make a go of it as a self-employed craftsman.

Having been trading for six months, he wanted some interim accounts prepared, and he wished me to examine his records to see if they were adequate.

This was the first time I had met him. He was a man of approximately twenty-five years of age, and the shop reflected his personality and appearance.

Mr Thompson was a small man and everything about him was neat, from his small, highly-polished brown shoes, to his short back and sides haircut. He wore a protective apron but I could see that his trousers were of good quality and his shirt was clean. His grey eyes twinkled as he shook my hand warmly.

'I shall be coming to you for advice quite a lot in the next few months, no doubt,' he said.

His records were awaiting my attention and while he was serving a customer, I looked around. There were several shelves containing cloth and various tools – all in apple-pie order. As I tried myself to be neat in my ways, I appreciated Mr Thompson's efforts in the presentation of his shop.

On examining the records, they were as I expected, perfectly balanced and a pleasure to check. I could not find one error. On my mentioning this to him, he seemed pleased, but was anxious to know if he had made a reasonable profit for the first six months of trading.

'I'll have to take your records away for a few days to prepare the interim accounts, but a preparatory look at your records indicates to me that you seem to be progressing well,' I said.

Seeing the standard of some of his work, the partly upholstered chairs by the side of the table where I was sitting, I would have been surprised if he had not made a success of his business, small though his shop was.

I made arrangements for him to bring his records in at a mutually convenient time and said goodbye. He raised his hand to me and smiled warmly. There's a man happy in his work, I thought as I walked back to the office.

My studies were progressing well and high marks were being obtained generally via the correspondence course tutors. The work was becoming less of a burden and on reflection this was due, I suppose, to the number of hours I was studying.

The concern for me was that my social life was suffering. This was unfortunate but all my relatives and close friends kept telling me it would be worth it when I passed my final exams and became a Chartered Accountant.

Rose seemed to accept and understand that my social life was confined mainly to weekends.

I WAS CHATTING to Rose at the office during one of the breaks and she asked me if I would like to call at her parents' home for tea, the following Sunday. This was the first time I had been asked.

'My parents would like to meet you properly,' she said.

It was quite clear to me that I was being put on the spot but I instantly told Rose that I would be pleased to come. I had already made up my mind about her and I didn't resent Mr and Mrs Turner wishing to get to know me.

I had by this time bought a Capri scooter from the proceeds of my insurance claim regarding the write-off of my B.S.A. sports car. A bit of a comedown, I thought, but at least I had mobility at a modest cost.

On arriving at Rose's home, I was greeted by Mr Turner at the garden gate. 'You can put your scooter at the side of the house,' he said.

I quickly removed my helmet and gloves and wheeled my scooter along the narrow path, looking at the garden as I went.

Mr Turner was obviously a keen gardener. On either side of the path were busy Lizzies, geraniums and roses, making a magnificent display and a riot of colour.

As I followed Mr Turner to the rear of the house and the kitchen door, Mrs Turner appeared. She joined her husband and myself in the small garden.

The lawn was neatly mowed and there were dwarf conifers surrounding it. In the centre of the lawn was a granite bird bath where I could see two blackbirds splashing and singing contentedly.

In one corner of the garden was a small shed, freshly creosoted, and in the opposite corner a greenhouse. I could see tomatoes and grapes through the panes of glass. Propped against the shed was a man's cycle. Mr Turner was a keen cyclist.

Rose peeped through the kitchen curtains and soon joined us. We spent five minutes or so looking at the garden and then went into the kitchen.

The rear of the house faced south and the sun was streaming in. The kitchen was brightly decorated with light blue ceramic tiles running halfway up the walls. A quantity of food and drink was spread over the table.

'Make yourself at home, Tom,' said Rose's mother, Lucy. Mrs Turner, a spotlessly-clean-looking lady, had on a quality cream dress with a small flowered pattern. She spoke to Mr Turner. 'Jim, take Tom's jacket and put it in the hall.'

Mr Turner was, as I've said, a small, wiry man, much shorter than Mrs Turner; he had bright sparkling eyes like Rose. His movements were quick and he spoke rapidly in a clipped way. I could see that Rose's parents were doing their best to make me welcome.

'Jim, have a word with Tom and Rose in the dining room, while I finish off getting the food ready,' said Mrs Turner.

I was always taught by my parents to respect my elders and I continued to address Rose's parents by calling them Mr and Mrs Turner. They did not suggest me calling them by their forenames.

Mr Turner turned towards me. 'How's your studying going, Tom?' he asked.

I knew Mr and Mrs Turner would be anxious to learn as much about me as possible, and I didn't mind being questioned. They wanted to see what kind of a young man their only daughter was going out with.

'My studies are going well and I am anxious to take my final exams,' I replied. The words 'Chartered Accountant' seem to convey to some people something very special and on reflection, I agreed it did mean attaining very high standards of work to become qualified.

Mrs Turner came from the kitchen into the dining room with a tray on which were placed two steaming plates, one of which she placed in front of me.

'I hope you like chicken, Tom,' she said.

I stared at my plate. There was enough food for two people. I would never eat it all.

We soon settled down, and I found talking to Mr and Mrs Turner very easy. Usually, I was quiet with people I did not know well, but I soon found that I was talking about a number of subjects. This I put down to the relaxing atmosphere created by my hosts. They were good, kind, considerate people and Rose was lucky to have them as parents.

When we'd finished our meal, Mr Turner turned towards the drinks cabinet. The dining room was partitioned off from the lounge. There was a sideboard, the drinks cabinet, a large table and six chairs.

'Like a liqueur, Tom?' asked Mr Turner. I thought hard about the last time I had drunk alcohol. 'A very small one, please.' I replied. 'You have probably heard about my office party celebrating my twenty-first birthday.'

A small lead cut-crystal glass was handed to me with the only comment: 'Take a few sips and see what you think.'

The quantity of liqueur was very small and did not harm me. In fact, I enjoyed it.

I was left chatting to Mr Turner whilst Mrs Turner and Rose cleared the table; I could hear them in the kitchen washing up. After about twenty minutes, they reappeared.

'Let's go and sit in the lounge,' said Mrs Turner.

We made our way to the comfortable room which was tastefully decorated and full of high quality ornaments and pictures. Looking round, I could see that the family liked tasteful possessions.

After a while, Mr and Mrs Turner rose from their armchairs. The time was about eight thirty and as it was Sunday, I didn't want to leave it too late before travelling home on my scooter.

'We'll leave you two young people to have a chat for a while. The crockery needs putting away,' said Rose's mother. She and Mr Turner moved towards the kitchen.

I was sitting on the settee with Rose and suddenly it dawned on me that this was one of the few times we had been alone together.

Rose, who was sitting close to me, suddenly looked coyly at me. Instinctively, I knew that she wanted me to kiss her and I responded straight away.

She had just a trace of lipstick on and her lips were soft and yielding. My heart started pounding and I know my pulse was racing.

We were in the middle of a passionate embrace when suddenly Rose's mother peeped around the door.

'I see you young people are enjoying yourselves,' she said with a gleam in her eyes. We sprang apart. 'Would you like a cup of coffee, Tom?' she asked.

My face felt hot, and really I wanted a cold drink and perhaps a cold flannel, but I soon agreed to her offer.

Mrs Turner quickly disappeared. Rose was smiling and then started to giggle. 'You enjoyed that, didn't you?' she asked, teasing me. I may have enjoyed the moment but I knew she had too.

A few minutes later, Rose's parents came through with the coffee. Eventually I decided it was time for me to depart.

'Thanks for a lovely meal. I really enjoyed your company,' I told them. Mr and Mrs Turner looked pleased as they closed the front door and left Rose to see me off.

Rose held my jacket and helped me put it on. I strapped my helmet on and sat astride my scooter, starting the engine. 'I do like you a lot, Tom,' she said. She kissed me and I rode down the driveway on to the road. She waved to me and her face spoke volumes. I knew she was happy.

As I rode home, I could not help thinking what a lucky chap I was. I was in good health, on the way to becoming a Chartered Accountant and had a lovely girlfriend.

My dreams were coming true.

Once I qualified I could start my own business. Capital would be required, but surely the bank would assist me. Rose could be my secretary. She could type and do clerical work. All these thoughts were buzzing through my head.

I put my scooter away in my father's garage, thinking what a very special day it had been.

The next day at the office, Rose came quickly over to me. 'Mum and Dad were so pleased to see you yesterday,' she said eagerly.

I had obviously made a good impression with them. It seemed my plans were fitting into place just right.

'Mum and Dad wondered if you would like to come with us to The London Palladium in six weeks' time,' she added.

I thought I would have preferred to have gone with Rose alone, but I did not want to offend her parents, so I readily agreed.

Mr Turner was quite wealthy (he had his own hardware shop) and had told Rose that he wished to pay for all travelling expenses and the cost of the theatre tickets.

Although I was still studying hard, my social life was improving and I was becoming very optimistic about my future.

THERE WAS GREAT consternation at the office. One of our clients, Mr Cave, a builder, had been caught defrauding the Inland Revenue. He was not one of the clients I had dealt with, but as part of my practical experience, I was to attend the Inland Revenue's office with Mr Davis.

Defrauding the Inland Revenue is a very serious matter. It had come to the Revenue's notice that Mr Cave had been receiving large sums of cash for building work and not declaring them. The Revenue had found out, by seeing another taxpayer's records which had clearly shown the cash payments to Mr Cave, whose own records showed no signs of the sums.

Mr Davis and I arrived at the Tax Office a few minutes before the appointed time and found Mr Cave in the waiting room.

He was in his working clothes and had not bothered to change, presumably coming direct from the building site.

Mr Davis had interviewed him and ascertained that he had clearly defrauded the Revenue and was going to be subject to additional tax, penalties and interest; the risk of imprisonment was there, too.

Luckily, I was to be a spectator, but I could not help feeling a bit nervous.

Mr Cave was a stocky man, about forty years of age, unshaven, with a large bushy black moustache. His hair was receding. His jeans, open-neck shirt and boots were spattered with mud.

He was a bulldog of a man and as I followed him and Mr Davis up the staircase to the District Inspector's office, I wondered what would transpire at the interview.

Mr Davis knocked on the Inspector's door and it was opened by a small, chubby man with a neat, clipped moustache; he wore a smart, dark grey suit.

He shook hands with Mr Davis and I was briefly introduced. I noticed he did not shake hands with Mr Cave.

Three chairs were arranged in a row, opposite Mr Sand, the District Inspector. We sat down.

There was a knock on the door and a thin man with glasses appeared.

'This is Mr Palmer, an Inspector from the Investigation Department and he will be taking notes,' said Mr Sand. We were introduced and the interview commenced.

Mr Cave admitted that he had received large sums of cash and not recorded them.

'You admit then that you have defrauded the Revenue, Mr Cave?' asked Mr Sand.

'I damn well said so.' Mr Cave turned purple and looked extremely aggressive. He thumped his fist on the desk when he spoke and his eyes were wide open and fierce looking. At one time, I thought he was going to attack Mr Sand.

Mr Davis tried to calm Mr Cave, saying, 'We are here to resolve the situation, not make it worse.'

Figures of the monies omitted from Mr Cave's records had been prepared by Mr Davis and agreed with the Inland Revenue. What had to be decided, at this stage, were the penalties. The tax and interest could be exactly quantified.

'In view of the seriousness of the offence, the maximum penalties will be sought by the Revenue,' said Mr Sand. 'Whether a prison sentence will be appropriate will be decided at a later date. That is the end of the interview.'

Mr Cave rose to his feet. He was trembling and walked slowly to the office door. I followed him, and Mr Davis was left to discuss the situation with the two Revenue Inspectors.

The interview had been a real eye-opener for me. Many people think accountants have boring jobs but the episode had shown the assumption to be erroneous.

I later determined that Mr Cave did not go to prison. He may have deserved to have done so, as he had deliberately set out to defraud the Revenue; but the large sum of money representing tax, interest and penalties virtually ruined his business.

A few years later, he was made bankrupt and ended up working as a labourer, so in a way justice had been done.

L EAVING THE OFFICE at nine forty-five one morning, I strolled at a leisurely pace along the high street.

My appointment to see Mr Jackson, a retailer of beds, was at ten, and therefore I had plenty of time. I called at Mr Kent's shop to buy some humbugs, some of my favourite sweets, and sucked one, putting the remainder in my briefcase.

Mr Fred Jackson was a friend of mine, about my age, and we got on well, although he used to be a 'Rocker'; he wore a leather jacket and rode a powerful motorcycle, whilst I rode a scooter.

In the 1960s, there were gangs of Rockers and Mods who often conflicted, their lifestyles being different. The Rockers presented an image to the public of leather-jacketed youths dashing about on powerful motorcycles, whereas the Mods usually dressed neatly and mostly rode scooters.

Even though Fred Jackson's lifestyle was different from mine, there was some basic common understanding between us; we simply liked each other. He collected motorcycles and had about ten, and one of his main hobbies was tinkering about with these machines; being covered in oil and dirt didn't seem to worry him at all. In fact, he revelled in it. I had been to his home on several occasions, and he delighted in showing me his motorcycles, some of which were rare.

He had tried diverse jobs, including being a taxi driver, selling jewellery at a market, and a commission agent for a firm selling vacuum cleaners. All of these ventures had failed. I had prepared accounts for him and each time they showed a pitiful financial position.

It was clear to me that Fred Jackson was a poor salesman, but he could not accept the fact.

He had been trading from a small shop in the high street, buying and selling modestly-priced beds for about six months, and I was calling to examine his records, to see if he was making a profit or not.

He had rented a lock-up shop, and had called to see me at the office when he commenced trading. He was full of enthusiasm.

I had seen it all before with his previous ventures, but I hoped that this one was to be different. Reaching his shop, I opened the door and walked in.

Fred Jackson was talking to a customer and he looked up and said, 'Won't be long, Tom, and I'll be with you. Go through to the office.'

His office consisted of a cubicle at one end of a large room. I squeezed past rows of beds and headboards and sat down to wait for him.

After a few minutes he appeared. 'Managed to sell another bed,' he announced. 'Had to give a discount of five pounds, though.' He laughed loudly.

He was a large man – about fourteen stone, compared to my ten stone – and he towered over me. His jeans were torn and his soiled shirt barely covered his pot belly.

I don't believe he had shaved for several days and he rubbed his stubbly chin thoughtfully. His dark brown eyes looked at me from a round, jovial face.

The fact that he seldom seemed to succeed in his business ventures didn't seem to worry him; he lived for the day.

Handing me a steaming mug containing coffee which he had quickly made as he was talking to me, he sat down and produced his daily takings and expenses book.

He didn't have a bank account. There had been some trouble with a local bank when he had overdrawn his account without authority, so he had never bothered to try and open another account at a different bank.

The front door banged. 'I'll leave you to it, Tom,' he said, and went off to see a customer who was peering at a double divan.

I examined his accounts book and it did not take me long to see that he was running the business on a shoestring.

Five minutes later, he trotted back, his pot belly wobbling. 'Sold another bed.' He beamed and rubbed his hands together.

'How much did the bed cost you?' I asked.

'No idea,' he replied. He rummaged through some invoices and delivery notes and after a few minutes produced the relevant document.

Although he was pleased that he had sold the bed, his face dropped momentarily when I informed him that the discounted sale price was less than the price he had paid for it.

Suddenly his eyes lit up. 'Not to worry. I'll make it up on the next one.'

I explained to him that to make a reasonable profit from the shop, the mark-up on each bed had to be a certain percentage, otherwise he would be running his business at a loss.

'Whatever you say, Tom,' he said, laughing. I think his mind was elsewhere – still thinking about his motorcycles.

Coming away from the shop after making a few notes for the file, I was somewhat disappointed. Another Fred venture down the drain.

A few months later at the office, there was a call for me. 'Fred Jackson here. I've given up buying and selling beds – no money in it. I'm going to go back to the market trading – selling fish.'

Another financial disaster, I thought, replacing the receiver on its cradle.

SITTING IN MR Brian Crane's office, surrounded by his receipts, invoices and books, I was in one of my reflective moods.

Accountancy to some people may appear to be dull but although there are long periods of routine work, there are often very interesting episodes.

Mr Crane owned a grocery store which had been converted from the old-fashioned counter system to the modern, open-plan, self-service mode.

I had been called in by him to examine his bookkeeping system and particularly to consider the problem of his reduced profit, since the introduction of the self-service system. He had unfortunately been losing goods through pilferage.

He had a worried look as he told me, 'I have begun to wish I had kept the old-fashioned counter system. At least I had full control over my stock.'

Mr Crane was about forty years old, a chubby man, neat in his appearance. His dark brown eyes looked at me sadly. He always wore an immaculate, white overall when working in the shop.

'I've had installed a two-way mirror to help solve the problem of pilferage.' He pointed to the closed, mirrored door of the small office.

The office was at the far end of the shop which had shelves on the walls and also in the centre of the floor.

Other than Mrs Crane, who worked in the shop part-time, he employed two assistants: a young lady, short, petite and cheerful; the customers liked her; and a young man, thin with a sallow complexion. He had been employed by Mr Crane directly on leaving school.

Mr Crane continued to discuss the situation with me. 'I know I'm losing stock but catching people stealing is difficult. I've instructed my assistants to be wary but if they are serving, and a number of customers come into the shop, the problem is not easy to solve.

'There are several customers I know who are taking goods and not paying for them, but I have to catch them with the goods outside my shop to enable me to prosecute them. If this pilferage goes on for much longer, I will seriously consider reverting to the old-fashioned counter system. The goods will be behind the counter and I will be able to keep an eye on them.'

He looked crestfallen and I knew he had spent considerable sums of money converting the shop.

Whilst speaking to Mr Crane, I was looking through the two-way mirror.

A middle-aged female customer was putting a tin of salmon into a pushchair containing a young child. There were other goods in the shop's wire basket but the tin of salmon had been put directly into the pushchair. I pointed the woman out to Mr Crane.

Instead of leaping out of his chair as I expected, he sat back, watching the customer. 'Yes, I saw her too. That woman is a thief but I haven't been able to catch her with any unpaid-for goods outside my shop,' he told me.

'Well, I certainly saw her put a tin of salmon in the pushchair,' I said.

'Perhaps this is time for action.' Mr Crane rose slowly from his chair. He was a courteous and refined man and hated disputes of any kind but his business was deteriorating, and he was being forced to act. There were several prominent signs in the shop saying 'Thieves will be prosecuted', but obviously some shoppers took no notice.

I watched Mr Crane as he followed the middle-aged woman out of the shop. She had paid for the goods in the wire basket, but not the tin of salmon.

I had made it plain to Mr Crane that I would prefer not to be involved and I stood by the door as an onlooker.

Outside on the pavement, Mr Crane was remonstrating with the customer. 'I saw you put a tin of salmon into the pushchair, but the till roll doesn't show any payment.'

By this time the woman, who was very poorly dressed, thin and haggard, was crying. The tears were flooding down her cheeks.

She picked up the child, who looked frightened. 'I haven't taken the tin of salmon,' she said vehemently.

Mr Crane rummaged through the pushchair. There was no tin of salmon, yet we had clearly seen the woman pick it up. Perhaps she had put it back on the shelf. No, Mr Crane and I had watched her very carefully through the two-way mirror as she walked towards the cash till.

Suddenly he spoke. 'What's this, then?' He had in his hand the tin of salmon.

The tin had been concealed beneath a false bottom in the pushchair. He had only seen the tin of salmon because the false bottom had not been secured properly, the flap being slightly ajar.

By this time, the woman was extremely distressed and the young child was crying as well.

'I should call the police,' Mr Crane told the woman, whose face was twitching uncontrollably. She was pleading, 'I'll never do it again.'

He was clearly undecided, but seeing the state of the woman, he made a decision. 'I don't want you back in my shop again.'

The woman, trembling, put the child into the pushchair and quickly walked away from the shop.

'I know the family, Mr Read,' he explained. 'The husband is out of work and there are five children. I just could not bring myself to call the police.' He looked sad as he spoke to me.

Collecting my working papers and writing implements, I put them in my briefcase.

'I've made up my mind, Mr Read.' Mr Crane looked strained. 'I'm going back to the old-fashioned counter system. I made more money and there was much less worry. This open-plan self-service system is too tempting for some people.'

Shaking hands with him, I said goodbye and returned to my office, thinking he was probably right.

The episode had upset me as well as Mr Crane. I had great difficulty in concentrating on my work.

A few weeks later, there was a telephone call for me. 'Mr Read, this is Mr Crane. I've reverted to the old-fashioned counter system. I know I've lost money incurred in modernising the shop, but I feel much happier, and as far as I can determine, the pilferage has stopped.'

When he brought his records in for the annual preparation of his accounts, I was not surprised to see that his gross profit had indeed recovered to its former healthy ratio.

With hindsight, it was clear that his shop was too small for the open-plan self-service system, but the most important point was that he was again happy in his business.

MY STUDYING WAS progressing well but in addition to the correspondence course, I had to attend a number of lectures in London.

The lectures were excellent and summarised essential points quickly, thus often eliminating many hours of perusing textbooks.

I was still using my pedal cycle, partly for exercise and partly for economic reasons. Shortage of cash seemed to be a constant worry. Rather than ride my scooter into the centre of London, I would sometimes use my cycle.

One day I had to attend a very important lecture and decided to travel to London, by cycle; I had done it before, without any problem.

To a young man in good health, cycling a distance of twenty miles was no effort at all.

I set off and arrived at the lecture rooms about fifteen minutes before the lecture was due to start.

As I had done previously, I locked my cycle to an iron railing at the rear of the building, where the lectures were held, and joined the crowded room with the other students.

The lecturer was very coherent and I learnt a considerable amount, taking notes as he spoke.

After three hours, the lecture ended and I walked out to the rear of the building to retrieve my cycle. I was horrified to see that it had been stolen. All that remained was the lock and the severed chain.

Being a cycling enthusiast, I had bought a specialist racing cycle, handmade, which was worth a considerable amount of money.

At that moment, however, all I could think of was how I was going to get home. Looking in my pockets, I found some loose change – insufficient to pay my fare. There was only one thing I could think of at the time. I was panicking somewhat.

Rather than risk the possible embarrassment of returning to the lecture rooms and explaining my predicament, I decided to call at the police station, which I knew was close by.

I located the police station and slowly climbed the stairs.

Being a trusting individual and perhaps at that time naïve, it had never entered my head that my cycle would be stolen. I had locked it merely as a formality.

The police sergeant at the counter looked up. 'What can I do for you, young man?'

I explained what had happened and was asked to give a description of the cycle.

'Do you think I will get my cycle back?' I queried.

'Little if any chance,' replied the police sergeant. 'This type of crime is happening all the time in London and we rarely recover stolen cycles.'

I explained to him about the fact that I did not have enough money to get home.

He was a kind chap, about fifty years of age, broad shouldered and tall. He had seen it all before. 'No trouble whatsoever,' he said sympathetically. The funds were soon provided and I signed the receipt. 'Send us the cash when you get home,' said the police sergeant and walked away.

Travelling home by train and bus, I felt sick with the thought that somebody had my prize cycle. It had become part of me during the last six years. However, there was absolutely nothing I could do about it, and I made my way home in a depressed state.

When I got home I explained the position to my parents. They were sorry for me and promised to assist me financially to buy another cycle.

That episode was the first of many which demonstrated to me that to trust everybody was naïve. I had learnt one lesson the hard way; but that of course was part of growing up.

MOST OF THE clients I had to deal with were situated close to the office, but as I had my own transport, albeit a scooter, I was being allowed to travel further afield to clients on my own.

Mr Fletcher was a gentleman farmer. His family had owned one thousand acres of land for many years.

I had prepared his accounts at the office for three years. When I saw him he asked me if I would like to visit his farm.

He usually brought his records into the office but speaking to him on the telephone, I arranged that I would collect his records from his farmhouse and spend time looking round the farm. There is a great advantage sometimes in seeing a client's business premises, as this assists the accountant in preparing accounts, especially from incomplete records.

Mr Fletcher's farm was about thirty miles from the office.

He had resisted selling part of his land for building and continued to grow wheat, barley, oats and beans and also kept some livestock, mainly pigs.

I found the farmhouse quite easily from the directions he had given me over the telephone, and stopped my scooter near a large wooden gate which bore the sign, FLETCHER'S FARM.

Opening the gate, which was heavy and had a leather strap securing it to the right-hand post, I wheeled my scooter through. I was careful to shut the gate after me.

Wheeling my scooter along the muddy drive, which had some shingle scattered over it, I soon faced the farmhouse. It was surrounded by large trees, some of which I recognised as oaks and sycamores. There were a number of rooks circling a rookery, making a considerable noise.

The farmhouse was fronted by a large shingle driveway. I approached the front door which was huge and appeared to have been made from oak. There was no bell, but a large brass knocker in the shape of a fox. After banging the knocker a few times, I could hear footsteps approaching and the door opened.

Mr Fletcher stood there, a man of about seventy years of age, but still very upright. He was tall – about six foot three. Overalls covered his gaunt frame. Looking at me intently from steel blue eyes set in a long, weather-beaten face, he was the first to speak. 'Glad you could come, Mr Read.' Politeness was one of his qualities which I really appreciated.

He was a wealthy man, but he treated people, whatever their jobs, as equals.

'Come through,' he said. 'You have never met Mrs Fletcher, have you?' She appeared, as we were walking along a large, wide, high passage.

Physically, Mrs Fletcher was a complete contrast to her husband. She was only five feet tall, a thin lady, neat and tidy with grey hair drawn tightly back and pinned. She greeted me warmly and directly asked me if I would like a cup of tea.

'Whilst you are making the tea, I'll show Mr Read some of the livestock,' said Mr Fletcher.

I followed him through a large room, which I noticed was the kitchen, outside to a yard.

The farmhouse was surrounded by fields of wheat and other crops, which seemed to stretch for miles. Although it was a hazy day, the sun peeped through, sending down cascades of light. The colours were breathtaking, the ears of wheat glinting in the sunshine.

What a lovely place to live and work, I thought. I knew farmers worked hard, but they were surely compensated by nature at her best.

I followed Mr Fletcher, and we reached some outbuildings. He was mainly an arable farmer, but liked to keep a few animals.

As he was about to open the door of one of the outbuildings, a Labrador appeared, wagging his tail. He was a magnificent looking dog with a beautiful shiny coat – the picture of health. He licked his master's hand with obvious pleasure. 'I've had him six years now and he's been no trouble at all,' said Mr Fletcher, stroking the dog affectionately.

He opened the door, and the sickening smell hit me like a brick wall.

I looked in. Various stalls were set out, about half a dozen, and each contained one or two pigs. Mr Fletcher did not seem to notice the smell and proceeded to empty some swill into the feeding troughs.

The pigs were squealing with delight and soon gobbled down the food.

'Do you like pigs?' asked Mr Fletcher.

'I've never seen any close up before,' I replied. I didn't want to offend him and left it at that.

'I've won cups for some of these,' he said proudly, closing the door securely.

The next building contained an old horse with sunken eyes. Even to my untrained eyes, I could see that he was old. He looked at Mr Fletcher, who produced a lump of sugar, from his coat pocket. I realised there was a great mutual affection. 'I can't bring myself to put him down. He used to draw the plough many years ago but I use a tractor, and in any case he's a pet now.' He continued to stroke the horse.

After looking at the barn containing the combine harvester, tractor and other implements, we walked towards the grain store. A large barn was used to store the grain and I stared at a huge pile of it. 'This lot will be gone by the end of next week,' Mr Fletcher said.

We walked back to the farmhouse where Mrs Fletcher had refreshing cups of tea waiting for us. She was kind enough to provide some home-made scones, covered in butter and jam.

I looked at Mr and Mrs Fletcher. Their children were grown up and had left the farmhouse but they were still happy and content. I could see that by their faces. They were communing with nature, and for many people what better life was there?

My long chat with Mr and Mrs Fletcher was over and I had not at any time mentioned financial matters. Mr Fletcher's records were always well kept and I took them away with me, picturing the farm in my mind.

Saying farewell to Mr and Mrs Fletcher, who were smiling, I walked towards the gate, mounted my scooter and rode off.

I WAS LOOKING forward to the trip to The London Palladium with Rose and her parents. Flanagan and Allen and The Crazy Gang were on at the theatre. I had often seen them on television, but never live. In fact, I had never been to a theatre before.

The Saturday on which we were going to The Palladium arrived and I started putting on my best clothes; my radio was playing a popular Beatles record. Shortly they were to take the world by storm, including the United States.

I looked in the mirror. The result was satisfying. At that time, I had an elegant light grey suit. I used to have my suits made to measure, by a tailor, who worked from a shed which was situated in his back garden. A brilliant white shirt and a light blue silk tie – a birthday present – and a pair of well-made black shoes completed the picture. I was not vain, but looking in the mirror, I was happy with what I saw. Making sure I shaved thoroughly, and using a good quality aftershave and cologne, I wandered downstairs, to wait for Mr Turner to collect me.

He had an Austin Somerset car and he promised to call for me at 6 p.m.

At six precisely, the doorbell rang. Mr Turner was standing there. 'Ready, Tom?' he asked.

I told my parents that I was going and walked with Mr Turner to his car. He kept the vehicle immaculate; it was black, highly polished, and as far as I could see, blemish-free.

We soon arrived at Rose's home and she and her mother quickly got into the car. They seemed excited by the occasion.

Mr Turner was not going to drive directly into London, but was going to leave his car at the official parking area outside Hayford Station.

Having parked the car, we were soon on the platform waiting for the tube train to arrive. Rose and Mrs Turner were talking nineteen to the dozen, and I was talking to Mr Turner.

The journey did not take long, and we were soon queuing outside the theatre. After about ten minutes, we were inside, found our seats and settled down to watch the show.

I had always thought that The Palladium was a very large theatre, but looking round I soon discovered it was not that big. There was a very cheerful atmosphere and Rose, her parents and myself were soon enjoying ourselves. This was a very special show, and watching it live was nothing like watching it on television. The Crazy Gang were up to their usual antics and I could understand why they had remained popular for so long. There was magic in the air.

The time passed so quickly and then the show was over. We soon found ourselves outside the theatre, walking towards the station. On the way home on the train, I sat next to Rose, but she was quiet. Perhaps it was because of the presence of her parents, I thought.

Glancing at Rose as she sat beside me, I noticed that she had put on some weight, since I first met her. The train was not crowded and there were one or two other girls sitting nearby. I could not help comparing Rose with those girls, who looked petite.

Trying to put the thoughts out of my mind, I told myself it was personality which mattered most; however the thoughts lingered.

Rose was then about a stone heavier than me. This was the first time that a slight doubt had crept into my mind about her, but I quickly tried to dispel it. After all, I told myself, there was the special chemistry which seemed to cancel anything else.

Mr Turner took Rose and her mother home in his car. They waved to me as Mr Turner turned his car to drive me home.

'Did you enjoy the show, Tom?' he asked me.

'It was splendid,' I replied. 'Thanks for taking me.'

Although I had, indeed, enjoyed the show, I was left with some thinking to do. I had made up my mind that Rose was the only girl for me, but why was there this slight doubt creeping in?

Deciding to shelve the matter, I resolved to give it some in-depth thought later in the week.

On the Monday following the trip to The Palladium Rose seemed her usual cheerful self. She was chatting to the other office girls, telling them about the show. As I looked at her my doubts began to fade. She was still the only girl for me.

H AVING COMPLETED MR Harding's annual accounts, I made arrangements to return his records to him.

Very seldom did he come into the office and now, having moved out of the area some forty miles away, he still expected me to visit him.

My scooter was being serviced. I found it would be cheaper to hire a car than to travel by public transport, so I contacted one of our local clients, Mr Brown, who ran a car hire business. I knew him well, as I prepared his accounts for him.

I telephoned him and he quickly said, 'Come over, Mr Read, and pick the car you would like to hire.'

I immediately walked to the car hire firm, a distance of only a few hundred yards. Mr Brown, a friendly, stocky man with heavy-rimmed spectacles, was standing outside his office waiting for me.

Inspecting the rows of new Ford cars, I chose a bright blue Anglia, as I thought I would be able to handle it quite well.

'Have you driven an Anglia before?' Mr Brown asked, looking at me kindly.

'I've only driven my father's car, an Austin Devon, and an old sports car which I owned for a short time,' I replied.

'These Anglias are very easy to drive,' he said, reversing the car I had chosen on to the forecourt. He quickly showed me the gear changes and left me to drive the vehicle away, adding, 'When you return the car just pop the keys through the letter box.'

Never having driven a new car before, I was slightly apprehensive. I put the gear lever into first, and moved off. The visibility was extremely good, the rear window sloping inwards and I immediately felt confident, driving down the main road towards the office with ease. I parked the car down a side street, near the office.

I reported to Mr Johnson that I was going to see Mr Harding. The managing clerk merely looked up, nodded and lowered his head, continuing with his work.

Driving the Anglia was a pleasure. The steering was light and I vowed that on qualifying, I would purchase a new Ford car.

I soon reached Mr Harding's old cottage, which was situated in a small picturesque village in the country. Parking the Anglia in the leafy lane I looked across at the building. It was made of lath and plaster and it had a thatched roof; I could see that it had been well cared for. Opening a small wooden gate, painted white, I approached the front door; the garden was a blaze of colour: roses, fuchsias, marigolds, geraniums and masses of plants which I could not identify. A winding cinder path led me to the front door, also painted white. On either side were two urns; each contained beautiful red and white fuchsias in full bloom. Swinging slightly in the breeze was a hanging basket full of lobelias, busy Lizzies and yet another fuchsia, a resplendent mauve and white.

There was no bell, but a small brass door knocker.

As I was about to knock, a large black cat appeared, peeping from behind the corner of the cottage; it purred contentedly and rubbed itself against my legs, arching its back as it did so. I knocked at the door.

A small woman of about sixty years of age opened the door and peered at me. She was very thin and her weather-beaten face was etched with lines. Her light blue eyes were kind as she greeted me. 'Come in, Mr Read,' she said, 'I'm Mrs Harding.'

I followed her along a narrow hall which was covered in grey lino and we reached the large kitchen bathed in sunshine. The kitchen door led to a large garden comprising a wide expanse of lawn, edged with flower beds, shrubs and trees. At the bottom of the garden I could see a large wooden workshop.

As I was looking around, Mr Harding came out of the workshop. He shook hands with me warmly. He was one of nature's gentlemen. Kindness was one of his qualities and I had never known him to say anything detrimental about anyone.

'Come through,' he said. He spoke in a whisper. Years of working as a blacksmith had damaged his respiratory system, and at times I had difficulty in understanding him.

Following him into the workshop, I noticed a marked deterioration in his physical condition. He was stooped, and had lost weight since I had last seen him. Looking over his shoulder at me, his thin bony face creased into a smile.

Some years ago, he had ceased to have anything to do with horses. Most of the local farmers had tractors and he was therefore faced with retiring altogether, or diversifying. There was a large demand for ornamental iron and steel gates; therefore he had decided to use his skills accordingly.

He proudly showed me the results of his efforts. Rows upon rows of gates were leaning against the sides of the workshop, some newly-painted, mostly in shiny black, and others primed and awaiting their final coats.

'That's splendid, Mr Harding,' I said, listening to him telling me of his success in selling gates.

'My order book is full,' he commented proudly.

However, my concern for him was his health. After all these years of scraping for a living, financially he was doing very well; but what was the use of money without good health?

The furnace was red-hot and Mr Harding proceeded to show me how he treated the metal and bent it into shape.

I stood back, away from the heat and the sparks. He lifted the metal up and plunged it into a pail of water. Perspiration was on his brow; his face, neck and chest were red.

'Time for a drink,' he said. I followed him to the cottage.

Mrs Harding was waiting for us. She knew that I seldom drank beer, a favourite of her husband's, and had made me a cup of coffee. 'Here you are,' she said. She smiled contentedly as she handed me the drink.

I sat down on one of the four chairs surrounding a small metal table and asked, 'Did you make these, Mr Harding?' He looked proud as I praised him for his efforts in making the ornamental table and chairs.

Sitting there with Mr and Mrs Harding, breathing in the fresh country air and listening to their pleasant tales, I had no desire to move, but I knew I soon had to travel back to the office. Reluctantly I rose from my chair and commented that I would have to be going.

They saw me to the gate. 'Nice car,' said Mr Harding, looking at the bright blue Anglia.

'I wish it was mine,' I commented. 'I've only hired it for the day.'

I said my farewells, thinking, If only all my clients were like Mr and Mrs Harding...

The drive home was enjoyable; I stopped at a lay-by to have my sandwiches and some coffee from a flask.

On reaching home, I parked the Anglia on the driveway and went indoors.

'How did you get on, Tom?' My mother was always interested in my work and listened to me as I related the day's events. As she worked in a chocolate factory part-time in the evenings, to supplement the family's income, I really appreciated her efforts, and also my father's.

I vowed their sacrifices would be repaid, when I became a Chartered Accountant.

There was no doubt in my mind that I would achieve my ambition, as I had constantly obtained very good results in the correspondence course; I was looking forward to taking my final exams.

The following day, I returned the Anglia to the hire firm and ruefully I looked back. I wished I could have had a new car like that, instead of using my scooter. I consoled myself, however, that the time would come.

I PICKED UP the internal telephone receiver in the office.

'Miss Williams for you,' said the receptionist.

'How can I help you, Miss Williams?' I asked.

'Would you be kind enough to call to see me? I am having difficulty in balancing my daily takings book,' she told me. She seemed somewhat concerned.

A mutually agreeable time for me to call to see her was fixed for the following day.

Miss Williams was a retired music teacher and ran a Dance School – Ballroom and Latin American – during the weekdays and at weekends. The place where she taught dancing was not far from the office.

Climbing the staircase to the dance floor, which was situated over two shops in the high street, I could hear a quickstep being played.

The music was quite loud and I heard Miss Williams shouting instructions to the pupils. On reaching the top of the staircase, I peered in.

There was a group of adults standing on the edge of the dance floor and Miss Williams was dancing with a huge man of about sixteen stone. She was clearly in charge and was actually pushing him into the correct positions. As she was only about nine stone, this required considerable effort on her part.

She had years of experience and knew exactly what she wanted to happen. The quickstep ended and the large man left the dance floor, perspiring profusely.

Looking across the floor, Miss Williams noticed me standing there. 'I'll be with you in a few minutes, Mr Read,' she shouted. 'Continue to practise the steps,' she said, motioning to the group of dancers and starting the record player.

She was a lady of about sixty years of age, greatly respected for her expertise in teaching dancing to adults and children; indeed, many of her pupils had attained very high standards, obtaining bronze, silver and gold medals.

I looked at her. Although small and slim, she was extremely strong and very confident in her abilities.

Following her to a small cubicle which was on the edge of the dance floor, I noticed her ramrod straight back, and her neat, short hairstyle; in fact everything about her was absolutely correct.

I had seen her dance on a number of occasions, and it was not surprising that many of her pupils achieved excellent results.

She showed me her daily takings book. I could see directly where the errors were occurring, and her eyes lit up. 'Each to their own, Mr Read,' she said.

She was very good at her vocation and she was appreciative of somebody like myself, who was well versed in accurate figure work.

'Are you interested in dancing?' Miss Williams looked directly at me, as she spoke. She had probably noticed me gazing at the couples as I walked towards the door.

'Well, yes,' I murmured.

'Did you say you were?' she asked.

I nodded and explained to her that my girlfriend, Rose, also might be interested in joining a dancing class; I promised to contact Miss Williams at a later date.

MY MOTHER HAD heard all about Rose, but she had never met her. For some reason, I kept putting off asking Rose home, but one day I was chatting to her in a park at lunchtime and suddenly she mentioned that she had never seen my parents. I arranged to pick her up on the following Saturday and take her to my home.

We had decided to go to a beginners' class at Miss Williams's Dance School at 7.30 p.m., and I picked Rose up from her parents' home at 6 p.m. I didn't know how my parents were going to react; were they going to like her or not?

Rose was looking, as usual, immaculate; she had on a yellow dress and a smart, light brown coat with a small fur collar.

Parking my scooter in the driveway, I made my way to the back door; Rose followed close behind me and suddenly we came face to face with my parents who were standing in the rear garden.

Seeing their faces, I knew instantly they were favourably impressed with Rose. She had this very special look which spoke volumes; quality speaks for itself, and she had it. My parents' eyes lit up as I introduced Rose to them.

'You will have to come to tea,' said my mother. She motioned Rose to sit on a chair in the kitchen.

Rose was a very confident young lady and was soon chatting to my parents in a very comfortable way; I could see that they felt at ease with her and I felt relieved.

'We had better be off,' I said, looking at my watch. 'The dance class starts at seven thirty.'

My parents said how pleased they were to meet Rose and I promised to make arrangements for her to come to tea.

When we were riding along on my scooter, Rose squeezed my waist. 'I really liked your mum and dad. Do you think they liked me?'

'I'm positive,' I replied enthusiastically.

As we were climbing the staircase to Miss Williams's dance class, I was having second thoughts about learning to dance; I had never danced a step in my life; supposing I made a fool of myself...

Rose had had a few lessons when she was a young girl at school and knew the rudiments of dancing.

We joined the beginners' class, having paid our fees to Miss Williams; she was, I noted, correctly recording the monies received.

She glanced at us. 'We are going to start with the waltz – some simple steps.'

Rose and I joined seven other couples, all of whom looked apprehensive. The sound of the waltz was clearly heard above the hullabaloo.

'Line up please – four couples each line,' said Miss Williams, using a very authoritative tone.

We all did as we were told.

'The gent holds the lady's back slightly above her waist with his right hand and holds the lady's right hand with his left hand. The lady places her left hand on the gent's right shoulder. The gent then pulls the lady gently towards him, until meeting in the middle,' she said.

By this time, I was already confused.

'We will try a few steps without the music,' said Miss Williams. 'Gent left foot forward, lady right foot back, gent right foot to the right, lady left foot to the left, then gent and lady both feet together. Repeat with alternative feet,' she continued, shouting the instructions.

Some couples were already tripping over each other. Rose was smiling and really enjoying herself. She didn't seem to mind if I was treading on her toes.

'Now for the music!' shouted Miss Williams.

This seems like hard work, I thought, again tripping over Rose's feet.

After a few attempts, most couples, including Rose and myself, were beginning to get the hang of it. Unfortunately, we found that when we came to a corner of the room, we could not turn.

'Don't worry about that. That comes with the next lesson,' said Miss Williams. She called the couples together. 'For the first lesson, that was quite good.' She had to give people encouragement, as otherwise they would be deterred from coming again.

As Rose and I were leaving the Dance School – the half-hour had gone so quickly – Miss Williams called us over and said, 'I think that you both will prove to be good dancers. Keep trying and you will be successful.'

We left the dance hall feeling happy. Dancing opens up a new social life, and we both went home chatting about the waltz, and looking forward to the next lesson.

'I enjoyed dancing with you, Rose,' I said. As we walked towards her front door, she looked back. Her eyes were bright and she was smiling again but I saw a look which I could not quite understand.

EVERY MONTH, I had to go and see Mr White, who owned a fish and chip shop in the high street. He was a very pleasant chap, but his trouble was he could not add up. Each time he added up a column of figures, he would get several different results.

It had become a recognised joke in the office whenever his records appeared, and to assist him, it was suggested by Mr Johnson to Mr White that monthly visits would be made to keep his records up to date and accurate.

Mr White was quite a character and well known about the town. Although he was in his late sixties, he was a fitness fanatic. Every morning he went for a six-mile jog. He swam at the local baths five times a week and cycled regularly. He also went dancing and had recently joined a yoga class. This was in addition to handling the shop with his wife, who was also in her late sixties.

As soon as I reached the shop door, the unmistakable aroma of fish and chips wafted towards me. My mouth started watering and I found myself licking my lips in anticipation.

I usually arranged my monthly visits for a time just before lunch, as I was always partial to fish and chips, especially when they were the best sold in the area.

Mr White looked at me over his thick-rimmed spectacles, which were covered in steam.

He was athletic, having broad shoulders and a straight back. His curly hair was jet-black, with not a streak of grey; I felt certain he did not dye his hair.

While he was serving a customer, he glanced again towards me. 'Go through, Mr Read. I'll be following you shortly.'

Mr White and Mrs White, who was at his side, had white overalls on, with just a few splashes of oil. I passed the fish and chips all golden and sizzling.

Walking along a dimly lit narrow hall, I turned left into a small room the size of a large cupboard. I had been there several times before and I knew it was Mr White's office.

The little cubby hole was a mess: clipboards with vouchers all out of date order; several books strewn about carelessly; a waste-paper bin lying on its side, its contents spilling over. Two old kitchen chairs fronted a battered table used as a desk.

As I picked up the books, Mr White appeared. 'Sorry to have kept you waiting. I see you have found the records.'

I sat down with him and went through the lists of monies received. An attempt had been made to add the figures up, but at the bottom of each page there were three or four different answers!

'I'll leave you to it,' he said and went back to his shop, relieved of the chore of the bookkeeping which he obviously disliked. As he turned away, he began to whistle cheerfully. He was returning to the part of his business that he liked.

Mr White was a prosperous man. His fish and chip shop flourished; he was popular with his customers. The fact that he couldn't add two and two together and get four didn't worry him unduly. He could employ the likes of me to get the bookkeeping side correct.

It did not take me long to balance his books and I was soon making my way out of the shop.

'Thank you for calling, Mr Read,' he said, and placed a newspaper-wrapped parcel in my hands. I knew by the heat and the lovely permeating aroma that it was his usual gift of fish and chips.

'Salt and vinegar added, as you like it.' His eyes glinted as he spoke. Here was a man happy at his work. 'See you next month, Mr Read,' he added.

His attention was immediately focused on his next customer. 'Can I tempt you with a nice piece of plaice instead of cod today?' He smiled down at a short, elderly lady just tall enough to look over the counter.

Strolling back to the office, I could not help reflecting what a full life Mr White was leading. He was living from day to day and enjoying every minute of it – except when it came to bookkeeping!

WHEN I GOT back to the office, I was introduced to a young man called Ken who was due to start work with us.

I had known for some time that he would be joining Davis & Co. as a new articled clerk. Up to that point, all I knew was his name and his age – nineteen, the same as Rose's – and that he had a motorcycle. I had gleaned this information from one of the typists who knew his family.

As soon as I met him, I liked him. He was about five feet nine inches, thickset, weighing about thirteen stone, and had dark, wavy hair and a cheeky smile. His nose had been broken. A thick, good quality leather jacket made him look smart.

'Pleased to meet you, Ken,' I said.

'Likewise,' he commented, grinning at me.

It was to be part of my office duties to teach Ken the rudiments of the practical side of accountancy; he had enrolled with the same correspondence course tutors as myself.

He looked particularly confident and I reckoned that Mr Johnson would not treat him as he had treated me. Ken looked as if he could look after himself; I later found out that his interests included boxing and judo.

Rose was standing by my desk when I was being introduced to Ken. I saw her look at him attentively and then turn away towards her own desk.

M Y FINAL EXAMS were approaching fast, and I was spending part of my weekends, as well as three to four hours every evening during the week, studying.

Although I tried to find some time for leisure, this was difficult in the weeks immediately prior to my exams.

All of a sudden, my exams, which were spread over several days, were virtually upon me. I had done my best with my studying and now I looked towards the first day of my exams.

'Good luck, Tom,' said my mother. She was standing at the front door as I walked towards my friend's car. I didn't want the worry of travelling to the exam centre in London and therefore I had arranged for my friend, Henry, who was on holiday, to take me, drop me off and collect me later when I had finished the exams for the day.

Henry and I did not say much during the journey to London. He was a good friend and realised that I wished to be quiet and had a lot on my mind.

We reached the exam centre in good time and after saying goodbye to Henry, I joined the other students, who were standing about outside. Some students were full of beans, chatting away; others were quiet like myself.

All of a sudden, the doors opened and we were walking into the large hall, where there were rows and rows of desks.

As one entered the hall, one had to give one's name and address and was then allocated a number of the desk which one had to occupy. Having taken my intermediate exams I knew the procedure and made my way to the desk with my number on it.

The exam papers were placed downwards and there were two adjudicators, one sitting at the head of the hall, the other wandering around.

'When I say "time", you may turn your papers over and commence,' said the adjudicator who was sitting at the top of the hall.

I looked at my watch – two minutes to go. One student near me fainted. He was assisted back to his seat. Another ran from the hall. For some reason, I did not then feel nervous at all. My preparation had been thorough, and I could have done no more.

'Time,' said the adjudicator. I turned the papers over.

The first subject was taxation, one of my best. Looking at the questions, I felt a surge of joy. My persistent studying had apparently paid off.

At least I knew I stood a good chance of answering the questions well; I began writing.

Several hours later, one of the adjudicators again called time and we had to immediately stop writing.

During the interval, several students left the hall and their desks remained vacant. There is intense pressure on students during the time leading up to exams, and some find that when the day eventually arrives, it proves to be just too much for them.

I wandered outside to get some fresh air.

Recognising a student I had spoken to on several occasions at lectures, I asked him how he fared. 'Terrible,' was his reply. 'I've been doing some cramming – six weeks prior to the exams – but I seem to have missed out on taxation somehow.' He looked despondent.

I continued sitting the exams. The procedures were the same for every subject and at the end of several days I felt drained, but I knew that I had done my best and it remained for me to wait for the results.

Rose was anxious to learn how I had fared taking my exams. I had felt quite confident after completing them, but it all depended on the examiners, so I was a bit evasive when replying. 'All right, I think. I've done my best,' I said. I left it like that. I had to sweat it out and wait for the results.

SEVERAL WEEKS PASSED and I got on with my office work. Suddenly the day arrived. This was it. Now was the time I found out whether I had passed my final exams or not.

I got up early. Sleep was impossible. Looking out of the front room window, I saw the postman approaching. The letter box clicked and there it was – the official envelope.

I picked it up and took it to my bedroom. My hands were shaking, but tearing open the envelope, I gazed down. I had passed – a Chartered Accountant.

I raced down to my parents. 'I've passed.'

They were soon celebrating and ringing several friends and relatives.

My old headmaster at the secondary school somehow got to know and telephoned me. He later wrote a letter to my parents, saying that the joy had welled up inside him. He was a very genuine and sincere man. I shall be eternally grateful to him, and to my English and mathematics teachers.

I would have a certificate for passing my final exams and a certificate of membership of the Institute of Chartered Accountants in England and Wales; I would also be entitled to use the letters ACA after my name. I felt ecstatic. The euphoria does wear off after a time but when I strode into the office however, I was still exuberant. There were congratulations all round, including some from Mr Davis and Mr Johnson, who looked at me in a different light from that day onwards.

As soon as I qualified, my salary was increased by Mr Davis to a reasonable figure, but it was made clear to me that he could not afford to pay me the money which I could expect to earn as a Chartered Accountant.

With his agreement, I decided to bide my time and look out for a suitable position. I would have liked to have immediately become self-employed and started my own business. I knew I was capable of it. I had proved to myself my abilities regarding the handling of clients.

When one becomes newly qualified, it is easy to think that running an accountancy practice is simple; of course it isn't, and qualification is just a beginning.

Nothing can replace the years of experience of being your own boss; there is no one to lean on; one survives or one does not.

Doing accountancy work is often fairly straightforward. Dealing with people and getting paid for the work done – that is a different matter.

After I passed my final exams I continued to go out regularly with Rose but I noticed she was becoming friendly with Ken.

They would tease each other and sometimes he would act roughly. I could not understand why Rose did not object to the rough treatment, but rather than get annoyed, she enjoyed it. 'Why do you let Ken tease you?' I once asked her.

She did not reply but looked away.

As I had now qualified, it seemed certain that it would not be long before my earnings would noticeably increase and I decided to acquire a new Ford Cortina on hire purchase.

This was quite a step for me to take, as my family always believed in the old maxim: 'If you don't have the cash, don't buy the goods.'

One of my friends, John Cook, had a brother who was a salesman for the Ford Motor Company and I made an appointment to see him at a local showroom.

'I have a new Ford Cortina that has just come in. Come and look at it,' he said. Mr Cook was not persuasive. He didn't have to be. I had already made up my mind. There it stood – light blue. I had to have it.

'Can I have a test drive?' I asked. Mr Cook, a salesman of many years' experience, knew I was going to purchase the car and therefore immediately agreed. 'Provided you keep the mileage under ten, certainly.'

I took the car round the block and returned, beaming. 'I'll have it.'

'Jolly good,' said Mr Cook. 'Come into the office and we will deal with the paperwork. I will arrange for the car to be undersealed free of charge.'

The total cost of the Cortina was six hundred and thirty pounds. I paid a small deposit, the balance being repayable over twenty-four months.

'When will the car be ready?' I enquired.

'Tomorrow,' was Mr Cook's reply.

I collected the car, as arranged.

I PICKED UP the internal telephone receiver and recognised the worried voice of Mr Jordan; he was a singer/entertainer at a night club and had recently been experiencing trouble with the local Tax Office.

He had received income tax assessment notices based upon estimated income figures, because he had not had accounts prepared for four years. The total tax being demanded amounted in total to two thousand pounds, about forty thousand pounds in today's money.

I had explained to him on several occasions that as soon as I received his full records – I had examined some for one year which he had brought to me a few weeks ago – I could probably substantially reduce his tax liability.

On interviewing him, I could see that he was highly strung; he was simply scared stiff of the Inland Revenue.

On the telephone he was becoming agitated. 'They want two thousand pounds, Mr Read! They are threatening court proceedings if I do not pay up in one month's time.'

'As I explained, Mr Jordan, you will probably not have to pay that sum of money, if I prepare your accounts.' I endeavoured to try to keep him calm but without success.

The next day there was a call from the Collector of Taxes.

'Mr Read, I understand that you deal with the tax affairs of Mr Jordan.' I agreed. 'One of my staff has found an envelope with two thousand pounds in it and the name Jordan on it. Do you know anything about this?' The Collector seemed bemused.

I confirmed that I did not, but promised to get hold of as much information as I could and phone the Collector back.

Directly, I telephoned Mr Jordan and asked him about the envelope.

'Yes, I went round to the tax office and pushed the envelope through the letter box,' he said.

I was staggered. No one in the office had heard of a similar incident. Apparently, Mr Jordan had worked himself up and acted on the spur of the moment.

'You had better come and see me,' I said. He agreed and I managed to untangle his tax affairs prior to my leaving Davis & Co. The major part of the two thousand pounds was repaid to him.

Friday came and I said my farewells to the staff of Davis & Co. I received various cards and a Concise Oxford Dictionary signed inside by all the staff. I promised to see Rose the following day.

Rose would be leaving Davis and Co. a few weeks later, but in the meantime would be assisting me during the evenings and weekends.

THE FOLLOWING WEEK, I had arranged to meet Rose on the Saturday and we decided to spend some time at a park.

About fifteen miles away from Hayford was a huge expanse of land called Cranfield Park. The area had been owned some years previously by the Cranfields, a very wealthy family, but was then opened to the general public. It was often frequented by young couples.

At about two thirty, I parked my new Cortina outside Rose's home, confidently strode up the path, and rang the bell.

I felt on top of the world. I was a Chartered Accountant with a lovely girlfriend, a new car, and a glittering future lay ahead of me.

Rose appeared at the door. 'Come in, Tom. I won't be long,' she said. I went directly to the lounge. Her parents were sitting there drinking tea.

'Congratulations, Tom. We are pleased for you,' they chorused. Their expressions displayed their delight at my success.

After a few minutes, Rose came down the staircase dressed in casual clothes. 'Ready, Tom,' she said, smiling, and I noticed a trace of lipstick and rouge. The scent of Chanel No. 5 wafted towards me.

Having said goodbye to Mr and Mrs Turner, Rose and I were soon seated in my car. As I started the engine, I noticed Rose looking at the upholstery. 'Nice car, Tom,' she said.

Cranfield Park was only a few miles from Rose's home and we were soon nearly there. It was a lovely day, the sky was cloud free and the sun was shining. Driving slowly along the leafy lane leading towards the park, we passed over a humpback bridge, under which a river flowed. It glittered in the bright sunlight. I parked my car and we walked towards the great area of greenery.

To get to the park, one had to pass an old church. Rumour had it that Dick Turpin, the highwayman, had used one of the outbuildings as a hideaway.

We walked slowly along a winding path, past numerous huge rhododendrons with large clusters of pink, trumpet-shaped flowers. The scene was idyllic.

We passed through an avenue of very old oak trees which grew beside a deep moat no longer filled with water. The soft leaf mould beneath our feet made walking a pleasure.

Suddenly we were out of the shade and into the sunshine. The parkland in all its glory lay before us. Finding a quiet spot, we spread a rug out on some freshly mown grass and sat down. The small hamper was placed to one side, the contents to be consumed later.

Rose gazed into my eyes. We lay down and all of a sudden we were kissing passionately.

I knew from the fervour of the moment that the special chemistry was still there. Neither of us had ever used the word love but for me there was no need to say it. I just knew.

Rose had never asked me if I loved her and I had never asked her if she loved me.

I knew subsequently I should have spoken the words and made my intentions about the future crystal clear. I didn't realise at the time but there is sometimes a fine dividing line between passion and love.

All of a sudden, Rose sat up and her eyes were glazed. She turned away, looking directly ahead and didn't speak.

'Is there anything wrong, Rose?' I asked. She turned to face me. She was flushed.

'Not at all – I was just admiring the view,' she replied.

However, her features told me different. The food and drink was spread out, and we had our picnic, hardly speaking; it seemed as if there was a wall of silence between us.

Rose was pleasant but I noticed a difference about her. It seemed to me that something important had occurred. Rose was somehow different and I didn't know why.

Apparently, in just a few minutes she had altered. I looked at her intently. Her eyes were still sparkling but her smile was not radiant.

As we slowly walked back to my car, inwardly I was sad. Sometimes something very important happens and one does not realise exactly what it is. I experienced that feeling then.

I drove Rose to her home, and she was still quiet.

She stood impassively at her garden gate and watched me drive off. There was a definite difference in her attitude. I tried to put the matter to one side, but it was at the back of my mind and I was unsettled.

After taking Rose to Cranfield Park, my mind had been working overtime. The following day I picked her up and we went for a short drive; I pulled in at a lay-by.

I looked deeply into her bright blue eyes. No words were spoken as I pulled her close to me. We kissed passionately, for a long time.

I reached into my pocket and pulled out a small felt-covered box. 'This is for you, Rose.' She was surprised and looked at me expectantly. Did I see a flicker of doubt? It was only a few seconds but it seemed an eternity before she reacted.

She opened the box and there was the ring I had bought the previous day.

She picked up the ring and asked me to place it on her finger. The expression on her face told me all I wanted to know.

'I do love you, Tom.'

'I love you, Rose,' I said.

These were the words she had been waiting for.

Sitting in the lounge in Rose's home, with Rose and her parents, we were discussing various matters, including the future.

'I understand that you have always wanted to start your own practice, Tom,' said Mr Turner. He had run his own hardware business from a local shop, for many years, and was well experienced in the practical aspects of running a business.

He had obviously given the matter considerable thought before mentioning the subject. He was that type of man – methodical and highly intelligent. He stared at me with his bright eyes.

I replied, 'That's right, Mr Turner, but the only thing that's holding me back is the lack of capital.'

'I have a proposition to put to you, Tom,' he continued. He pulled his favourite armchair closer towards me. 'If you are not interested, then please say so and that will be the end of the matter. As you know I have run my own business for a number of years and it is well established. I understand that it is your intention to work for another firm of accountants but if you had the opportunity, you would prefer to be your own boss.'

My attention was fully focused on his comments and I listened closely.

Having recently qualified, I had given the matter of possibly starting my own accountancy practice direct thought, but having spoken to the local bank manager who was quite prepared to advance me on a long-term basis a substantial sum, without security, based upon my qualifications, I had hedged somewhat.

'I have some good investments and various funds in building society accounts,' said Mr Turner, glancing at his wife, who smiled at him encouragingly.

'Would you consider accepting a loan of five thousand pounds from me with no strings attached? I would not expect interest but if you get established then you could pay me a nominal amount.' Mr Turner paused and went on, 'There is a small lock-up shop, near my hardware shop.'

This lock-up was only half a mile away from the home of Mr and Mrs Turner and had recently been advertised to lease. It had been an off-licence, but the previous tenant could not make a success of his business and after eighteen months of trading had to close down.

At this juncture, my imagination was running riot. Mr Turner's proposal seemed very attractive to me but the main stumbling block would be the quick introduction of clients. I mentioned this to Mr Turner, who again had done his homework.

The five thousand pounds would, he reckoned, suffice to pay for the office furniture, equipment, etc. and leasing payments, together with other overheads, and tide me over until the nucleus of a clientele could be established.

'You can certainly take over my accounts preparation and there are a number of business acquaintances of mine who would be interested in changing their accountants,' he said. He seemed full of enthusiasm and I was beginning to feel confident.

It would be a risk, but a calculated one. If I started out working for another accountant, I might find myself in a rut. The opportunity of starting my own business could not be missed.

'I will certainly give the matter serious thought, Mr Turner. Thank you for the offer.'

I had already basically made up my mind but I was never one to make hasty decisions and promised to let him know the following day, Sunday.

At home, I discussed the matter with my parents and they were full of encouragement, particularly my father. 'Go for it,' he said. My delight with their reaction was very apparent and on the Sunday I telephoned Mr Turner to ask him if I could come round to see him again.

Rose opened the door. 'Come in, Tom. Dad is waiting for you in the lounge.' She was smiling and patted my arm reassuringly.

Mr Turner came towards me and ushered me into the lounge. He was astute and I believe he already knew by the expression on my face that I was going to agree to his proposal.

He picked up a small envelope from the coffee table and handed it to me. Opening it quickly, I took out the cheque for five thousand pounds. 'Thanks, Mr Turner,' I said.

'I've got some details of the lease of the lock-up shop for you,' he said. He handed a bulky package to me.

'The rent is only four hundred pounds a year,' he said. 'There are no fittings. They have all been removed but the electricity, gas and telephone are all ready to be connected.' Mr Turner was thorough.

'If you agree, Tom,' said Rose, 'I will give up my job at Davis & Co. and work as your secretary.' She was brimming over with enthusiasm. Her parents were wealthy. They had been left substantial assets by their parents. This seemed like a dream which was coming true.

Rose was trained as an accounts clerk and a typist, and her assistance would be invaluable.

After coffee and biscuits with Rose and her parents, I made my way to the front door.

I had a lot to organise.

Rose kissed me at the garden gate and I promised to telephone her the following morning.

The next morning I made several telephone calls and wrote various letters. Firstly, I telephoned the estate agents to ensure that the lock-up shop was still available, and the answer was in the affirmative. The owners were quite agreeable for me to obtain the lease, and I would be sent the necessary documents directly.

I telephoned the Institute requesting an application form for the practising certificate and I wrote a letter to support the call. The issuing of the certificate would be a formality.

Close to Mr Turner's shop was an office equipment and stationery shop and on speaking to the owner, Mr Gage, a man I had met before when purchasing personal stationery, I made arrangements for me to call to see him, and discuss my requirements for my office.

Events were proceeding at breakneck speed but I was enjoying every minute of it. I had a goal and that was to become my own boss; the adrenalin began to flow and I did not notice any pressure.

The venture was to be a completely new experience for Rose and myself. She was just as enthused as I was.

Over the next few days, I went to see my bank manager, paid the five thousand pounds from Mr Turner into my business account in the name of 'Tom Read & Co., Chartered Accountants,' and obtained my new paying-in and cheque books.

The bank manager was most cooperative and made available an overdraft facility of two thousand pounds, without any security whatsoever. He knew I had qualified and that was sufficient for him.

I wrote a letter to the local Tax Inspector, advising him that I had ceased to be employed and would be commencing self-employment shortly.

The picture began to look rosy; my only qualm was whether I would get sufficient clients to keep me busy. As it turned out, I needn't have worried on that score.

Calling at Rose's home, I found that her father was at his shop, but her mother greeted me warmly. 'Come in, Tom. I'm glad that you seem to be getting on well with the arrangements for your new accountancy practice.'

She moved towards the kitchen. 'I'll make you and Rose a cup of tea and you can discuss matters with her.'

Rose came through from the kitchen into the lounge; she kissed me and sat close to me on the settee. 'Can I see the list, Tom, please?' She knew I was bringing a note of the office equipment and stationery requirements and I gave it to her; she went quickly through the various items.

'I think you have covered most things,' she said. I knew what I needed for my work but the typing side I left to Rose who had made out her own list, including a typewriter, and the accessories.

We had our tea and biscuits and explained to Mrs Turner we were going to see Mr Gage to let him know our proposed purchase of equipment, and so on. He had promised to give us generous discounts. This was good business sense, as he knew that if we were satisfied initially, we would use his shop on a regular basis in the future.

Mr Gage was serving a customer when we walked through the entrance to his shop.

'Won't keep you long, Mr Read.' He smiled warmly at Rose. He had known her since she was a youngster.

Looking around Mr Gage's shop I could see he was a tidy man; everything seemed set out very neatly. We were examining a typewriter when he came over. Mr Gage was a middle-aged man about my height, but broader. His hair was receding. In fact he was nearly bald in places, but he had a bushy black moustache flecked with streaks of grey. He dressed well. His dark charcoal-grey suit was immaculate. A light blue shirt with gold cuff links and a red tie kept in place with a gold clip completed the picture.

I showed him the list. 'Come through to my stockroom, Mr Read, please.'

I followed him, with Rose alongside me.

'I believe I have all your requirements in stock, apart from the headed notepaper and business cards which I will have to obtain from the printers. They'll only take a few days.'

Going through the list, we chose desks, chairs, filing cabinets, cupboards, stationery, pencils, pens. One or two suggestions regarding extra items were made by Mr Gage and we added them to our lists. The discounted prices were noted against each item and I was well satisfied.

I had made an estimate of the total cost and I was pleased that Mr Gage's total figure was much less.

By this time I had arranged with the estate agents to obtain the keys of the lock-up shop. I had paid the deposit and signed the necessary papers.

I shook hands with Mr Gage, who promised to deliver the items as soon as I required them.

We made our way to the lock-up shop; Rose and I had already looked at it. It was bare but clean. There was little that needed doing; a slight improvement to the decorating – that was all.

My new office was squeezed between a confectionery shop and a newsagent's. At the back was a tiny kitchen, with a small cooker sufficient to make the occasional hot meal.

We had already purchased a kettle. There was a small toilet and washbasin. Heating was by way of two electric fires installed in the walls. Each fire had three bars and therefore we would be able to regulate the heat. Rose and I were pleased.

Her father had examined the premises before speaking to me and I would have been very surprised if they had proved to be unsatisfactory.

Whilst working at Davis & Co. I had, with the permission of Mr Davis, secured a few private clients – mostly close friends and relatives – and therefore I was not completely without the nucleus of a practice.

It was not going to be easy, but there were a number of prospective clients in the pipeline, and with the balance of money left over after I paid for the office equipment, etc., I would have sufficient funds to keep Rose and myself going for at least a year.

Dreams do sometimes come true and although at that time I had no experience of running my own business, I had advised many other people; I was very optimistic about the future.

'When do you think we should start the business, Tom?' Rose enquired.

I had given this serious consideration, and once all the office furniture and equipment was in place and the stationery was available, we could start as soon as clients' records commenced arriving.

I had two new clients recommended by Mr Turner, who were bringing their records in to me directly, and this work would last Rose and me about two months. Then it would depend on whether further clients were obtained or not.

Rose and I decided we would commence business in two weeks' time.

One item I had nearly forgotten and that was my nameplate: 'Tom Read & Co., Chartered Accountants – Sole Practitioner, Tom Read, A.C.A.' Mr Gage promised to have this delivered to me by the end of the week.

I was excited at the prospect of seeing my own nameplate outside my own office.

My excitement was transmitted to Rose, who said, 'This is a great adventure, Tom.' We gazed at each other, perhaps with rose-tinted spectacles. There were problems ahead, but of course we were enjoying the exultation of the moment.

THE OFFICE FURNITURE, equipment, stationery and so on was being delivered. As Mr Gage's shop was not far from my office, he arranged for two of his assistants to bring the various items round without the intervention of a delivery van.

Standing just inside my office with Rose to one side of him, Mr Gage was assisting us in the correct positioning of the desks, chairs, filing cabinets and cupboards.

There were two telephone points, so there was no problem with the desks. There were two large window panes. Conveniently, Rose being left-handed and myself right-handed, we could both make use of the daylight, by placing the desks on either side of the front entrance.

'Are you happy with the position of your desk, Rose?' I asked. As she looked up, I could see that she was content. She was pleased for me, but also pleased for herself. There would be no 'boss' to worry about. It was my intention that we would work together as equals.

She sat in the swivel chair, which could be used as a typist's chair or for accounts work. She swivelled the chair round, laughing as she did so.

'I think that is just about right,' she said.

'Mr Read,' Mr Gage called, 'the cupboards look all right against that wall. What do you think?'

I could easily get them moved later, if necessary, and confirmed that they would be quite satisfactory.

Two filing cabinets were placed, so either Rose or myself could get to the clients' files. An open double bookcase was placed in position, to hold my textbooks, journals and certain stationery.

In a matter of an hour, all the furniture and everything else was in place.

We surveyed the scene; it actually looked like an office.

'There you are,' said Mr Gage. He moved towards the open door with his two assistants. 'I'll leave you to it.'

'Thanks, Mr Gage.' Rose and I waved to him, and he beamed back at us. He was pleased that he had sold a number of items to us, but I think it went far beyond that. A young couple starting up a business and he was there to see it – this genuinely made him content.

I N MY OFFICE as we were clearing the coffee cups and saucers away, I was whistling and Rose was humming a well-known tune.

In the small kitchen we looked at each other. Suddenly Rose came over and put her arms around me and kissed me. 'That was for good luck and fortune, Tom,' she said.

I knew we would both try our best to make a success of the business. Rose's standards of accounts work and typing were high; with our combined expertise, I looked forward to the future with optimism.

My Ford Cortina was parked just outside my office, and I was carrying some textbooks and journals towards the front door when a small van pulled up.

A young man with a bright red pullover strode over towards me. He had in his hand a small parcel. 'Are you Mr Read?' he asked. I nodded. 'Mr Gage asked me to put your nameplate up. Where do you want it put?'

Rose was peering through the doorway. 'What do you think, Rose?' I called. I was exhilarated but I wanted Rose to share my exhilaration. We both agreed that just to the left of the front door on the brickwork at eye level would be ideal.

After ten minutes, the young man with the pullover walked towards us in my office. 'I've finished, so I'll be off.' I thanked him and he drove away.

Rose and I stood on the pavement and read, 'Tom Read & Co., Chartered Accountants – Sole Practitioner, Tom Read, A.C.A.' The pride exuded from me. There it was: a shiny brass plate with my name on it. Rose took my hand and squeezed it. We slowly walked back to the office, both of us looking forward to the future.

The euphoria gradually subsided, after my parents, Rose's parents and some close friends and relatives had been over to see the office. I was looking forward to 1st July.

Although Rose and I would have to work hard to establish my practice, we decided not to neglect our social activities.

We had been attending Miss Williams's dance classes once a week, and had moved from the beginners' class to the amateur bronze medal, Latin American class. It usually took most couples about a year to reach the standard to enable them to take the test, to see if they were entitled to a bronze medal.

Rose and I seemed to be progressing well, in the cha-cha-cha, jive, rumba and samba.

Every month, on a Saturday, there was a proper dance held at the ballroom owned by the chocolate-making company where my mother worked. I had peered through the large windows on a number of occasions when I had picked up my mother after her evening work, but I never thought I would be dancing there.

I had purchased two tickets for the dance, after confiding with Rose that she wanted to go. She was delighted and we were both looking forward to our first official ballroom dance.

We had by this time purchased proper dance shoes with special non-slip soles and heels. Small bags were available to carry these shoes, together with other items such as wire brushes to roughen the surface of the soles and heels.

The dance was due to commence at 8 p.m. and we were advised to get to the ballroom at about seven thirty, to enable well-positioned seats to be obtained.

At six thirty, I said farewell to my parents and drove off to Rose's home. I was wearing a pair of close-fitting light grey trousers with a dark blue blazer covered in small gold buttons; a white shirt and red tie completed my apparel, with the addition of my gold initialled cuff links and a tiepin.

I had spent the morning cleaning and polishing my car, which was proving to be reliable and extremely comfortable; I was pleased with the purchase.

As I arrived outside Rose's home, I saw the net curtains pulled to one side, and she waved to me. She opened the door. 'Come in, Tom, I'm nearly ready.'

Mr and Mrs Turner were in the lounge. 'You look smart, Tom,' said Mr Turner with his eyes twinkling.

Rose wore a short, light blue dress with a plain gold brooch. Her hair had obviously been done at the hairdresser's; the auburn colour shone and a touch of make-up completed the lovely picture. She was young and full of vitality.

When dancing, we seemed to complement each other; she was a delight to dance with and had a natural easy movement, essential for a good dancer.

'Ready, Tom,' she said, and held my arm. 'See you about eleven thirty,' she added, looking at her parents as they watched us climb into my car. I tooted the horn and we were off.

This was an exciting time for both of us; although we had been to the occasional social dance, we had never been to a proper ballroom event.

On reaching the chocolate factory security gates, we soon found a parking space near the ballroom, which was situated away from the main factory building.

A number of workers were regular dancers and it was very convenient for them to call at the ballroom.

'Have you got your dance shoes?' asked Rose, as she was closing the passenger door. I nodded and proceeded to lock both doors.

As we were walking to the doorway of the ballroom, there were footsteps behind us. Looking round, I saw Colin and Dawn Brand, a young couple who lived near my home.

'Hello, Tom,' they said. I introduced them to Rose and we walked along. I knew they were keen dancers and had obtained gold medals in ballroom dancing and were in the silver medal Latin American class at Miss Williams's Dance School.

He was a mechanic and she worked as a nurse at a local Nursing Home. Colin was a tall, upright, smartly dressed man of about twelve stone. I had never seen him miserable. He was always telling jokes. Dawn was about three inches shorter than her husband, a neatly dressed lady with her hair drawn tightly into a bun, tied back with a white ribbon. They were splendid dancers, as I realised when I saw them at the dance school.

We went through into the brightly-lit ballroom, showing our tickets.

'Do you want any raffle tickets?' said the plump man sitting at the table. They were a shilling each, so I bought two.

'You can sit with us if you like,' said Dawn, pointing to a vacant table. About eighty tables were set out with chairs, all around the wooden dance floor, which was properly sprung. As I walked across it I could understand why non-slip dance shoes were essential.

We settled ourselves down and I looked around. Several tables were already occupied and people were hurrying about, securing seats.

I recognised a number of people from the dance club and several others.

There was a hubbub of noise. At one end of the dance floor, away from the actual dancing area, was a bar and already people were queuing for drinks.

Colin rose from his seat and said, 'I'm going to get some white wine for Dawn and myself. Would you like me to get you anything?'

'I'll have an orange juice, please,' replied Rose, raising her head, as she put on her dance shoes.

'Lemonade for me, please.' I began to put my dance shoes on as well.

We were joined at the table by another couple, Derek and Pauline Jenkings, also from the dance club. Music was provided by a small band, composed of a pianist, drummer and a guitarist.

There were already several couples on the dance floor. A quickstep was being played. They were obviously experienced dancers and looked extremely confident.

I listened to the excellent music. When I first started dancing, I found that I could distinguish the beat quite easily. I had played the piano when I was younger, and no doubt that was an assistance.

In no time at all, the dance floor was crowded. A waltz was being played. Rose and I gazed at each other. I was feeling a little nervous but I thought I must ask her for a dance. After all, that was why we were there. 'Shall we have a try, Rose?' I asked.

She got up from her chair. I pulled her gently towards me, listened to the beat of the music, one, two, three, and then we were off.

When doing ballroom dancing, couples basically move around anticlockwise. There are spins and turns, but one ends up going round anticlockwise.

Rose and I were only dancing the basic steps of the waltz, but I found the sensation stimulating. It is a lovely feeling to have a nicely scented woman in your arms, dancing around on a properly sprung floor. It felt as if I was floating.

We had been taught to turn at the corners, and we were really enjoying ourselves. The waltz came to an end and a cha-cha-cha commenced.

'Let's try the steps we have been learning, Rose,' I suggested.

The band was playing well and after a few hesitant steps, we were soon dancing the basic steps of the cha-cha-cha. I could hear the beat quite distinctly. We were on the edge of the floor and as the music came to an end, we made our way back to the table.

Miss Williams was sitting at one of the tables. She smiled and asked, 'Enjoying yourselves?' We replied that we were, and after having a brief chat with her, sat down at our table.

Dawn looked up. Her words were encouraging.

'I was looking at you dancing the cha-cha-cha. Your timing was good.'

My cheeks felt hot and I looked at Rose. She was flushed but smiling.

Although drinks were provided, food, at this particular dance, was not. It was usual for people to bring their own. We didn't realise that, but were offered some snacks by Colin and Dawn.

Dancing is very therapeutic and we were feeling the benefits already.

Suddenly, the band commenced playing a jive; this happened to be my favourite of the Latin American dances, and I was anxious to try out the steps we had learnt at the dance club.

As soon as I got up from my seat, Rose was at my side and we quickly walked on to the dance floor. I picked up the beat directly and although I was perspiring slightly, I was soon enjoying myself tremendously.

There were only about a dozen couples on the floor, as the jive is rather a vigorous dance.

The band played for a lengthy time; they could no doubt see the dancers were enjoying themselves.

The jive finished, and the foxtrot commenced. I walked Rose back to the table; we had not yet been taught that particular dance.

Colin and Dawn were dancing; I thought how well they danced. They were raising and lowering themselves in time to the music, and they presented themselves well. I could see other people at the tables casting admiring glances at them.

I was determined that Rose and I would aim to reach their high standards. Little did I know that we would eventually obtain gold medals in Ballroom and Latin American dancing.

Time went very quickly and it was approaching the end of the dance.

The pianist stepped forward on the stage. 'Time for the raffle, ladies and gentlemen.' All the raffle tickets were put in a container, shaken and a young lady was asked to pick out the winning tickets. 'Number 106.' I looked down at my ticket. No luck – Rose neither. 'Number 65.'

Rose stood up holding her ticket. She had won. 'You go and get the prize, Tom,' she said.

I walked over to the pianist. There was a good selection of prizes. I chose a large box of candies and, clutching it tightly, walked carefully across the shiny dance floor to Rose and gave the box to her.

I shall never forget the look on her face. It was pure joy.

The function ended with 'Auld Lang Syne' and we joined the throng of chatting people leaving the ballroom. What a splendid evening it had been. We had been introduced to a different world – the world of Ballroom and Latin American dancing.

Wandering outside into the fresh air with Colin and Dawn, Rose and I were just about to walk towards my car when Colin spoke to me. 'Tom, I understand that you have commenced your own accountancy practice,' he said. He wasn't going to mix business with pleasure, but he asked me if he could make an appointment to come and see me.

I was hopeful that in due course word would get around about my new business but this was quicker than I dared hope for. 'Here's one of my business cards,' I said and handed him one from half a dozen I kept in my back pocket. 'Give me a ring any time when I'm at my office. I start on 1st July.'

He tucked the card into his jacket pocket. 'Thanks, Tom.'

We said our farewells to Colin and Dawn, and got into my car. The windows were misty, so I spent a few minutes ensuring they were clear, and then started the engine.

Rose pressed my hand appreciatively. 'I really enjoyed that dance, didn't you?' she asked, and I agreed enthusiastically.

We were chatting all the way back to her home. It was about eleven thirty when I pulled the car up. She leaned over towards me. 'Thanks, Tom.' She was clutching her box of candies and kissed me warmly. 'I'll see you on Monday,' she said.

Part Two

I WAS AGAIN immersed in a client's incomplete records, but this time I was sitting at my own desk in my own small office. Looking around, I surveyed the scene with great satisfaction. My certificates for passing my final exams to become a Chartered Accountant, and the right to practise, were mounted just behind my desk and I stared at them with pride. It had taken me six years of persistent studying to achieve my present professional standing and the hard work had been rewarded.

At the age of twenty-three, in 1963, I had qualified, and shortly after had acquired the lease of my office which was squeezed between a confectionery shop and a newsagent's in the bustling town of Hayford, Middlesex.

My fiancée, Rose, was assisting me with typing, during the evenings and weekends; momentarily she was still working full-time at the firm where I had been an articled clerk. As soon as I commenced working in my own office, a few weeks after I qualified, the intention was for Rose to leave her employer, Davis & Co. and commence working full-time with me. However, after further discussing the matter with her and her parents, Mr and Mrs Turner, it was decided for her to continue to work for Davis & Co. until I was well established.

Rose and I had set out my office with the usual desks, chairs and cupboards and so on and as I looked across the room towards Rose's empty chair, I thought of her working at Davis & Co. and wished earnestly she was with me. However, that time would come, I assured myself. I put aside my dubious thoughts and endeavoured to concentrate on balancing a set of accounts; I was five pounds adrift somewhere and I began to recheck my calculations.

As I concentrated on my task, there was a ring at my front door and I looked up from my desk. A thin, stooped, elderly man with a cap and a worn, ripped mackintosh, the lapels of which were turned up, entered. His long thin face creased into a warm smile and he came towards me with his hand outstretched.

I looked at him closely as he shook my hand. It was Mr Harding, a client of Davis & Co. He had once been a blacksmith but had resorted to making ornamental iron and steel gates. His business had prospered but unfortunately his health had deteriorated.

'Mr Read, I am so pleased to see you again.' I reciprocated his good wishes as I ushered him towards one of the two chairs opposite my own armchair. He removed his old torn cap and placed it on the floor.

'How are you, Mr Harding?' I asked, looking at his wrinkled, sallow face.

His grey watery eyes looked sad as he replied, 'I'm afraid that I haven't been at all well of late. I've lost weight and although my business is prospering I get very tired and find the work hard.'

I felt sorry for him as I knew that he was extremely conscientious and had been delighted to succeed in supplying numerous satisfied customers with quality gates made to order.

'I have a question to ask of you, Mr Read, but if the answer is no, I will quite understand.' By this time I had made coffee and had handed a cup to him.

'Milk and sugar, I believe, Mr Harding?'

'Yes please, Mr Read.' He sipped the hot liquid, sucking his unkempt moustache with his bottom lip.

'Did you know that Mr Davis has been very ill, Mr Read?'

I had heard that my principal continued to suffer from high blood pressure and haemophilia. Mr Harding continued to chatter on between sips of his coffee, brushing a few crumbs from a biscuit into his hand and on to his plate.

I had left the employment of Davis & Co. shortly after qualifying, and as Mr Davis and I had not mixed socially, I had not seen him for some time. I visited the offices of Davis & Co. but rarely saw him. Rose had told me that he was going to retire prematurely due to ill health, but I didn't know when.

'I received this letter from Davis & Co. yesterday,' said Mr Harding. He handed me a crumpled envelope and I read the contents of the letter; I noted that Mr Davis had decided to retire in two months' time and his practice was to be taken over by another firm. Rose had gleaned this information through the grapevine but now the news had been confirmed.

Mr Harding looked at me intently. 'You handled my accountancy and taxation affairs for me well when you were at Davis & Co. Would you take me on as your client?'

A surge of pleasure coursed through me and I endeavoured to refrain from blurting out my joyful reply. Instead, I sat back in my armchair and considered the matter. If Mr Davis was retiring, a number of other clients might seek my assistance. I was ecstatic.

'I shall be pleased to act for you, Mr Harding, subject to the usual etiquette letter sent by me to Davis & Co., and a favourable reply; there shouldn't be any problem.'

We again shook hands warmly. Mr Harding beamed back at me. There was mutual respect and liking for each other – the basis for a good professional relationship.

'As soon as I hear from Davis & Co. I will contact you, Mr Harding; in the meantime I advise you to call to see Mr Davis and make known your wishes,' I said.

Mr Harding rose stiffly from his chair and hobbled to the front door. We said our farewells and I hardly noticed the noise coming from the hurrying pedestrians and the fast moving traffic as I closed the door. I had already the nucleus of a practice and I could foresee new clients coming to me from Davis & Co. I was delighted at the prospect, and rubbed my hands together with enjoyment. My thoughts raced ahead.

M Y LIGHT BLUE Ford Cortina was parked outside my office and I was striding confidently towards it, carrying my new shiny brown leather briefcase, when I heard Rose calling my name. We faced each other. She was wearing a yellow dress with a flowered pattern; her small black shoes were, as usual, highly polished. She never used much make-up – just a touch of powder and lipstick. Her auburn hair shone and wisps blew in the breeze resting lightly on her forehead. The scent of her favourite perfume, Chanel No. 5, wafted towards me. Briefly touching my hand and kissing me good-naturedly, she looked at me with her bright blue sparkling eyes.

'I called you several times, Tom, but you couldn't have heard me,' she said softly. Her whole countenance radiated the vibrant health of youth.

I gripped her hand and led her to the passenger door of my car. 'I was rather absent-mindedly thinking of my next client,' I explained.

Rose usually walked to work. Davis & Co.'s offices were not far from her house and my office was about a mile away. She often saw me in the mornings as she passed or called at my office and that morning we decided to have a chat, sitting in my car for ten minutes or so. It was approximately eight thirty.

As we sat in the front seats of my Cortina, a group of youngsters – Mods – on Vespa scooters raced by, tooting their horns and shouting to each other. One young lad thumped the side of my car as he went by, grinning maniacally. He was gone in a flash but after examining my car I could not find any evidence of damage.

'Young whippersnapper!' I said to Rose, who laughed at my temporary annoyance.

'They are only high-spirited,' she said, handing me the local daily newspaper. She turned the radio on. Victor Silvester was playing 'We'll Meet Again'. We both enjoyed his music, which was often played at the dances we went to.

Rose pointed to an article on the front page of the newspaper and I read it with interest.

During the last few weeks, there had been numerous cats reported missing in Hayford and there were rumours that they had been taken for their furs; this had not been proved however. I handed the newspaper back to Rose; she kissed me and got out of the car, saying, 'See you at seven, Tom.'

She began walking towards the offices of Davis & Co. and I noticed her confident, upright posture. Most evenings she called at my office to do some typing for me.

It was intended eventually that she would assist me with the accounts work, but this would not arise until she worked full-time within my practice.

I started the engine of my car and began driving towards the home of one of my clients. His name was Mr Edwards, and being elderly and disabled with severe arthritis in one leg, he was unable to visit my office.

M R EDWARDS'S HOME was situated about four miles from Hayford; I soon arrived, parked my Cortina, locked the doors and strode up the brick pathway towards his detached house.

The gardens were neat and tidy; the lawn was freshly mown. There were numerous rose bushes, busy Lizzies, geraniums and lobelias; a touch of morning dew was still apparent on the leaves, glistening in the early morning mist. Mr Edwards employed a part-time gardener.

I reached the end of the pathway and looked over my shoulder. The road was at a much lower level than the house and I could hardly hear the busy traffic. Looking up at the imposing detached building, I noticed the impressive bay windows on either side of the large oak door which had a multicoloured glass panel above the huge brass letter box.

I knocked twice with the moulded brass door knocker. A small dog barked and peeped inquisitively through a neighbour's sparse hedge.

In due course, the door opened and Mr Edwards greeted me. 'Come in, Mr Read.' He extended his hand towards me and the grip was firm and reassuring. 'I'm very pleased to see you, Mr Read; it must be six months since we last met.'

He was a large man in his mid-seventies, nearly bald; he had a round, rosy face with twinkling eyes.

'Come through to the lounge.' He banged the front door shut with his thick walking stick. I followed him as he limped along the wide hall and turned right into a cavernous, sumptuously-furnished room. 'Please sit down, Mr Read,' he said, and ushered me towards a huge dining room table surrounded by four leather-bound chairs; the dark green velvet curtains were drawn aside and sunlight cascaded into the room. I sat down at the same time as Mr Edwards, who placed his walking stick on a nearby armchair.

On the table there were various papers in neat piles. It was my duty to complete his annual tax return. He had a considerable investment income and a sizeable pension from a local engineering company where he was formerly a director. In no time at all, the tax return was completed. Mr Edwards was meticulous and had provided all the required information – unlike some clients I could call to mind.

'How about a hot toddy, Mr Read?' I knew that he liked a whisky with hot water and sugar; his usual comment was, 'To keep the cold out.'

I seldom drank, having suffered from alcoholic poisoning when I was younger, but I didn't wish to offend him and replied, 'Just a small one, please.'

He quickly provided the hot toddies and we sat there as I listened to him reminiscing. His life had been a full and interesting one but now he was virtually housebound.

We got on to the subject of gardening; he used to be an enthusiastic gardener but his arthritis prevented him from doing anything to his garden, apart from simple tasks. There was one job which he could perform, however, and that was the pruning of his old grapevine.

'Have you ever seen my back garden, Mr Read?'

'I can't remember you ever showing it to me,' I replied.

He rose ponderously from his chair, grasped his walking stick and shuffled over the carpet's thick pile towards the hall. I followed him and we reached an outer door which he opened. The door led to a narrow pathway and then to a large, moss covered greenhouse and a ramshackle shed. There were a few sad looking vegetables: cabbages, carrots and parsnips in one corner of the small walled garden; the remainder of the ground was uncultivated.

On reaching the greenhouse, Mr Edwards slid the metal door open. I looked in with interest. Although I was not a keen gardener, I could understand why so many people enthused over this pastime.

A huge grapevine confronted us. 'This is fifty years old,' said Mr Edwards proudly, taking off one or two dead leaves as he spoke. 'I planted it when I was twenty-five years of age on moving into my house with Mrs Edwards.'

She had died six years ago and he now lived alone.

The grapevine had numerous bunches of grapes, some ready for picking. He produced a pair of secateurs from the corner of the greenhouse and snipped off four large bunches. 'Please accept these with my compliments, Mr Read.' There were some paper bags handy and he put the grapes in one, commenting, 'These are lovely and sweet and will last a week – if you can keep them that long.' He laughed and gave me a friendly wink.

'What's your secret, Mr Edwards?' I asked. I wondered how on earth he could have produced such beautiful grapes over a period of fifty years.

'I've told only a few people but the answer is: half a bullock.' He rubbed the side of his nose, as he spoke.

I looked at him incredulously. Whatever did he mean?

He proceeded to explain. 'Before I planted the vine, I was talking to an old gardener who advised me to visit the local abattoirs and obtain half a bullock which was of no use to them. I was told by the old gardener to dig a deep trench just outside the greenhouse, bury the half carcass and then plant the vine. This I followed to the letter and the result has been splendid bunches of grapes every year.'

The half carcass had provided the nutrients for the vine, ever since it was planted!

I followed Mr Edwards back to his kitchen door, through the hall and to the front door.

We shook hands and said our farewells; age made no difference as we were on the same wavelength. I looked forward to our next meeting.

IT WAS LUNCHTIME and I walked from my office to the offices of Davis & Co. to meet Rose. We often met at 1 p.m. just outside one of the local bank's premises; Davis & Co. occupied the first floor and the bank, the ground floor.

I called to Rose across the busy road and she just about heard me above the hubbub of traffic noise. She waved to me and I scampered towards her, avoiding a Morris Minor, a Ford Anglia and a trolleybus.

When I was an articled clerk at Davis & Co., I usually went to Ron's Café, a local workmen's café, which provided substantial meals for modest prices. Ben, another articled clerk, often accompanied me. He had taken his final exams for the third time and failed in two subjects. In his second attempt, he had also failed in two subjects but different ones from the third attempt. This meant that he had to take all the exams again. Examinees were not allowed to retake individual subjects. He felt like giving up, but I had a chat with him and convinced him to persevere and to have one more attempt; I promised to assist him with his studies.

Rose and I strolled hand in hand at a leisurely pace along the high street, endeavouring to avoid the other hurry-scurry pedestrians. I asked her how she was progressing with accounts work; eventually we would be working together in my office.

'I'm getting on well – in fact at times I like the work as much as typing,' she said. She was typing for me in the evenings and it made a refreshing change to prepare accounts at Davis & Co. In my opinion she was an excellent typist; always neat and methodical. She would be of great assistance to me in my practice.

We reached Granger's Restaurant and wandered towards a small table, close to a large plate-glass window through which one could see the high street. Ron's Café was still frequented by Ben and myself sometimes, but when I was with Rose we tended to go to restaurants. Ron's Café was a bit rough-and-ready and seldom did one see a female customer there; the workmen's language was rather colourful. Ben understood that at certain times Rose and I wished to lunch alone.

Mr Granger stood before us as we entered his restaurant and ushered us towards the table we had chosen. There were few other customers in the restaurant. Mr Granger was a small, bumptious man, about forty years of age, with a jovial face, a thin black moustache, a brush cut, smart dark jacket and trousers and highly polished brown winkle-pickers.

'Please follow me,' he said, foppishly.

We sat down at the table; he handed us a menu, bowed slightly and quickly walked away. We looked at the menu. Rabbit pie was a favourite of mine but Rose had been disillusioned by the thought of the disease myxomatosis; she decided to have the roast beef and Yorkshire pudding. I was not deterred, however, and decided to order the rabbit pie.

When I was a young lad my holidays were sometimes spent in the Suffolk countryside and the locals used to shoot rabbits, especially at harvest time. The farmers and many of the villagers stood at the edges of the cornfield until a small amount of wheat or barley remained to be reaped. Then all of a sudden the rabbits still within the last remnants of the standing crop would make a dash for their lives. Unfortunately for the rabbits, very few survived the accurate shooting of the farmers and the villagers.

As we were waiting for our main course, a group of Teddy boys sauntered past the restaurant. They wore drainpipe trousers, long wide-shouldered coats, shoelace ties and displayed prominent DA haircuts. Most Teddy boys had ceased to gang together by the late 1950s but there were a few groups in towns like Hayford in the early 1960s. They shouted to each other and one stared at Rose through the plate glass window and cheekily thumbed his nose at her. She laughed and made the same gesture to him.

Rose enjoyed her main course but I felt rather queasy. She had some peaches and vanilla ice cream but I decided to miss the sweet. We finished with coffee.

As we left the restaurant, Mr Granger gave us a mock salute, smiled wryly and turned away.

'Peculiar chap, Rose,' I commented; Rose agreed.

I walked back with Rose to Davis & Co. I was still feeling slightly sick. 'Cheerio, Rose – see you this evening,' I said.

'Don't forget those accounts you want typing,' she replied. I assured her that they were safely in my briefcase. We were both looking forward to working together in my small office and I hoped that it would not be long before my practice was well established and she could join me. When I reached my office I was as sick as a dog; I decided to stop working and made my way home.

The next morning I saw Rose at my office at eight thirty; she started work at Davis & Co. at nine. She closed my office door with a bang and greeted me excitedly, holding a copy of the local newspaper.

'Look, Tom,' she said, pointing to a large caption on the front page: RESTAURANT OWNER CAUGHT BY HEALTH OFFICE – CATS' SKINS AND HEADS FOUND IN RESTAURATEUR'S DUSTBINS.

My eyes were drawn to the name of the restaurant: Granger's. I held my stomach, which was turning; I again felt sick at the thought of the 'rabbit pie' I had eaten so ravenously the previous day.

Reading the newspaper article in depth, I ascertained that Mr Granger had paid some youngsters to comb the district for stray cats and as there was a shortage of rabbits due to the myxomatosis, he had substituted the cats in the rabbit pies; no one, including myself, had apparently been any the wiser.

I later determined that Mr Granger was heavily fined and his restaurant was immediately closed. Eventually it reopened, under different ownership; he left the district under a cloud. I never saw him again and indeed had no wish to.

Whenever I see rabbit pie on the menu I avoid it; I think of Mr Granger's wry smile as we left his restaurant. The whole episode until that time was a joke to him, but little did he realise that shortly afterwards the game would be up and he would be fined and ostracised for deceiving his customers so atrociously!

MISS WILLIAMS, THE retired music teacher, was now my client, having asked me to act for her when she knew Mr Davis was retiring. She ran her dance school (Ballroom and Latin American) during the weekdays and at weekends. The place where she taught dancing was situated over two shops which were about one hundred yards from my office.

Rose and I had attended Miss Williams's dance classes once a week for several months; we had reached the stage where Miss Williams considered that we had the required standards to take tests to see if we could obtain amateur bronze medals in Latin American dancing.

I telephoned Miss Williams to ascertain if she could call to see me to ensure that she was maintaining her business records correctly. In the past she had experienced some difficulty in balancing her accounts book.

'Mr Read, will two thirty this afternoon be all right for me to call to see you?' Her authoritative tone was distinct. I looked in my desk diary.

'That will certainly be fine, Miss Williams.'

'Thank you, Mr Read.'

I heard her replace the receiver.

At precisely two thirty Miss Williams rang my office doorbell and entered. She was small and slim with a ramrod straight back and a neat, short hairstyle; as usual everything about her appearance was absolutely correct. She gripped my hand firmly and I noticed her glancing around my office. I endeavoured to keep my office tidy and liked books and papers to be placed in a certain order. Her eyes lit up as she surveyed the scene.

'You have a nice bright office, Mr Read,' she remarked. I had hung a few attractive pictures and all the office furniture was brand new.

I asked Miss Williams if she would like to sit down and she graciously accepted my offer, thanking me when I made certain that she was comfortable.

She produced her accounts book and, reaching over my desk, asked me to make the test checks. 'Do you consider my entries have improved, Mr Read?'

I looked at her bright, greenish-blue eyes as she smiled at me. She had great presence and I had to concentrate to deliberate over her bookkeeping. I looked at the entries and checked a few casts.

Her bookkeeping had vastly improved compared to when she asked me to call to see her at her dance hall. I had then suggested to her various improvements and she had obviously taken notice of my advice.

'Your bookkeeping has improved tremendously, Miss Williams.'

She looked at me and her face reflected her pleasure. Did I see the possibility of her eyes becoming slightly tearful? No I must have been mistaken – or was I?

'I am so pleased, Mr Read,' she said gently. She was the type of person who liked to achieve the best she could at whatever she tried; as persistence was one of my attributes, I admired her for her tenacity in obtaining a high standard of bookkeeping, a task she didn't really enjoy.

I handed the accounts book back to her and she put it in her smart leather shopping bag.

She rose quickly from her chair, saying, 'Mr Read, now I'm here I will tell you before your next dance class that the tests for bronze, silver and gold medals are to be held three weeks come next Sunday.'

I held my breath. Just over three weeks! I was seeing Rose that evening and I wondered what her reaction would be. We had been trying our best to dance as well as we could, but the moment of truth was approaching.

I couldn't wait to see Rose's face when I told her the news.

Miss Williams was walking quickly towards my front door. 'I'll see you and Rose at the Saturday dance, Mr Read,' she said. She always called me 'Mr Read' when she saw me in connection with her accountancy or taxation affairs – keeping the professional distance – but resorted to 'Tom' when involved with dancing activities.

I saw her to the front door and she again shook my hand warmly. The niceties of life never failed to impress me. It was raining slightly and she produced a fold-up umbrella from her handbag. We said our farewells and she daintily made her way to her Mini motor car.

As I was walking along the high street in Hayford, I was in one of my reflective moods. Mingling with the other pedestrians, many of whom were hurrying to their different destinations, I was undisturbed by the noise and bustle; I was content with life.

Some months ago, I was studying hard for my final exams and now I was a Chartered Accountant with my own small practice; I was doing the work which I preferred: dealing with personal tax cases and smaller businesses. I liked to see people achieving, from a grass-roots level.

As I strode along, I saw a man in the distance walking towards me. He seemed familiar but I could not quite place him. Then, as we came face to face, I realised it was Mr Johnson, the bane of my life, the ex-managing clerk at Davis & Co. He had lost considerable weight and his face was haggard. His swarthiness and pugnacity were still apparent, however; he was still wearing his heavy three-piece dark grey suit, which now hung loosely on him. I noticed his grubby, frayed shirt cuffs. His large bulbous wart-covered nose made me shudder. This was the man who had endeavoured to make my life a misery when I was an articled clerk at Davis & Co.

As soon as he knew that Mr Davis's practice was being taken over by another firm, he had left to commence employment at a commercial company in Hayford. However, shortly after his new employment he had argued with the owner and had been sacked.

His dark bushy eyebrows rose when he caught sight of me. 'How are you, Tom?' he asked, averting his eyes when I looked directly at him. I used to dream of unspeakable acts of revenge concerning this bully, but now I had qualified and was a Chartered Accountant with my own practice, somehow I felt sorry for him. Most bullies are cowards at heart.

I decided reluctantly to let bygones be bygones, although I could never forget the way he had treated me as a young man. Young people are particularly vulnerable regarding intimidation at workplaces. If they try their best, they should always be assisted to develop their careers – not thrust aside inconsequentially.

We shook hands and I said, 'My practice has really taken off well; my clientele is increasing weekly.'

Mr Johnson's upper lip trembled. 'If you ever want a managing clerk, you know where to come.'

Not on your life, I thought.

The tables had been turned, yet where I had the opportunity to make the man feel more inadequate, I didn't take it. To see him reduced to being unemployed, his ego deflated, was sufficient for me.

As he slouched away, shoulders hunched, his military bearing no longer apparent, I wondered if he would ever be employed again. He was in his late fifties so it was unlikely; also his temperament was against him.

In the offices of Davis & Co. he had ruled the staff with a rod of iron and most of them were frightened of him. My fear had disappeared. Life sometimes has a habit of twisting the knife in the wound and what had happened to him was a prime example.

I continued my walk, returning to my small office where I sat down in my comfortable plush armchair and began to balance a set of accounts. Somehow a deep feeling of contentment came over me and I looked to the future with optimism.

M R FLETCHER WAS now my client, having transferred to my practice from Davis & Co. He was a gentleman farmer – his family had owned one thousand acres of land for many years.

His farm, mainly arable, which I had visited before when I was as an articled clerk at Davis & Co., was about thirty miles from Hayford. He also kept some livestock, mainly pigs.

The telephone rang and, picking up the receiver, I recognised Mr Fletcher's voice.

On the previous occasion I had visited his farm, I had made the journey on my scooter. This time I was a Chartered Accountant with my own practice and a new car. I knew this would not make a ha'p'orth of difference to him, as he judged people by their characters and not their jobs. This was one of the reasons I liked him; he treated everyone, whatever their job, as an equal.

'Would 2.30 p.m. tomorrow suit you, Mr Read?' he asked in his distinctive, cultivated voice.

I looked in my desk diary. 'That will be fine, Mr Fletcher.' I could hear him coughing slightly and then he said, 'I look forward to seeing you.' I heard the click as he replaced his receiver.

The following day, I called at my office after an early lunch and collected Mr Fletcher's file. I browsed through the draft accounts I had prepared, made certain I had listed the queries to enable me to finish the accounts, put the file in my briefcase, locked my office door and walked to my Cortina.

I commenced my journey to Fletcher's Farm. The sun was shining from a cloud-free azure sky. Although the farm was only thirty miles away, I decided to stop at a lay-by. My briefcase was on the back seat and I leaned over, retrieved the case and pulled out my flask of coffee. I was my own boss and if I wanted to stop to reflect, why not? Drinking my coffee and eating my chocolate biscuit, I sat there contemplating my achievements and the future.

Since leaving school at seventeen, I had been studying hard for six years — often two or three hours in the evenings and also at weekends — but the hard work had resulted in success. My small practice was flourishing and expanding fast — perhaps too fast. Although my social life was enjoyable, my work schedule was taking over.

I found the work extremely interesting and stimulating, especially the tax side, and my clients fascinated me. Every one had different facets. The right balance must be achieved however, between work and play, and somehow there was, I felt, an imbalance; it was up to me to make the right adjustments.

My reflections over, I started the engine of my car and proceeded to complete my journey to Mr Fletcher's farm. I remembered the way from the last time I had journeyed there. All of a sudden a large wooden gate came into view and a prominent sign announced 'Fletcher's Farm'. I got out of my car, opened the heavy gate, drove my car through and closed the gate.

The last time I came, I had to wheel my scooter along a muddy driveway but this time the shingle-covered private road was dry. Driving slowly, I came to the large, impressive farmhouse surrounded by huge oak and sycamore trees. Noisy rooks were again circling the rookery.

After parking my Cortina on the gravelled courtyard, I surmounted the few stone steps leading to the magnificent oak front door and knocked, using the large, shaped brass knocker.

'Good morning, Mr Read.'

Looking over my shoulder, I saw Mr Fletcher standing at the foot of the stone steps.

He was seventy years of age and had a military bearing; a tall man – over six feet. His steel blue eyes looked kindly at me from his long, sunburnt face.

'I saw you drive up,' he said. 'I've been setting some rabbit snares over there.' He pointed to a grassy area opposite the farmhouse. As he was speaking to me, Mrs Fletcher appeared, carrying a tray with cups of tea and her lovely home-made scones, covered in butter and jam. The last time I visited the farm I was lucky to consume some and she must have remembered how appreciative I was. Knowing how punctual I was, she had prepared the tea and scones ready for my arrival. Both she and her husband were examples of the polite people I admired. They were courteous and refined.

Mrs Fletcher was a small lady, slim, and wore a bright yellow apron. Her grey hair was drawn tightly back and tied with a blue ribbon. 'There you are,' she said. 'You have your tea and scones before Bob takes you on a tour of the farm.' She playfully tweaked Mr Fletcher's arm as he stood patiently by her side. He smiled warmly and pressed her hand affectionately. They were happy and content with their lives.

To the right of the farmhouse, facing south, there was a patio, a small fountain and a lawn edged with a multitude of flowers; there were four chairs, a wooden table and a bench seat. I followed Mr and Mrs Fletcher.

'Sit down, Mr Read, if you please,' said Mr Fletcher, taking the tray from his wife.

'I'll see you later, Mr Read; I'm baking some cakes,' she said and smiled at me. She went through the kitchen door which faced the patio.

Taking Mr Fletcher's file from my briefcase, I soon cleared the queries with him to enable me to finalise his accounts, replaced the file and listened to him as he picked up the rabbit snares.

'Would you like to see how we catch rabbits?' he asked. He knew that my knowledge of farming was limited, being town bred. I was always interested in my clients and eagerly rose from my chair. I followed him to the rear of the farmhouse where two hutches were placed. Surely he didn't keep rabbits as pets? He opened one of the hutches and put his hand in and withdrew a ferret, holding it by the scruff of its neck. It was white and had beady eyes. I later ascertained that ferrets are small half-domesticated polecats. Often farmers would keep them to catch rabbits.

Handling the ferret with care he stroked it. As I put my hand out to touch it, he quickly restrained me. 'I wouldn't do that, Mr Read; she'll bite as she doesn't know you.' I immediately withdrew my hand.

We strolled towards the grass area opposite the farmhouse and I noticed mounds and holes, presuming them to be burrows. Mr Fletcher had placed some nets over the holes; he bent down and put the ferret down one of them. All of a sudden a rabbit appeared and rushed straight into one of the nets.

'That'll do for lunch tomorrow,' he said, giving the rabbit a quick strike at the back of the neck; the rabbit ceased to struggle and went limp.

I didn't comment, thinking of the last time I had eaten 'rabbit pie'. I decided not to relate my dreadful experience at Granger's Restaurant to Mr Fletcher. He seemed satisfied with the rabbit he had caught and placed it in a bag hanging from his trouser belt. Retrieving the ferret, he strode back to the hutches and I followed him.

I heard the sound of machinery in the distance. 'That's the combine harvester, Mr Read,' said my host.

Looking across the sunlit fields of wheat which stretched for miles, I could see in the distance the combine surrounded by clouds of chaff and dust.

'I get a contractor in to harvest the wheat nowadays,' he added. Mr Fletcher's eyes glazed momentarily as I assumed that his thoughts strayed to earlier years when he was younger and capable of combining all day, if needed. For a moment it seemed that he had forgotten my presence; then suddenly he perked up, looked at me and smiled wistfully.

There was another noise – a shrill one; this time quite close.

'What's that, Mr Fletcher?' I asked.

'I'm having a tree felled; it's died back so much it's become dangerous and particularly as it's close to the road, it must come down. I hate getting rid of trees but I don't have any option.'

He looked sad as he spoke, and no doubt wishing to relax, took his old briar pipe out of his jacket pocket, filled it with tobacco from a tin of Gold Block, lit it with a match after several attempts in the slight breeze, and puffed away contentedly.

'Sorry, Mr Read,' he said, as clouds of smoke encircled me. 'I had forgotten that you don't smoke.' After a few minutes, he extinguished his pipe, and tapped the ash from the bowl.

As we were walking towards the tree which was being felled, I looked up at the tree surgeon who was standing high in the branches. He had a chainsaw and was cutting through parts of branches. After the pieces were cut they were lowered by rope to another man who was standing at the foot of the tree.

I looked with much trepidation. The tree surgeon was actually walking along some of the thicker branches. 'Won't he fall?' I queried.

'He is an expert,' said Mr Fletcher, protecting his eyes from the bright sunlight with his hands. 'You look closely and you'll see that he has a harness on. If he slips the harness will prevent him from falling to the ground.'

We passed the tree but kept well away. It was dangerous work felling trees but I could see that the men knew exactly what they had to do.

I somehow guessed what was coming next. Mr Fletcher had to show me his pigs. They were a delight to him, as I ascertained from my last visit.

Smut, the Labrador, greeted us, wagging his tail with delight. He was a magnificent looking dog with a beautiful shiny coat. First he approached Mr Fletcher, who stroked him affectionately. It was obvious that they were friends and delighted in each other's company.

The sickening smell wafting towards us told me that we were nearly at the pigsties. Mr Fletcher opened the door leading to the sties and my reflex action was to step backwards quickly.

There were more pigs than last time; there was a huge sow with her litter of ten piglets all sucking ravenously at their mother's teats. Emptying some swill into the feeding troughs Mr Fletcher looked at me and then at the squealing pigs. 'Beautiful, aren't they?'

I agreed enthusiastically. How could I say to him I hated the sight of them? It would have broken his heart, especially as he had won numerous cups at shows for his prize pigs.

We strolled back to the farmhouse, breathing in the fresh country air. I had a brief chat with Mrs Fletcher, said my farewells, got in my car, waved and drove away.

M Y THOUGHTS WERE interrupted as my telephone rang. I was halfway through casting a column of figures; it often happened. I picked up the receiver. 'Fred Jackson here, Tom,' said a voice. He was a friend of mine, about my age. We had known each other since we attended primary school; our working lives had ended up completely different. Although he was bright and articulate, he had not felt any strong desire to work towards a qualification and left school at sixteen years of age without any GCEs. Although his lifestyle was completely different from mine, there was a basic common understanding between us; we simply liked each other.

He ended up as a Rocker and I was close to becoming a Mod. Whilst as a young lad he rode a powerful motorbike with heavy leathers and didn't mind getting covered in oil, grease and dirt, I rode a smart Capri scooter and was concerned about my modern stylish clothes.

Having no desire to study after he left school, he had drifted from one job to another – mostly self-employment, but never making much money, whatever he tried. However, it didn't seem to bother him, and as long as he had his beloved motorbikes to tinker with, he seemed happy. He'd been going out with various girls over a long period of time but they got tired with his motorbike activities coming before them. He seemed totally unconcerned.

The last time he had contacted me was shortly before I left Davis & Co., and he had told me he was selling fish at a local market.

'Tom, you remember I was selling fish at the market?'

'Yes, I do,' I replied.

'Well, I've given that up. I lost money on the venture.'

Not again, I thought.

'I've got some good news,' he said. 'Won some money on the pools.'

'How much?' I queried, expecting him to say about fifty pounds.

'Twenty thousand pounds,' he replied.

That was a small fortune in 1963. My brand new Cortina had cost me six hundred and thirty pounds.

Some people are financially lucky in life. They don't seem to try to accumulate money but they fall on their feet. This was the case with Fred Jackson. He was quite content with drifting from one job to another and then he had received this tremendous windfall. There was no jealousy on my part, however; I liked him and was pleased about his good luck.

'What are you going to do with the money, Fred?' I asked.

'Well, I would like your advice; I want to commence a business, buying and selling motorbikes. There's a motorbike shop up for sale in the high street,' he said. I knew the place.

'Could you draft some new accounts books for me and tell me the best investments?'

'Leave it to me, Fred; I'll give the matters some thought. I'll ring you tomorrow.'

He gave me a telephone number where he could be reached and replaced the receiver.

I sat back relaxing in my armchair and contemplated. What a bombshell! Fred Jackson was worth a small fortune.

From obscurity to fame overnight. My job however was to act as his accountant to the best of my ability and this I intended to do. Rising from my chair, I took a new accounts book from my stationery cupboard and soon drafted the headings. Another new client; my list was increasing rapidly.

The next day I telephoned Fred Jackson.

'I've been to a solicitor,' he said. 'The owner of the motorbike shop has agreed to sell the premises and all the stock to me for eight thousand pounds.'

'That's great, Fred; could you call to see me this afternoon?' He agreed and an appointment was made for two thirty.

At 3 p.m. he arrived – typically late, but the delay was not unexpected; I had arranged to have my coffee break and do some studying, reading magazines until he arrived.

My office doorbell rang and Fred Jackson strode towards me. He was a large man of about fourteen stone and he towered over me as I went to greet him. He had obviously bought a new shirt and trousers, as his old ones were torn and soiled. However, his pot belly was still visible squeezing through his tight shirt. He had shaved, which was unusual. His dark brown eyes looked at me from a round jovial face. We shook hands, with mutual affection. I often wondered why we liked each other as we were so different in lots of ways. We did like each other and that was that.

'What do you think about my windfall, Tom?' He laughed loudly as he eased his large frame into one of the chairs opposite mine.

'I'm really pleased for you,' I replied.

I suggested he went to the bank to get expert advice regarding investing the majority of the money remaining after purchasing the motorbike shop and stock.

'Yes, I'll do that, Tom. I've already opened a new bank account.' Apparently the bank manager had welcomed him with open arms.

For some time Fred hadn't had a bank account because some years ago he'd overdrawn without authority, and from that time had used cash for his various trading activities.

'Would you like a coffee, Fred?' I asked him.

'Thanks, Tom. You have your coffee neat and I'll add something to mine!' He withdrew from his back trouser pocket a small bottle of rum and placed it on the table. He knew that I didn't drink alcohol often.

We sat there for a couple of hours reminiscing – me a Chartered Accountant with a new practice and him a wealthy man with a new business on the horizon. As they say: 'It's a funny old world.'

THE SUNDAY FOR the dance tests – bronze, silver and gold – had arrived. Pupils were to be tested at the ballroom where the monthly dances were held. I always looked forward with pleasure to the ballroom dances but this was different – mistakes would matter. Rose and I had been asked to arrive at the ballroom owned by the chocolate-making company where my mother worked at 11 a.m. The factory would be closed but the security guard at the gates had agreed to work overtime.

Those pupils taking their tests for the bronze medals would be examined first.

I arranged to pick Rose up at her home at 10 a.m. and I arrived there five minutes before the appointed time. I was wearing a pair of my close-fitting light grey trousers, a dark blue blazer covered in small gold-coloured buttons, a white shirt and a light blue tie; my gold initialled cuff links (a gift from Rose) and a tiepin completed my apparel.

I rang the doorbell; the door opened and I was greeted by Mr Turner, who said, 'Come through, Tom.'

We walked along the hall and into the lounge.

Mrs Turner was sitting on the settee, listening to their Dansette radio.

'How are you, Tom?' she asked, putting her knitting on her lap.

'A little nervous, to tell the truth, Mrs Turner.' I usually got a bit edgy before an exam or test but the nerves disappeared when the exam or test commenced.

'Rose won't be long,' said Mr Turner. He turned to the drinks cabinet. 'I won't offer you a drink, Tom, but I'll get one for myself. I'm feeling nervous thinking about the test!' He smiled at me warmly as he lifted the glass of sherry to his lips. 'Sorry, Lucy, would you like a drink?' he asked his wife.

'No thanks, Jim,' she replied, and picked up her knitting.

As I was about to sit down, Rose appeared.

'Hello, Tom,' she said. She didn't look nervous at all and her bright blue eyes sparkled. To me, she looked as if she was keen to take the test.

She was wearing a cream blouse with a dark blue miniskirt. Silk stockings showed off her shapely legs. Her well-made black shoes were polished. She smiled at me; her face was peach-like with a touch of powder and lipstick; auburn hair tied with a white ribbon and small pearl earrings completed the classy picture. I had been told by Miss Williams that our presentation would be taken into account by the examiner.

After having a chat with Mr and Mrs Turner, I looked at my watch and said, 'We had better be going, Rose.'

She immediately made her way to the hall where she collected our coats. 'See you later, Mum, Dad.'

I also said my farewells and we walked towards my Cortina. Rose got into the car and after I made sure that the passenger door was shut safely, I backed out of the driveway on to the road. I tooted the horn and we waved to Rose's parents, who were peeping through the net curtains.

Within five minutes, we arrived at the chocolate-making factory and were ushered through by the security gateman.

Parking my car, I was not surprised to see numerous other cars already parked. Many pupils would be taking their tests that day. We made certain that we had our dance shoe bags, which also contained the wire brushes for ensuring the surfaces of the dance shoes were kept clean and non-slip, then we locked my car doors and walked towards the ballroom. The atmosphere was tense as other couples also made their way towards the main entrance.

'Hello, Tom,' said Jane, a young lady of Rose's age. She was small, dark haired and petite, and smiled at me as Rose and I joined her and her partner, Bert. I had danced with Jane on several occasions at social dances and found her extremely attractive and easy to talk to. My fanciful thoughts quickly evaporated and I started to think of the test and, in particular, how Rose and I would fare.

Colin and Dawn Brand, neighbours of mine, were already seated just inside the ballroom, which was partitioned from the dance floor by a wide screen. There were chairs up to the screen and the wine bar, which was closed. Some younger pupils were endeavouring to peep through a small hole in the screen to see two of the pupils being tested. I could hear a jive being played.

Most of the chairs were occupied but there were two vacant next to Colin and Dawn so we sat next to our friends.

'How are you feeling?' asked Colin. 'You look as if you need stiff drinks.'

Rose spoke. 'Now I'm here I feel nervous, although I hadn't felt so before.' Nerves affect different people in various ways.

'Don't worry too much,' said Dawn. 'We feel nervous and we've taken a number of tests.' They were taking their gold bars in ballroom dancing.

Rose and I put on our dance shoes, being very careful to ensure that the soles and heels were clean and roughened with the small wire brushes.

I noticed Miss Williams standing at the edge of the screen, looking cool and relaxed. She had seen it all before, time and time again. Cha-cha-cha music was being played and suddenly it stopped.

The two pupils who had been tested – they were in our class at Miss Williams's school of dancing – squeezed past the screen and started talking to her; she was ramrod straight and dressed neatly in a dark blue dress. The pupils, David and Jean, sat down; they looked despondent.

Miss Williams walked briskly over towards us and said, 'Hello, Tom, Rose. All ready for the fray?' She laughed and joked, endeavouring to calm us. 'Your test will be at eleven thirty,' she added, giving us our papers. She walked back to her official position near the screen.

I looked around. Some pupils were laughing and chatting – others quiet and sombre. The place was crowded. Looking at my watch I saw that it was eleven twenty-eight – two minutes to go!

Suddenly Miss Williams beckoned to us and we joined her at the side of the screen. 'Try your best and you need have no fears.' She gently pushed us through and on to the dance floor. Rose and I walked towards the table where the examiner was sitting, gave him our papers and awaited his instructions.

The examiner, a man of about forty-five years of age, was impeccably dressed in a dark grey pinstripe suit, white shirt and red tie. He looked at us kindly over his half-moon spectacles.

'Please take the centre of the dance floor and commence dancing the jive,' he said.

Rose and I had practised the jive and cha-cha-cha repeatedly until we knew the sequences exactly. I held Rose's hand and took her carefully to the centre of the dance floor. Her hand was trembling and I looked at her face – usually smiling, but now tense and wan. We commenced dancing. My nerves had disappeared but Rose was shaking like a leaf. 'Calm down, Rose,' I whispered. We completed the jive sequences and looked towards the examiner.

'Kindly commence the cha-cha-cha.' After a faltering start, my confidence was conveyed to Rose, who soon settled down; I felt that we had danced as well as we could.

'Thank you,' said the examiner, 'that will be all.'

We met Miss Williams at the screen.

'How did you get on?' she asked. We explained about the false start in the cha-cha-cha. 'Don't worry. It happens to most pupils,' she said, and smiled encouragingly. 'You danced more than adequately. I saw you through the gap in the screen.' She smiled and turned away to talk to the next pupils to be tested.

'Let's go home, Rose,' I said. We waved to Colin and Dawn and left the ballroom. We gasped the fresh air as we walked towards my car. My face was hot and I wiped the perspiration from my brow. Rose looked flushed.

'I'm sorry I got so nervous, Tom,' she said. She was sad.

I pressed her hand reassuringly; I had no idea that she would be affected by nerves. She always seemed so calm, but I had not previously experienced her reaction to taking exams or tests.

We drove back to Rose's home in virtual silence. The bronze medal test was only the first stepping stone in Latin American dancing, but it was important for us to do well. Dancing was our main social activity.

Rose's parents were sympathetic when we arrived home.

'We'll just have to wait and see,' I said, endeavouring to look on the bright side. I had taken many examinations and I knew that nothing could be done to affect the result.

Later in the day, I was still at Rose's home having had lunch with her and her parents when there was a telephone call.

'It's Miss Williams,' said Mr Turner, handing me the receiver. Rose was upstairs, freshening up.

'I thought you would like to know the results of your test and also Rose's.' Miss Williams sounded exuberant. 'You have both passed with excellent marks – highly commended.'

'Thanks very much, Miss Williams,' I said. I replaced the receiver and I felt a rush of adrenalin. I was so excited.

Rose came hurtling down the stairs. She'd heard my voice on the telephone.

'We've passed with honours,' I said. Rose's face displayed her rapture. We both took further dance tests but that first one was very special.

ROSE HAD DECIDED that she would like to drive a car. 'What do I have to do to learn, Tom?' she asked. I was taken aback. It never occurred to me that she would wish to drive; I was the driver. Male chauvinism, I suppose.

'Well, you could have lessons from a professional driving instructor. They are quite expensive though; or I could try to teach you.' I nearly bit my tongue off. What had I said? My father had taught me to drive and I had been lucky, perhaps, to pass at the first attempt.

'Would you teach me, Tom?' she pleaded. She looked at me with her bright blue appealing eyes, coyly. How could I refuse her demure appeal? I wondered what I had let myself in for. I'd taught a friend of mine to drive and he had passed his test first time also, but quite a few hours of practising were required. Teaching Rose would be a different kettle of fish. How would she react when I told her what to do? It was very easy for a lay teacher and a pupil to get overheated and quarrelsome when driving lessons commenced.

'We'll see how it goes. I'll pick you up on Saturday afternoon at 2 p.m., if that's all right, Rose?'

She agreed and I could see that she was excited. I must admit I had considerable trepidations thinking about my Cortina's gearbox and clutch! A learner is bound to make errors. That is part of the learning process and my car would suffer. However, I had agreed to teach her and I would keep my promise.

Saturday arrived and I called at Rose's home. After parking my car, I strolled along the garden path and saw Rose drawing aside the net curtains. Her mother and father were also looking through the window. Opening the door, Rose greeted me with her usual welcoming kiss.

Rose's father wore a freshly laundered brilliant white shirt, red tie and smart brown trousers. I looked down at his multicoloured slippers – no doubt a present from Mrs Turner or Rose.

'Hello, Tom,' he said. He was always friendly towards me; we had gelled as soon as we had first met, and we often had long discussions about topical news reports.

Standing next to him was Mrs Turner. Although she was slighter built than Rose, she had similar features – prim, spotlessly clean and very tidy looking. 'Like mother, like daughter,' came to my mind.

'How long will you be?' Rose's mother asked, looking at us anxiously. She was concerned as Rose had never previously driven a car.

'We'll be about two hours, Mrs Turner,' I said. 'I'm not taking Rose on to the public roads yet. I know a large lay-by which is not used that often and Rose can practise using the gears and clutch.'

Mrs Turner relaxed a little and turned towards Mr Turner who put his arm around her protectively and smiled reassuringly.

'I'll do my best to teach Rose properly,' I added. I always endeavoured to be positive but I must admit I was feeling somewhat anxious myself.

I looked at Rose; she set my pulse racing. She was wearing cream slacks, a white blouse, and her auburn hair was tied back with a red ribbon. Good quality flat shoes, ideal for driving, completed the picture.

'Ready?' I asked.

Rose nodded. 'I'm really looking forward to my first driving lesson, Tom.'

We walked arm in arm along the garden path to my car.

'I'll drive to the lay-by, Rose,' I told her.

'All right, Tom,' she said, and smiled her ingratiating smile which I knew so well.

We waved to Rose's parents who were standing at the garden gate. I put my car into first gear and slowly drove down the road. The lay-by was only about a mile away and on reaching it I drove off the road and stopped my car.

I got out of my car and opened the passenger door, saying, 'You sit in the driver's seat, Rose.'

She looked at me a little nervously but got out and was soon sat next to me with her hands on the steering wheel. I moved her hands gently to the right positions.

We had been through the Highway Code several times and Rose was quick to learn the theory. This was different; she was actually going to drive my car!

I had turned the ignition off. First I went over the controls with Rose: the footbrake, clutch, accelerator, handbrake, gear lever and ignition.

'Rose, we'll now go through signalling and the use of the mirrors,' I went on. My car had the usual inside mirror and two wing mirrors. 'Before you move off you must look in the mirrors to ensure that other vehicles or cyclists are not behind you. Only when the road is clear should you signal and commence driving.' We went over this simple but most important routine.

'Make sure that the gear lever is in neutral,' I said, and pointed, showing her what I meant. 'The handbrake must be on.' Again I showed her. 'You can now turn the ignition key to start the engine.'

'Like this, Tom?' she asked. The engine started.

'That's fine,' I said, and she smiled. She was enjoying herself.

'Push your left foot down to the floor with the clutch (the left pedal),' I said. This she did. 'Then, holding the handbrake, slowly let it free from the ratchet. Slowly lift your left foot off the clutch and slowly press the accelerator (the right pedal). To stop the car press the clutch and the foot brake (the middle pedal).'

Coordination at first is not easy. 'Like this, Tom?' asked Rose. She lifted her foot off the clutch and pressed the accelerator. The car jerked forward a few feet and stalled. 'What did I do wrong?' She looked frightened.

'Don't worry,' I said, 'it happens to most learners at first – it certainly happened to me.' She still looked apprehensive. 'Turn the ignition off, put the gear lever in neutral and the handbrake on and we'll sit quietly for a few minutes. Then you have another try.'

After relaxing for a while, Rose tried the routine again, and this time the coordination was better – slightly jerky at first, but eventually the car moved forward slowly and smoothly.

'The car is moving, Tom.' Rose shrieked with delight.

'Concentrate, Rose – keep the car straight,' I prompted. She was veering to the left.

After about fifty yards, I gave Rose further instructions. 'Take your right foot off the accelerator, press the footbrake and the clutch.' This she did and my car came to a halt. 'Pull the handbrake up, Rose, and turn the ignition off.' She did so and coyly looked across at me. I was perspiring and wiped my forehead with my handkerchief. 'That was fine for the first attempt, Rose.' I remembered when I first drove my father's car. Rose had driven at least as well as me, if not better.

'We'll have a break, Rose.' I turned the radio on. The Beatles record, 'I Want to Hold Your Hand' – No. 1 – was playing. I reached over to the back seats, found the flask of coffee, poured out two cups and gave one to Rose; she was sitting quite calm.

'What do you think, Tom?' she asked.

'I believe that overall you have done well for your first attempt,' I replied. Coordination is all important when driving and I believed that Rose, who was highly intelligent, was a natural and would prove to be an excellent driver.

We tried driving up and down the lay-by for about an hour and eventually she was consistently driving in first gear smoothly. I tried her with second gear up to fifteen miles per hour and there was no problem whatsoever. Deciding to draw the first driving lesson to a close, I asked Rose to stop the car.

We exchanged seats and I drove back to her parents' home. Rose was chatting away and was looking forward to her next lesson. 'When will you give me another lesson, Tom?'

'Next Saturday,' I replied. I was expecting the experience of teaching Rose to be difficult, as it had been when I had taught her to swim, but I had been pleasantly surprised. Many females make excellent drivers and it looked as if Rose was going to be one of them.

I HAD BEEN asked by a clergyman to act for him regarding his tax returns and to advise him regarding tax matters generally. Occasionally he came to see me at my office and sometimes I went to see him at his rectory in Hayford.

The Rev. John Hammond was a highly intelligent and kind man, well thought of by his parishioners and many others, including tramps who would call at the rectory at all times of the day and night and impose themselves upon his hospitality and generosity. He provided hot meals and drinks and the money for these provisions came out of his own funds. I do not hesitate to say that I have never met a more benevolent man. One's religious faith or lack of it did not matter to him; if one was agnostic or atheist, this was immaterial to him. He was interested in the well-being of his fellow man. I never heard anyone say anything detrimental about him; his parishioners flocked to his sermons.

Sometimes one meets a man who has a very special quality of making one feel better just by talking to him. The Rev. Hammond had this aura, difficult to pinpoint, but it was there.

Speaking to him on the telephone, his kindness was immediately noticeable by the tone of his voice. I arranged to meet him at his rectory in the afternoon at 3 p.m. 'That will be fine, Mr Read; looking forward to seeing you again,' he said. I heard him humming a well-known tune as he replaced the receiver.

The church was not far from my office in a turning off the high street; I decided to walk there. Two of my other clients, Mr and Mrs Grange, lived in a flat opposite the church and I had visited them recently.

As I confidently approached the rectory which was next to the church, I breathed in the fresh air and looked skywards. Clouds were gathering; rain was on its way. I always kept a light mac in my briefcase for that eventuality, so I was unconcerned. Climbing the few concrete steps towards the rectory front door, which was painted green and peeling badly, I was about to ring the bell when I heard a gruff voice saying, 'I was here first, young man.'

I looked round; sitting on the ground just behind an overflowing dustbin was an old man with a long grey beard and moustache. His baggy trousers and shirt were torn and he wore an old, grey, musty, stained coat, the frayed edges of which lay in the dust; mud spattered Wellington boots completed his apparel.

He rose from his temporary resting place and picked up a rag bundle knotted together with string. Slowly, with the aid of an old scratched walking stick, he managed to stagger to his feet. I stepped back quickly. His breath was bad and the smell of alcohol drifted towards me. His bright brown beady eyes squinted at me from under dark bushy eyebrows. A 'dewdrop' remained poised on the end of his long nose until he slowly wiped it away with his coat sleeve. His fingernails were black and his hands were dirty.

'What do you think you're doing, pushing in front of me?' he snarled. He grimaced, staggered past me and rang the bell.

The door opened and there stood the Rev. Hammond. He looked first at the tramp and then at me. 'Won't keep you a moment, Mr Read. I'll just make Joe comfortable.

I've got some hot tea and biscuits for him in the kitchen. Go through to the lounge. You know where it is.'

I followed him and the tramp down the wide gloomy hall and I turned right into the lounge. I noticed the Rev. Hammond's writing bureau open with his tax return and other papers neatly set out. I sat down and waited for him.

After a few minutes, he greeted me properly. 'Sorry about that, Mr Read. Old Joe gets drunk and I let him rest for a while in the kitchen until he sobers up.'

The Rev. Hammond wore a black cassock and a white clergyman's collar. His round face had rosy cheeks and his light grey eyes stared at me perceptively. He never turned anyone away who needed his help – not even dirty unwashed belligerent tramps. 'They are all God's creatures,' he used to say. 'Provided that they don't harm anybody, I welcome them.'

He placed a tray on which cups of coffee, a bowl of sugar, a jug of milk and biscuits were visible, on to a small coffee table. 'I believe you take milk and sugar, Mr Read. Please help yourself.'

We chattered about current affairs for about half an hour and then he turned towards his bureau and the tax return. 'I don't understand these tax papers at all. I think I've accumulated all the details which you will require. Please check them for me.'

I checked them accordingly, soon completed the simple tax return, and asked him to sign it.

'Each to their own, Mr Read,' he said, and smiled kindly. He had joined the ministry when he was middle-aged. He had held a top executive job in commerce for many years but decided to train to be a clergyman after his wife had died following a long period of illness.

I was putting his completed tax return into my briefcase when Joe, the tramp, came through the lounge door. He didn't knock.

'I'm going now. Thanks for the food and drink,' he said. He looked towards the Rev. Hammond, hobbled away leaving a cloud of alcoholic fumes behind him, banged the front door and was gone.

'It takes all sorts, Mr Read.' The Rev. Hammond graciously saw me to the door and clasped my hand warmly with his two hands. 'Pop in and see me any time – it doesn't have to be about business matters,' he said kindly.

I left him standing at the rectory door, waving to me; I came away greatly uplifted.

M Y PRACTICE WAS becoming well established, and I was endeavouring to improve my social life, particularly with Rose. We often went to Cranfield Park, fifteen miles from Hayford. The area had been owned by the Cranfields, as I mentioned before, but subsequently was opened to the general public.

At the park one Saturday, we were discussing our social activities. Most of our spare time was spent going to dance lessons, ballroom dances on a Saturday evening, or swimming at the local baths.

We were walking leisurely past the old church where Dick Turpin, the highwayman, was rumoured to have hidden from his pursuers, along the winding path where huge blossom-laden rhododendrons grew. Reaching the familiar avenue of ancient oak trees growing beside the old dry moat, we delighted in experiencing the soft, springy leaf mould under our feet. The heavily laden oak trees spread dark shadows, but we left them behind us and strode into the brilliant sunshine. We were soon running on to the broad grass of the vast expanse of parkland which opened up before us. We raced to our favourite spot and quickly spread our picnic over a large tartan woollen rug.

'Shall we go to Mills' Circus at Earls Court next Saturday, Rose?' I asked, looking at her as she was pouring the coffee into the plastic cups.

'I'd love to, Tom,' she replied.

Tube trains would take us into London and there would be no necessity for me to drive into the City.

We were lying on the woollen rug when Rose gave me one of her looks which I knew so well. No words were spoken; we embraced and were enjoying the pleasure of the moment when our bliss was abruptly interrupted.

'What are you doing?' asked a little boy, kicking his blue rubber ball towards us.

We sat up quickly and stared at him. He was about four years of age, had red cheeks and wide open innocent eyes. Pulling his orange socks up, he ran to pick up his ball. Rose got up from the rug and kicked the ball back to the little boy who ran towards a lady shouting, 'Mummy, Mummy!'

Soon there were other children surrounding us, playing various games, so we gathered up the remains of our picnic fare, put everything into the hamper and made our way back to my Cortina.

'Nice little boy, Tom,' said Rose, giving me a very meaningful look. Sometimes a look speaks volumes and that was one of them.

THE FOLLOWING SATURDAY, I picked Rose up at her home and we walked to the tube station. We were both looking forward to seeing Mills' Circus, as we hadn't been to a circus since we were children. It didn't take long and we arrived at Earls Court. We showed our tickets to the young lady with bright red lipstick, at the entrance to the circus, and made our way to our seats. I had paid for seats right at the edge of the ring.

What struck me first was the smell. Most circuses have it and that one was no exception. No matter how the cleaners strived to keep the place clean, various odours lingered; it was all part of the special atmosphere.

There were lions, tigers, elephants, acrobats, clowns and other acts, including a speciality, Leslie Bainbridge.

The top-hatted ringmaster was introducing the next act. I looked at the programme. Leslie Bainbridge came into the ring. He specialised in sleight of hand tricks with cards and other objects. Sometimes he asked members of the audience to assist him. Smartly dressed in a dinner jacket and dress shirt, standing in the centre of the ring, he looked towards Rose and me. 'Now here's a nice looking young couple,' he said, as I expect he did to numerous couples. 'I wonder if the young gentleman would assist me.' Rose pushed me. 'Go on, Tom.' I nervously and reluctantly climbed over the edge of the ring towards Mr Bainbridge.

'May I ask your name?' he said, looking at me.

'Tom,' I replied.

'That's a nice short name,' he said. 'Please sit down.' I did so on a small chair next to a table; both items had been brought on whilst we had been conversing. 'That's a good quality watch,' he went on. I looked at my wrist. My watch had gone. Next he said, 'Fancy coming to a high-class establishment like this without a tie.'

I looked down – no tie. 'Would you stand up please?' I stood up and felt my loose trousers. My belt had disappeared. 'Do you have any money on you?' I felt in my inside pocket. My wallet was missing.

'Are these what you are looking for?'

I turned round. On a table were my missing possessions. There was a round of applause from the audience and I saw Rose in fits of laughter.

'Thank you! May I ask you all to thank Tom for his participation in my act and for being such a good sport.'

Mr Bainbridge bowed to the audience, gave my possessions to me and led me to the edge of the ring. I made my way back to my seat, cringing. I have never seen Rose laugh so much.

Tears were streaming down her face. 'You should have seen your face,' she said. Then she kissed me affectionately and pressed my hand. She was enjoying the moment.

The circus acts came to an end with all the performers parading round the ring and as Mr Bainbridge passed, he smiled at us and winked. I had not felt a thing when he had taken my watch and other possessions. I wondered whether in the past he had been a real pickpocket. One could only guess!

Rose and I made our way home full of good humour and contentment. What a day that had been – a special one. The visions would remain vivid for years to come.

THE TELEPHONE AT my office rang and a voice said, 'John White here.'

I recognised him instantly. He was the owner of the fish and chip shop in the high street. 'What can I do for you, Mr White?' He was sixty-eight years of age, and a fitness fanatic – jogging, swimming and cycling virtually every day. He also belonged to a yoga class.

'Could I come round to see you, please? I've got myself in a mess with my bookkeeping. Since you left Davis & Co., nobody has been to check my books.'

He had transferred to my practice from Davis & Co. when he knew Mr Davis was retiring. Whilst at Davis & Co. I used to go to his fish and chip shop – the best in the area – on a monthly basis, but with my small practice it was easier for him to call to see me.

'I shall be pleased to see you, Mr White. If you bring your accounts book and bank statements, I'm sure I will be able to sort out the problem for you. Would 12.45 p.m. tomorrow suit you?'

Mr White paused. I heard him talking to someone – probably Mrs White. 'That'll be all right, Mr Read. See you then.'

Mr and Mrs White had a young assistant who helped prepare the potatoes and fish prior to frying, so Mr White was able to spend more time away from his shop.

A few minutes after twelve forty-five the following afternoon, my doorbell rang and I looked up from my desk. Mr White stepped into my office.

'How are you, Mr Read?' he asked cheerfully. His grip was firm. Broad-shouldered and upright, with jet-black curly hair, he looked ten years younger than his true age. Peering directly at me over his thick-rimmed tortoiseshell spectacles, he said, 'Nice office, Mr Read. I like the way you have set it out.'

He was wearing a camel-hair coat which he removed and placed on a chair, and I noticed his brilliant white shirt, green tie and his silky grey mohair suit. He looked more like a bank manager than a fish and chip shop owner.

'I've taken the afternoon off,' he said. 'Left the missis and our assistant, Terry, to run the shop. They'll cope all right. After I've seen you about my bookkeeping, I'm going swimming.'

He placed his sports bag on the floor. There was an article in the local newspaper about how he and others had completed a marathon swim for charity. I had seen him swim. I was a keen swimmer myself; his front crawl was excellent. I'm sure he could swim for hours if he wanted to. Usually he swam for about an hour up and down the pool; real evidence of his fitness.

He passed his accounts book to me. His arithmetic was poor. He just could not add up accurately. I made a quick check, located the errors within a few minutes and passed the book back to him.

'I was watching you add up,' he said. 'I bet you could beat an adding machine.'

I looked at Mr White with pride and said, 'Some colleagues and myself, when we were at a commercial firm conducting an audit on behalf of Davis & Co., had a competition with an adding machine operator, and in fact we proved to be the faster.' I was referring to the old type of manual adding machines, but I doubt whether I could beat the modern electronic ones.

Mr White picked up his sports bag and laid it on his lap. He reached into the bag and handed me a newspaper-bound parcel which was warm to the touch. The aroma of fish and chips spread through my office.

'I hoped they would remain hot, Mr Read.'

He knew by experience that fish and chips would stay hot for a reasonable time, provided they were wrapped up properly.

'Thanks very much, Mr White; I won't have to bother with sandwiches now,' I said gratefully.

As Mr White was leaving my office, Rose came through the door. She'd walked from the offices of Davis & Co. and we intended to have some sandwiches in my office.

'This is Mr White, Rose. Mr White, please meet my fiancée.'

His eyebrows rose as he looked at Rose admiringly and said, 'You have a good taste for quality, Mr Read, and this time I don't mean my fish and chips!'

His smile broadened until it changed into a grin. Then he was laughing loudly. His amusement was infectious, and at the office door Rose and I laughingly said our farewells to him.

SITTING AT MY office desk on a Friday, I had just finished drafting a particularly difficult letter to the local Tax Inspector. If the valid points in my letter were conceded, it meant that my client would be saved several hundred pounds, and therefore my facts and figures had to be very accurate.

I replaced my client's file in a filing cabinet, put the comprehensive letter into a tray for Rose to collect and type later in the evening, made myself a cup of coffee and sat back in my chair to enjoy my break. Munching a cream biscuit, my thoughts started to stray and I began thinking about the Saturday dance.

The doorbell rang and my fanciful thoughts quickly evaporated. Colin Brand opened the door and greeted me. Colin and his wife, Rose and myself, often socialised, particularly in the dancing circles. Being gold medallists, they were well known for their splendid dancing and also their general demeanour. I had given him one of my business cards shortly before I commenced my own practice and now he and his wife were my clients.

He was a car mechanic and she was a nurse at a local nursing home. Colin was perhaps five feet ten inches tall, upright and weighed about twelve stone. He was often telling jokes – some a little dry, many humorous – but you had to be in tune with his sense of humour. Occasionally he offended people, but not intentionally I am sure.

This was the second time he had visited my office. The first was shortly after I had commenced my practice.

'How's tricks, Tom?' he asked. He picked up a newspaper from a rack, unfolded it, placed it on a chair and sat down.

'Don't want to mess up your smart new chair,' he said, smiling broadly. His overalls were oil stained and his thinning hair was windswept.

When he was at a dance, he and his wife, Dawn, were immaculately dressed, but when working he was altogether different. I had looked in his small van once and his tools and materials were scattered haphazardly – a right pig's breakfast! It was difficult to reconcile his working life with his social life.

'Everything tidy – even the paper clips are in line, Tom,' he remarked. His eyes twinkled as he looked round my office, which I always endeavoured to keep neat.

He couldn't understand my attention to detail and I couldn't follow his messy way of working. Once we were at a dance however, these differences were forgotten and we had a common interest. Dancing was a great leveller.

Colin was a good mechanic, untidy it was true, but he knew his trade well and worked with two other men from a lock-up dilapidated warehouse half a mile from my office.

'There's my records, Tom. I'll leave you to add two and two and make five.' He laughed loudly, knowing full well the high standards of accuracy required of a Chartered Accountant.

Although his records were incomplete and his arithmetic was poor, he had a knack of making money on the Stock Market. I had seen his investment portfolio which had expanded over the years and he had become a very wealthy man. He knew which investments to purchase and sell at the right time. This had nothing to do with being good at mathematics, but was based upon being streetwise.

'See you on Saturday at the dance. Don't forget your shoes,' he said, grinning at me. He meant my dance shoes, remembering that once I had left them at home. He strode to the door, looked over his shoulder, gave a friendly smile, waved and was gone. I resumed my letter writing.

I WAS WALKING along the high street in Hayford with the intention of calling at Mr James's grocer's shop to purchase various provisions. I still lived with my parents, although I was courting Rose.

I was about one hundred yards from Mr James's shop when a trolleybus passed me. Suddenly it stopped. I looked up; the trolley wheel (a wheel attached to an arm used for collecting the current from the overhead electric wire) had come off the wire. This sometimes happened and it had to be refastened. A small crowd of pedestrians had gathered. Several passengers stepped from the platform, off the bus; a young clippie – a redheaded girl with a snub nose – also alighted; she was dressed in a dark uniform and had a ticket machine hanging from her neck.

The driver of the bus, a large fat man with a peaked cap and a uniform, climbed down the steps from his cab and shouted to the clippie, 'Trolley wheel off again, Grace?'

'Yes, Bert – afraid so.'

He looked up at the top of the bus and said, 'Won't take long to attach it.' He got a long pole from under the bus.

A disgruntled stocky man with a bald head and rimless spectacles expressed his disgust. 'I've got half a mile to go. Might as well walk it.' He glanced at me as he quickly brushed past.

I continued on my way. Thank goodness I didn't have to rely upon public transport. I was pleased that I had bought my Cortina.

Reaching Mr James's shop which was located between a clothier's and a stationer's, I never failed to be impressed by the high standard of his window dressing which was always attractive and tidy. Groceries were displayed in neat rows – there was only one window and a small door. Mr James kept his premises well decorated in a white glossy paint and the impression conveyed to me was one of elegance and neatness, a reflection of his own character. A large brass sign, H. JAMES – GROCER, was placed over the doorway.

Mr James saw me looking in the window and beckoned to me.

An old-fashioned bell tinkled as I opened the shop door and strode towards the counter. A mixture of intriguing scents enveloped me: the aroma of freshly ground coffee, fresh cheeses and hams, sultanas, raisins… the list was endless. To enter the shop was an intriguing experience.

Mr James, a round-faced cheerful man, often smiling, with a spotless, clean, white overall on, looked up from a book which seemed to be his takings record. He came from behind the counter. His wife was cutting some slices from a huge ham, using a circular saw.

A young assistant, a lad of seventeen years of age, small, thin, bright-eyed and cheerful, was serving an old lady with some Cheddar cheese. Mr James, shaking my hand with his usual gusto, said, 'I'm really pleased to see you again.'

It had been only a few days since I'd seen him but it didn't matter to him. He was one of nature's gentlemen and he never failed to greet me in a similar fashion, whenever he saw me.

'Have you got your list?' I gave him a note of the provisions I required. 'Mrs James will get those ready for you – come through to the lounge.'

I said hello to Mrs James and I followed Mr James along a narrow hall and through a door into a small, comfortably-furnished room which looked on to a garden crammed full of rose bushes, geraniums, fuchsias – resplendent red and white – with multicoloured pansies and numerous other flowers bordering a circular, bright green freshly-mown lawn.

A window was open and I immediately noticed the scents, particularly a honeysuckle with fragrant yellow flowers, and a rambling red rose creeping its way along the window ledge; the cuttings from the lawn piled in one corner of the garden added to the fragrances wafting towards us. A robin cheekily tapped at the widow.

'He's making known his presence,' said Mr James. He scattered some breadcrumbs through the open window on to the lawn below and the bird quickly flew down and pecked away, oblivious to its spectators.

Mrs James, a short lady with jet-black hair pinned back, popped her head round the door, saying, 'I've put all your groceries in a box, Mr Read. I'll make some coffee. Would you like some chocolate biscuits?' I quickly agreed. She smiled and said, 'I won't be long.'

As she left the room, Toby, the Yorkshire Terrier, left her side and bounded towards Mr James. The little dog licked his master's hand, stood on his haunches and was soon rewarded with a special bone-shaped biscuit from a tin placed on a high shelf. Toby ate his biscuit where he sat and looked at us with his bright button-like eyes.

'He's a grand little chap,' said Mr James. 'Never been any trouble – a true friend to the wife and me.'

There was real affection. The little dog had made a world of difference to the lives of Mr and Mrs James, who were childless.

'Do you remember two years ago when I asked you about starting your own practice?' I nodded. 'Now you've done it. I'm so pleased for you,' he said, and he meant it! He always expressed his confidence in my abilities; he had the gift of making people he was with feel important. Certainly he and others had instilled in me the will to persevere until I qualified as a Chartered Accountant.

There are some people who possess wonderful qualities, difficult to pinpoint sometimes, but one always knows of their existence. Mr and Mrs James were prime examples of these special people.

As soon as Mr James knew that I had commenced my own practice, he was one of the first to transfer from Davis & Co. and the nucleus had been formed.

Mrs James came in with a tray on which was placed the cups of coffee and biscuits.

'Lazing about,' she said good-humouredly. She got behind Mr James's chair and playfully ruffled his hair as she teased him. He got up from his chair and squeezed her waist, saying, 'Get back to the shop and make us some money, woman!'

It was so pleasing to see a couple content. They had a prospering business but that was partly because of their healthy and convivial attitude, which they conveyed to their customers.

I rose from my chair reluctantly. 'I must be going,' I said. 'Thanks for making me so welcome.'

Mr and Mrs James saw me to the shop doorway. The box of groceries was handed to me and I noticed a tin of ground coffee which I had not ordered placed on top.

I waved to them. 'Back to the grindstone,' I said and made my way towards my office, relaxed and happy.

Q UEUING AT THE bank I used in the high street I heard a voice. Looking round, a man with a straggly beard flecked with grey greeted me. 'You don't remember me, do you?' said the stranger. I looked at him closely. The face was familiar but I could not place him. 'You called on me when I rented an old converted shed two years ago; I was trying to make a go of it as an artist.'

He was a small man, well-dressed in corduroy trousers, a casual shirt and polished brown shoes. Then it dawned on me. It was Mr Dome, the man I called to see when I was an articled clerk. The old shed was at the rear of a shop in the high street. At that time, he was poorly dressed. His clothes were soiled and his face was spattered with paint. It was no wonder I did not recognise him. His appearance had been transformed.

'When I last saw you,' he went on, 'I was virtually down in the gutter – no money, no prospects and I was starving. You were kind to me and I have not forgotten you.'

He stared at me benevolently; drawing from his pocket a tin of loose tobacco, he rolled a cigarette and was soon inhaling the smoke deep into his lungs.

'As you know, I had to leave the area and I owed the owner of the shed some rent. I've repaid the debt and I've bought a detached house off the high street. An old aunt of mine left me thirty thousand pounds in her will. I hadn't seen her for twenty years.'

He smiled, and gone was the desperate look of despondency I remembered when I last saw him when he was unwashed, distraught and battling to survive.

I remembered that some of his paintings were very good, but he didn't have the capital to promote his business. Now his financial position had changed dramatically.

'At the rear of the detached house I've bought, I've had an extension built and I use it as my studio. Would you mind acting as my accountant? A friend of mine told me that you have your own practice,' he said.

We had by that time completed our transactions at the bank and were walking along the high street. I noticed he was limping and I remembered that he had a false leg. When I saw him in the old shed, I had tripped over his false leg, not realising that I had bumped into metal. He had many years ago been involved in a motoring accident and was forced to have one leg amputated.

It is strange how a person's fortunes can quickly change. Mr Dome, a struggling artist – virtually penniless – and later a wealthy man.

'My paintings are being exhibited in London, Paris and even America,' he told me. He was not boasting but I could see that he was proud. I had read about an artist called Dome who had become internationally successful, but I didn't connect the name with the smelly, poorly-dressed man I had seen in the ramshackle shed when I was an articled clerk.

'I shall be pleased to act for you, Mr Dome. Do you have an accountant at the moment?'

'No, I don't but I do have a good bookkeeper who has maintained my records since I moved back into the area, six months ago. The tax man has been notified that I have recommenced my business.'

I fixed a mutually agreeable time for Mr Dome to call at my office and I asked him to bring his records with him. I was anxious to determine his overall trading position, but judging by the high prices he was obtaining for his paintings and the injection of substantial capital into his business, it seemed that he would be highly successful.

'I look forward to seeing you Thursday,' I said. We shook hands and he turned away. Although he was limping, he looked smart and confident.

More grist to the mill, I thought. Another new client to add to my clientele.

MY APPOINTMENT TO see my dentist, Mr Jack Palmer, was at 2.30 p.m. I had been experiencing a slight ache in a tooth and reluctantly decided the time had come to have it attended to.

For some months Mr Palmer had been my client, previously being at Davis & Co. Reaching his surgery I gave the appointment card to the receptionist, who said, 'Please wait on the landing, Mr Read.'

I climbed the few steps, picked up a magazine and sat down. There were three other people in the waiting room: a middle-aged man with a red pullover, thin face and moustache – he looked worried and was holding the side of his face; an old lady with grey hair and dressed in dark blue – she looked totally unconcerned and possibly had dentures; and a young lady. I recognised her directly. She was Jane from the dance classes. We sometimes met at the monthly dances. She was very attractive and I found talking to her stimulating.

She looked up from a book she was reading. Our eyes met. She was slim, dark-haired and petite. 'Hello, Tom. I'm here for a six monthly oral check-up,' she said.

I got up from my chair and went and sat by her. 'I wish I was in the same position,' I said. 'I believe I shall have to have a filling.'

I hoped I didn't look as edgy as I felt. Jane was wearing a light blue miniskirt and a pale lemon top; her small round face was carefully made-up with powder, pencilled eyebrows and a dark red lipstick. Her hair was tied back with a cream ribbon.

She was a splendid dancer, particularly in Latin American, where she had obtained her silver medal with high marks. I had danced with her on several occasions and as she was lighter than Rose, she was easier to spin and twirl, particularly in the jive where the required movements were sometimes very fast. We were chatting away as if we had known each other for years. Her dark brown eyes seemed to have hidden depths and I found myself fantasising. Then I thought of Rose and pulled myself up with a jerk.

I was engaged to her. Why was I thinking like I was? I felt somewhat guilty. My fanciful thoughts were suddenly interrupted.

'Mr Read, please come through.' It was Mr Palmer.

'Cheerio, Jane. See you next Saturday,' I said. I knew that she was going to the monthly dance at the chocolate-making factory's ballroom.

'I'll be pleased to see you, Tom,' she said. Her eyes held mine for a few seconds and then I turned away towards Mr Palmer, who was holding a door open for me.

'Come in, Mr Read; please sit down.'

I took off my overcoat, hung it on the door which he had closed and lowered myself into the dentist's chair.

Mr Palmer was a slim man, over forty years of age with shiny black hair, and he had on a brilliant white gown. His multicoloured silk tie was visible and the scent of his expensive cologne was apparent.

'Let's have a look,' he said. 'Open wide.' He looked into my mouth, prodded about and located the aching tooth. 'I'll have to fill that. Won't take long.'

His nurse placed an antiseptic mouthwash near me and stood behind the chair. Working very efficiently, after ensuring I didn't want an injection to numb the possible pain, he quickly filled the tooth. It was only a small filling and my qualms about pain were unfounded.

'There you are – all done,' he said. He helped me on with my overcoat. 'I'll be calling to see you, Mr Read, next week. My receptionist will telephone you for an appointment. I need to discuss my tax return with you.'

I had prepared his annual accounts which had disclosed a substantial profit. As he was highly qualified, excellent at his work, some of which was very dangerous, he deserved every penny he earned. I shook hands with him and made my way to the waiting room. I was very disappointed to note that Jane had gone.

Endeavouring to put the fanciful thoughts of her out of my mind, I walked back to my office; however, the thoughts lingered.

Reaching my office, I pulled a file out of the cabinet and tried to concentrate on a particularly difficult tax case. Gradually the interest in my work took over and I settled down to write one of my comprehensive letters.

I WAS WALKING back to my office after calling to see Colin Brand, the motor mechanic, at his business premises, when I came face to face with Mr Rawling, the butcher. His tiny shop was down a dowdy side street, off the high street.

He greeted me, shaking my hand vigorously. 'How are you, Mr Read? I hear through the grapevine you have your own accountancy practice. You kept my records up to date when you were at Davis & Co., but nobody has been to see me since you left.'

No wonder, I thought. He had been visited by the Health Office a few months previously and his shop had been closed down for eight weeks until they were satisfied that the hygienic conditions were satisfactory. I remembered visiting his shop on a monthly basis when I was articled at Davis & Co.

His shop used to be a quaint place, the floor covered in sawdust which usually remained in place for weeks. Flies were attracted to the plucked chickens and turkeys which basked in the sunlit shop window. A piece of sticky paper dotted with flies and the occasional wasp, was tied to a dusty light fitting. To reach the counter, one had to pass cobweb-shrouded rabbits and hares which gave off a musty smell.

Mr Rawling was an untidy man, tall with unruly greasy black hair, and often he cut up meat and picked it up with his dirty hands; his fingernails were black; an unpleasant odour wafted towards me from his bloodstained overall. The last time I had visited his shop, he had an old tabby cat which used to have complete freedom to roam where it pleased, often leaving its hairs adhering to joints of beef and lamb.

All this was history, as the Health Office had insisted that he cleaned and modernised his shop, or he would be prevented from trading.

'Could you do my accounts for me, Mr Read?' he asked. 'I've modernised my shop. If you have time, I could show you.' As we were walking along the high street and his shop was only a few minutes away, how could I refuse?

'Certainly, Mr Rawling,' I said. We were soon at his shop and I looked in amazement. Gone was the filthy old sign, 'Rawling – Butcher'. Instead there was a modern, shiny, white-painted board. The door had been cleaned and the plate-glass window was sparkling. As he entered the shop, I followed him with interest. The old light fitting, display shelves and counter had all been replaced. No longer was there sawdust on the floor, which was now covered with shiny new lino. It seemed to be another shop I had entered.

'What do you think, Mr Read?'

Mr Rawling's face showed his pleasure. Taking off his jacket, he put on a clean white overall. His brown shoes were highly polished, his unruly hair was plastered down and his hands were clean, apart from his fingernails, which were still black. Some things don't change.

'Splendid, Mr Rawling,' I replied. What a transformation from the last time I had visited his shop. I shook hands with him and made an appointment for him to see me at my office.

'Thanks, Mr Read. You'll keep me on the right track.'

I left him at his shop door and he was smiling broadly. He was back in business!

As I meandered back to my office, I bumped into Ken from Davis & Co. He was an articled clerk and had joined the firm shortly before I had qualified. He weighed about thirteen stone and was slightly taller than me, with dark hair and a broken nose. He wore a thick leather jacket; I saw his powerful Norton motorbike parked at the kerbside. He was a Rocker, and at weekends usually wore all the special gear.

'How are you getting on, Ken?' I asked.

'Fine, how's yourself?' he replied. He had lost none of his self-confidence. 'My studies are going well. I take my intermediate in six months' time,' he said. He met my gaze unflinchingly.

'I wish you the best of luck,' I said. As I turned away to continue my walk back to my office, Rose appeared from a fashion shop carrying a small paper bag.

'Hello, Tom,' she said. 'Have you any typing for me tonight?'

'Yes – six letters,' I replied.

Ken was standing near his motorbike as we were chatting. He came over and asked, 'Give you a lift back to the office, Rose?'

She looked at me indecisively, saw the expression on my face and said, 'That's all right, Ken. I've still got some more shopping to do.'

However, the words did not match the look she gave him. I had seen a change in Rose. A fleeting glimpse, perhaps, but I sensed the vibrations between Rose and Ken.

I wandered back to my office; my mind was working overtime. The subconscious often comes up with the answer very quickly and this was a prime example. Rose was slipping away from me and inwardly I knew that I had to let her go.

IT WAS SATURDAY morning; Rose and I decided to visit the local swimming pool. I was a very keen swimmer from an early age; the exercise was excellent, especially for someone in a sedentary occupation, working in an office.

I had taught Rose to swim the breaststroke and front crawl. It had not been easy as at first she was apprehensive about the water. Gradually she gained confidence, when she found she could float easily.

I picked Rose up at her parents' house and we soon arrived at the pool. She was quiet during the short journey. 'Everything okay, Rose?' I asked. With her blue eyes looking at me like that, I knew before she spoke that something was amiss.

'I didn't sleep much last night, Tom.'

I parked my car and leaned over to the back seats and got our sports bags containing our swimming costumes and towels. Walking over towards the pool, we found that there was no queue; we bought our tickets and made our way to the separate changing rooms for males and females.

'See you in the pool, Rose,' I said. She nodded and I noticed she lacked her usual exuberance. Something material had happened and she had changed. It was like a light switch being turned off. Gone was the radiance and the sparkle. I knew that there was a barrier between us.

Locking my cubicle door, I went through the showers to the pool and saw Rose swimming the breaststroke in the deep end. By now she was an excellent swimmer and did not need my assistance. I waved to her and she returned my greeting in a half-hearted way. As I swam towards her, she pulled herself up to the edge of the pool and said, 'The water's warm today, Tom.'

I felt that was said to make conversation. Looking at Rose in her colourful costume, the one she had bought specially the first time we had gone swimming together, I thought how lovely she looked; but this time the magic was missing.

We swam a few lengths doing the front crawl together but it seemed to me as if we were automatons.

We were joined at the shallow end by Ben and Ken, the two remaining articled clerks at Davis & Co. We had arranged to meet them, when I had called at my old firm, the previous day.

'Hello, Ben, Ken,' Rose and I chorused. They returned our greetings and wandered off to the deep end. Ben, short with freckles and tousled hair dived in and did a bellyflop. He surfaced, grinning.

Ken, well muscled, broad-chested, climbed to the top diving board, stood there for a few seconds and dived – a magnificent swallow dive. I thought that I was a good diver – usually headers off the side of the pool – but I couldn't compete with that.

Rose and I had swum to the deep end, pulled ourselves up and sat on the edge of the pool. She was still quiet. I had looked at her face when she saw Ken surface after his dive and her smile was radiant; her bright blue eyes were sparkling. 'I've got a bit cold, Rose. I think I'll get dressed,' I said.

'All right, Tom, I'll meet you in the pool café. We can have coffee and biscuits.'

I made my way back to my changing cubicle, unlocked it, dressed and sat in the café, waiting for Rose. Eventually she appeared.

'Where's Ben and Ken?' I asked.

'They've gone home. Ken has given Ben a lift by motorbike,' she replied.

We had our hot drinks and biscuits but the talk was stilted and awkward. We did not discuss our swimming as we usually did; I looked at Rose. She was distant. I endeavoured to suppress my thoughts. I could not at first face the truth but it was stark and I had no option.

I took Rose home; we hardly spoke. Reaching her parents' house, I said, 'Cheerio, Rose.'

'Goodbye, Tom,' she replied.

Her eyes said it all. I knew instantly I had lost her.

The magic had gone. It was like a candle burning brightly, then unsteadily and finally melting away rapidly. The flame had been extinguished. The romance was over.

I felt moved but not devastated. Jane came into my mind and a feeling of tranquillity enveloped me.

It was clear to me that Rose and Ken were destined for each other and there was absolutely nothing I could do about it. I accepted the inevitable. In some inexplicable way, I was happy for Rose.

I WAS SITTING in my office before I started work. I usually made a point of commencing at 9 a.m., but now I was thinking about my life. I had been studying to become a Chartered Accountant since I left school at seventeen years of age and had achieved my aim when I was twenty-three. Although I had obtained the qualification I had been seeking and had a thriving personal tax accountancy practice, my close relationship with Rose was no more. She had found somebody she loved with much greater intensity than existed with me and although I was pleased for her, I had to get on with my own life.

I thought Rose was the only girl for me but I had been wrong. Doubts had sometimes crept into my mind, and on reflection, she must have felt the same way. There are varying intensities of love but true love leaves no important questions unanswered. The couple know they are right for each other and the proof is there when they are often happy in each other's company. Although I thought I loved Rose, there should have been no doubts, but they sometimes surfaced.

My reflections over, I made myself a cup of coffee, put my briefcase on my desk and opened it to extract a file I had been working on at home. As I pulled out the file, two tickets for the monthly dance at the chocolate-making factory fell to the floor. I picked them up. This time it wouldn't be Rose I was taking, but Jane. My thoughts of Rose evaporated and the picture of Jane came into my mind. I had no doubts about Jane whatsoever and I hoped she would feel the same way about me; I would find out in due course.

I opened the file and commenced my work and was soon immersed in an interesting tax computation.

The phone rang just when I was in the middle of adding a column of figures. 'Mr Grange here.' His voice was quiet but distinct. He played the piano accompanied by a drummer and a violinist and the group toured the local area, visiting clubs. 'Could Mrs Grange and I call to see you? As you have your own practice we would like you to act for us.'

Endeavouring to keep my voice calm, I said, 'I should be pleased to act for you; when would you like to call to see me?' I heard him flicking over some pages – probably his diary.

'Tomorrow at 11 a.m. be suitable, Mr Read?'

Looking at my diary, I saw that I was not seeing any other clients at that time. 'That'll be fine, Mr Grange.'

'See you then,' he said. He replaced his receiver.

My practice was expanding fast but as I found the work so interesting and the clients intriguing, I was extremely pleased.

Mrs Grange was a professional model, working mainly in studios in London. Her photographs – she was stunning – were featured in magazines nationally.

When I was at Davis & Co., I usually went to see Mr and Mrs Grange at their flat, which was opposite a church and the rectory occupied by the Rev. Hammond, to collect their business records and have a social chat with them. They made me so welcome and I always felt content in the happy atmosphere which pervaded their flat.

The following morning, I set out the papers which I needed on my desk. At precisely 11 a.m. the doorbell rang and Mr and Mrs Grange greeted me. She was about my height; she had an hourglass figure with a close-fitting lemon dress, gold necklace and black, highly polished shoes. Her peach-like face had just a touch of make-up and long blonde hair cascaded down her shoulders.

'I'm pleased to see you again, Mr Read,' she said, shaking my hand daintily. I noticed her perfume which reminded me of orange blossom flowers.

Mr Grange shook my hand firmly. He looked up at me. At five feet eight, I towered over him. He was a dwarf.

'Hope you've got some cushions for me to sit on,' he said. He laughed and any chance of a tense atmosphere disappeared. Having a gift of making people around him feel good more than made up for his lack of height. He was a kind and happy person and his band was very popular at the clubs where customers either listened or danced to his music. He was wearing a specially made grey suit with a fleck of blue in it, a white shirt and a red tie.

They sat down opposite me. I had remembered to place two thick cushions on his chair. I completed the papers and confirmed that I would be willing to act for them, subject to the usual etiquette letter to Davis & Co.

'Did you know that my band would be playing at the next monthly dance at the chocolate-making factory? I believe you are a keen dancer,' said Mr Grange, giving me one of his broad smiles.

'I knew that a band was going to play but I didn't know it was yours,' I replied.

'There are going to be competitions, I understand from Miss Williams,' he added.

He looked at me with his twinkling eyes.

Apparently the evening was going to be divided into two hourly sessions of social dancing and intermediate one half-hour of Latin American competition dancing, mainly the jive and the cha-cha-cha. I thought directly of Jane. We had been practising the jive, which was my favourite dance, and I felt sure she would wish to compete. I made a mental note to phone her later in the day.

As Mr and Mrs Grange made their way to my office door, I could not help noticing once again how happy they were. Their physical differences did not matter to them. We said our farewells and I told them that I would see them at the dance with my new dancing partner, Jane.

After they had gone, I picked up the phone and rang Jane's firm. She was a typist at a local solicitor's.

'Would you like to compete in the jive competition?' I asked.

'Love to, Tom. See you this evening.'

She was typing for me part-time and usually picked up the draft letters and accounts shortly after she ceased work at five thirty.

I felt like a break and put my radio on. There was a report about The Beatles: John Lennon, Paul McCartney, George Harrison and Ringo Starr. Their plane had touched down at Kennedy Airport and they had been met by hordes of fans. The group were to continue to take the States by storm. I sat there listening for a while and then changed the radio station to some pop music.

I took the list of my clients out of my desk draw and added the names of Mr and Mrs Grange.

My practice was expanding fast and my social life, which had dipped momentarily, was now recovering. I had a new girlfriend, Jane, and my optimism about life had returned. I again looked to the future with great expectations.

WHEN I WAS an articled clerk at Davis & Co., I had interviewed a young man of about my age. He was over six feet tall, broad with an upright posture. Smartly dressed in an expensive suit and wearing top quality shoes, he looked supremely confident. An established client of Davis & Co. had recommended the young man, Mr John Lanes, to call at my old firm and he had been introduced to me; it was up to me to advise him on bookkeeping, prepare his accounts and calculate his tax liability.

He had tried various jobs, including being a part-time barman, but he had seen an advertisement in the local paper for a double glazing salesman, applied for the job and was successful. At Davis & Co., we had an interview room, which was used mainly by the senior articled clerks when interviewing clients; I remember seeing Mr Lanes, who had brought a box of receipts, invoices and bank statements, placed them on the desk and asked me to assist him.

'Is this all you have?' I asked, thinking what a pig's breakfast it was.

'I've never been self-employed before. You tell me what to do and what you require and I will follow your advice,' he said.

Mr Lanes and I had mutual respect for one another from our first meeting and over the years had become friends.

When I first met him, he was puzzled about not being able to claim for the cost of his expensive suits and shirts, but accepted my comments and always asked for me to complete his accounts.

He had heard that I had my own practice; immediately he went to Davis & Co. and stated clearly that he wished to continue with my services. They had no objections and he was now my client.

Since being a double glazing salesman, he had become very successful. His annual commission was high. He lived quite close to my office and sometimes I called to see him. At other times he called to see me at my office. I looked out of my office window. It was drizzling but I had promised to call to see him at 3 p.m.

Taking my raincoat from the stand, I put it on, picked up my briefcase and locked my office door. It would only take five minutes to walk to his bungalow; he had recently purchased it by obtaining a hefty mortgage from a building society. The branch was in the high street. Having been self-employed for over two years and obtained excellent references from the double glazing company and his bank manager, there had been no problem obtaining the mortgage.

By the time I reached his home, the drizzle had stopped and the sun peeped through the clouds. I opened the double iron gates and walked up the driveway towards a narrow path leading to the smart, magnolia-painted pebble-dash bungalow. I passed his dark green Jaguar car. Raindrops remained on the glossy paintwork, which had been waxed thoroughly. He had made a wise decision to give up being a barman and become a double glazing salesman!

'Hello, Mr Read,' he said. 'Please come in.'

I was about to ring the bell, after noticing the impressive double bay windows and well-decorated cream coloured front door, but Mr Lanes had seen me approach. Opening the door wide, he shook hands with me self-confidently and led me down a wide hall, which was papered in an embossed gold colour. He turned right into a large lounge, sumptuously furnished and with an expensive looking oil painting.

'Please sit down,' he said and I did so at the highly polished table. 'I'll get my records, Mr Read.' He strode briskly over to a bureau and handed to me a document file. All his papers were neatly filed and the accounts book had been balanced. 'A little different from when I first visited you, Mr Read!'

He smiled, as he sat down. He and I remembered the shoe box he had brought to the interview room at Davis & Co.

'A small whisky, Mr Read?' he suggested.

'Thanks very much,' I said. My system could now tolerate a small amount of liquor.

We were sitting there talking about cars, sport and dancing – any subject except accountancy, when a young lady came into the room. She was about my height, dressed elegantly in a light blue medium length skirt and cream top. She was a stunner. Her small round face had just the right amount of make-up and her red hair had a bubble-cut style.

'Pleased to meet you again, Mr Read,' she said. She held out her hand and I was enveloped in the delightful fragrance of an expensive perfume. We had met, albeit briefly, at a dance. Hers was a face one did not easily forget.

'Like a drink, Diana?'

'No thanks, John. I have just had an orange juice.'

They had been friends for about six months and they seemed well suited. I hoped so. She was easy to talk to and I was pleased for Mr Lanes.

After a while I reluctantly rose from my chair.

'Well, I must be going. I've got to get back to my office. I have another appointment at 4 p.m. Thanks for making me welcome.'

It was pleasing when one could see a young man making a success from a new venture. Mr Lanes had persevered and his persistence had been rewarded!

Saying my farewells, I waved to John and Diana and made my way back to my office. The sun was shining and I was thinking that it was great to be a Chartered Accountant. It was the key to meeting all sorts of interesting people. Not all were as pleasant as Mr Lanes and his girlfriend; but life is not a bed of roses.

I reached my office in good spirits, made myself a coffee and awaited my next client.

Although my office was well set out with a number of small cupboards and bookcases, clients' records were accumulating and I decided to have a large fitted cupboard made by a local carpenter.

Mr Stanton's name came to my mind; when I was articled at Davis & Co. Ben and I would visit his business premises to check his records every three months. He maintained a full set of double entry books, including sales and purchase ledgers, which he always ensured were balanced to the penny. He was meticulous in his carpentry business, which he had run for approximately twelve years. I had found out when I had first visited his office that, apart from ordinary carpentry work, he and his employees also made coffins for the local undertaker. When Ben and I had visited his office I was unaware of the coffin making and having asked Ben to direct me to the toilet, he had pointed to a room; when I walked in I was surrounded by coffins. I quickly retreated. I often joke about that episode but my heart was thumping at the time and I had since repeatedly got my own back on Ben for his prank.

I still have the expertly crafted wooden bowl which Mr Stanton gave me when I first called at his office. Ben was given a similar one. My bowl stands in a prominent place among my prized possessions and always reminds me of Ben's mischievous nature.

Mr Stanton pulled up in his small grey Ford van and parked outside my office. I watched him get out of the vehicle, go to the back and take out his toolbox. He was a small, thickset man, over forty years of age with freckles and ginger hair. Banging the rear doors of the van shut, he looked over towards me and waved. I opened my office door and we shook hands.

'Pleased to see you again, Mr Read,' he said.

'Thanks for coming at such short notice,' I replied, as I ushered him in.

'You have some good furniture in here,' he said, looking around my office with approbation.

'Yes, I bought all the items from Mr Gage,' I replied, pleased with Mr Stanton's opinion.

He had called a few days previously to measure up and ascertain the quality of timber I required. Putting his tool bag down, he said, 'Won't be a minute – I'll bring the wood in.'

I decided to make some coffee in the small kitchenette at the rear of the office. I placed a cup of coffee and some biscuits within reach of Mr Stanton, saying, 'I'll leave you to it. I'll be writing a few letters.' They were routine and did not require much concentration.

'Thanks, Mr Read. The fitting of the cupboard won't take me long.'

Glancing across at him, I noticed the perspiration on his brow. He worked non-stop until the job was completed and asked, 'What do you think, Mr Read?'

I stopped writing and walked towards the new cupboard. It was splendid: excellent workmanship and first-class materials. The wood was solid teak. 'I'm very pleased with it,' I said.

He smiled. My words of praise had been his reward. The payment for the invoice to come was secondary to him. He said, 'I'll just sit down, if I may, Mr Read. I've got a headache.'

'By all means,' I replied. 'Would you like another coffee?'

'Just a glass of water, please. I suffer from migraine occasionally. I'll sit here quietly for a few minutes.'

He held his hand over his forehead and sat down on a sofa which backed on to one of the walls. I sat in my chair and recommenced my letter writing. Ten minutes later, I looked across at Mr Stanton; he had not moved. This was getting eerie. I crept over towards him. Perhaps he had experienced a heart attack and died. At his side I could not see any movement. Then I noticed he was breathing shallowly, so he was alive. He was asleep! I suppose it was nature's way of relieving the pain caused by the migraine. I continued with my work and after about an hour, he woke up.

'I must have dozed off. I'm sorry, Mr Read!'

'That's all right. At least you finished my cupboard,' I joked, endeavouring to put him at his ease. 'I'll make you a coffee.'

His colour had returned and he no longer looked wan.

'How long was I asleep?' he asked, looking at his watch. 'Over an hour! I don't know what you must think of me.'

I tried to pass the event off as immaterial. In fact I had been scared stiff. I thought he had died.

Finishing his coffee, he handed me the cup and said, 'Thanks, Mr Read. I'd better be going. I think that I'll take the rest of the day off.' He looked the picture of health again, but I knew that the migraine had taken its toll.

'Thanks for being so understanding, Mr Read,' he said gratefully. He picked up his toolbox, shook hands with me and made his way to my office door.

'Are you sure you'll be okay to drive?' I asked.

'Yes, I'll be all right now. That sleep did the trick.' He looked at me a little sheepishly and said, 'Cheerio.' He walked to his van, put his tool bag in the back, got in, waved and drove off.

I looked at the cupboard he had made – a work of art! However, minutes after he had finished it, he was fast asleep.

Putting the matter to one side, I continued with my letter writing. It had been another eventful day.

THE PHONE RANG. I picked up the receiver.

'This is Mr Partridge,' said the caller. He sounded concerned. 'I've received a letter from the tax man stating that I have omitted something from my tax return. I don't know what they're on about.'

His voice faltered and I interrupted him. 'Don't worry. Come round to my office. Will 11 a.m. be all right?'

He confirmed that it would be and replaced the phone. I wondered what the problem was. Having only recently taken over the case from another accountant I was not worried about my work because I hadn't done any for Mr Partridge yet. Retrieving his file from the cabinet, I examined the copy of the last tax return, which had been completed by his previous accountant.

I telephoned Mr Partridge and said, 'When you call to see me, please bring with you all your bank statements for the last two years, together with all your investment passbooks.'

'I'll do that,' he said. 'See you in half an hour.'

A few minutes after 11 a.m., he rang the office bell; I opened the door and shook hands with him. He was a small, thin man, smartly dressed in a good quality brown serge suit, cream shirt, red tie and a gold tiepin. He was about sixty-five years of age with a small moustache, and his long face showed his consternation by his deeply furrowed brow. Removing his trilby, he placed it on one chair and sat down on the other. He gave me a forced smile and wiped the perspiration from under his deep brown eyes.

'I don't like receiving letters like this, Mr Read,' he said, handing me the Inspector's letter which I read thoroughly.

'Let's go through your last tax return item by item, Mr Partridge.'

He handed me his bank statements and investment passbooks and I ticked off each entry on the copy of the last tax return.

Mr Partridge had taken early retirement; he was a bachelor and had been left substantial assets by his late widowed mother. He used to be a cabinetmaker, a job which required considerable skill and accuracy.

He was accurate in his private affairs as well; however, something had gone wrong.

Picking up a building society passbook, I looked at the interest. There was no entry on the tax return. 'Mr Partridge, I believe I have located the omission,' I told him. He looked at me and his top lip trembled. I handed the book to him.

'Yes,' he replied shakily. 'I opened that account three years ago. I must have forgotten to give it to Mr Plumb (his previous accountant). I'm so sorry. Will I be fined?'

He looked perplexed and worried. The omitted interest was only five pounds twelve shillings and sixpence, but it was not the amount that was important to the Tax Inspector, it was the actual omission. If one item had been missed, there might be others.

'If you're absolutely positive that there have been no other omissions, I am sure that the Inspector will understand that it was an honest oversight,' I said. I tried my best to reassure Mr Partridge, who got out his handkerchief and blew his nose exaggeratedly.

I finished checking all the other investment passbooks and the bank statements, and could find no other omissions.

'You leave this to me, Mr Partridge. I'll give the Inspector a ring and explain matters to him. You'll have to sign a certificate saying that you have disclosed all your income and that should suffice.'

Mr Partridge looked relieved and was thankful when I made him coffee and handed him a cup, from which he drank eagerly. He licked his small moustache with the tip of his tongue. Picking up his trilby he shook my hand firmly.

'You have taken a weight off my shoulders. I'll see you in two weeks' time when you complete my next tax return,' he said brightly.

As I saw him to the door, he looked a different man from the one I had greeted half an hour earlier. The pallor had gone from his cheeks and his eyes were no longer sombre. He waved to me cheerfully.

I telephoned the Tax Inspector, explained what had happened and as expected, the certificate of disclosure was sent which Mr Partridge completed. Another satisfied client, thank goodness, I thought.

HAVING JUST COMPLETED a particularly complicated set of accounts, I sat back in my office chair, drinking my morning coffee; I took the local newspaper out of my briefcase and looked at the page containing details of the films showing at the local cinemas. There was a good film on at the Odeon and I decided to telephone Jane to see if she would like to go with me the coming Saturday.

'Is Jane there?' I asked.

The telephonist at Jane's firm sounded cheerful. 'I won't keep you long. I'll put you through.' A click, a short pause and I heard Jane's voice.

'Hello, Tom. Are you phoning about the typing?'

'Not this time, Jane. Would you like to go to the flicks – I mean pictures – tomorrow?'

Jane didn't answer straight away and I heard other female voices over the phone. Then she said, 'I'd like that very much, Tom.'

'I'll pick you up at 7 p.m. then; I don't need any typing done this evening,' I said.

Settling down to my work, I soon got interested in preparing the tax computations applicable to the accounts I had prepared, and put to one side my thoughts of my social activities.

The following day, I spent a couple of hours in the morning cleaning my Cortina and doing a few domestic chores for my parents during the afternoon. I strolled down to the nearest confectioner's and bought a box of chocolates to give to Jane. When I returned from my stroll, I washed and changed into my best suit – a grey pinstripe with a fleck of blue in it, a brilliant white shirt and a multicoloured tie. Highly polished black brogues completed the picture. I looked in my high wardrobe mirror and combed my hair, after using plenty of Brylcreem. Jane had bought me some good quality cologne, so I used a little of it.

I shut my bedroom door and walked down the staircase to the kitchen calling, 'I'm off now, Mum, Dad.' They smiled and waved as I opened the kitchen door and made my way to my Cortina.

I tooted to them and was off. They were happy I had another girlfriend.

Jane lived about five miles from my parents' home and I soon arrived. I parked my Cortina in the road, which was a cul-de-sac. Her red Triumph Herald 13/60 was on the driveway and I looked at it with interest. It was small but very smart and had a number of unusual features, including a bonnet which sloped inwards from each side and white rubber bumpers.

The rear wings were extremely sharp and there were plenty of chrome strips, including one down the centre of the bonnet. Jane was often talking about her Herald and I understood it could turn on a sixpence. The turning circle was about twenty-five feet. She had promised to let me drive next time we used her car.

'Hello, Tom,' said Jane. She shut her front door after calling to her parents. 'I saw you looking at my car.' She walked daintily towards me.

'You keep it in good order,' I said. It certainly was a nice looking car and matched Jane's personality to perfection.

She was wearing a yellow dress and a small brown top coat with a fur collar; her dark brown shoes were patterned and shiny. About two inches shorter than me, she was just right as a dancing partner. Her face was small and I could see that she had paid attention to her make-up – a little powder and her usual dark red lipstick. I liked the way she tied back her dark hair with a yellow ribbon.

The cinema was only half a mile away and we decided to walk there. Rain was not forecast and it was a pleasant evening. Chatting away as if we had known each other for years instead of months, we soon arrived at the cinema. Joining the queue, we gradually moved along until we reached the ticket office. I recognised the plump, round-faced lady with a snub nose. 'Two tickets, please,' I said. She smiled as she gave me my change.

I was glad she didn't comment when she looked first at me and then at Jane. The last time he came he was with an auburn-haired girl, she probably thought.

We sat down on one of the comfortable settees. Every time I came to the Odeon, I noticed the plush, thick carpets and the elegant ceiling and wall light fittings.

I put my arm around Jane, who did not object at all; she snuggled up to me. She was warm and her favourite perfume wafted towards me. I was getting really comfortable when the audience from the previous sitting streamed out. We got up from the settee and went through to the upper circle. The usherette's torch directed us to the rear seats, which were already nearly full.

'There's two vacant seats, Tom,' said Jane, clutching the box of chocolates which I had given her earlier. She held my hand as we sat down. The lights dimmed and we started looking at the film. I say started, because after a few minutes the film ceased to have any interest for either of us.

We had other things on our minds. Very soon we were kissing passionately and, glancing along the row of seats, I could see that other couples had the same ideas as us.

The lights came on and I looked at Jane, who was smiling and content. This time the feelings were reciprocated; this time they were right. There were no doubts – and I felt it was mutual. 'Ice cream, Jane?' I asked.

'Thanks, Tom,' she said. She looked flushed but was eating her chocolates with relish. 'Have one before you go, Tom.'

I chose one with a nut on top and walked quickly down the aisle. I was overjoyed. Jane was happy. I was happy. All was well with the world! Ignoring the smoke-laden atmosphere in the cinema, I collected the two round Lyons ice cream cartons and the little wooden spoons and quickly made my way back to Jane.

'There you are, Jane,' I said.

'Thanks, Tom.' She spooned up the ice cream blissfully. The lights dimmed and we resumed our passionate kissing. I had no idea what the film was about, but I couldn't have cared less.

After the film ended, we made our way out of the cinema, hand in hand, into the fresh night air.

'We didn't see much of the film,' I said. I looked at Jane sheepishly and she looked up at me. We embraced again.

'Well, we didn't really go to see the film, did we?' Jane murmured, giving me one of her gorgeous smiles.

'Are you looking forward to the dance next week?' I asked. Jane quickly replied, 'Yes, I am, especially the jive competition.'

On reaching Jane's home, we kissed under the porch and she squeezed my hand appreciatively. 'See you tomorrow. I'll drive round to your home,' she said. We were going to Cranfield Park where a number of couples went, especially on a Sunday.

'Cheerio, Jane,' I said. One last kiss and she quietly shut the door. My last glimpse of her face was one of contentment. I got in my Cortina and slowly drove away. I was back in the driving seat!

E VERY YEAR THE chocolate-making factory where my mother worked had a carnival. The firm employed several hundred people and all the employees and their families and friends were invited. There was a special tent where entrants exhibited all sorts of home produced or made items, ranging from vegetables and fruit to various artefacts.

My mother, who was a chargehand, was a keen hand-knitter and for the first time had been persuaded by some of her colleagues to submit eight garments she had knitted. I had submitted a drawing of a squirrel. I had liked art at school, although I had not taken the subject in the GCE ordinary level exam.

I had arranged to pick Jane up at her home and take her to the carnival which was to be held Saturday afternoon. Phoning Jane on Friday evening, I explained that casual clothes would be suitable.

'That's all right, Tom. I'll wear my jeans and a top. I'm really looking forward to tomorrow.'

'Jane, I'm taking part in the hundred yards sprint,' I told her. Apart from the general carnival, part of the day was to be allocated to sports competitions.

'See you tomorrow, Tom,' she said and put down the receiver.

The following day, I backed my Cortina from the driveway of my parents' house and drove off to Jane's home. We would be meeting my parents at the chocolate factory's grounds later in the day. There were about six acres of grassland at the rear of the factory.

Jane stood at her garden gate as I drove up. I opened the passenger door for her and she quickly sat down. She was, as promised, wearing a pair of jeans and a pink top. She was a brunette and she had tied back her hair, this time with a red ribbon; her lipstick matched the colour of the ribbon. She looked a picture.

'When's your race, Tom?'

I looked at my watch which showed 2 p.m. 'Three thirty,' I replied.

We soon arrived at the factory gates and drove through; there was no attendant.

I parked my car, and Jane and I got out. I locked the doors and we strolled towards the marquee, mixing with the throng who had the same aim as us.

The man sitting at a small table just outside of the entrance to the marquee looked up as we approached. He was broad-faced with a large bushy moustache.

'Two tickets at a shilling each – two shillings please – all for charity,' he said. He gave us a wide smile, and winked at Jane. She winked back and we all laughed. This was a special day and I intended that Jane should enjoy herself.

Entering the large tent, we looked around. There were stalls of all descriptions. All the exhibits were set out: one for best potatoes, another for best carrots and so on. A large part of the tent was devoted to fruit and vegetables, as gardening was a popular pastime and the competition was fierce.

'Look, Jane,' I said. My father had entered some beetroot which he had grown on his allotment. 'Dad's won second prize.'

As we were gazing at the card pinned to my father's exhibit, he walked over towards Jane and me with my mother. They had never seen Jane before although they knew all about her from me.

'Hello, Mr and Mrs Read,' said Jane and held out her hand. My father's eyes lit up and my mother smiled.

'Have you seen your prize, Dad?' I asked.

'Yes, I've seen it. Not bad for an old-timer.' I knew he was very pleased, but he rarely showed his feelings.

Wandering along the stalls, we came to the art exhibits. I looked for my drawing – third prize.

'That's good, Tom,' said Jane. I was a little disappointed, having got first prize the preceding year. However, I endeavoured to hide my disappointment. I looked at the first and second prized exhibits. They were better than mine, so I had to accept the result as fair.

We reached the stall containing the knitting exhibits. I glanced at my mother's face. She was overjoyed.

She had submitted eight knitted garments. I pointed and said, 'Look, Mum.' She had won a prize – then another, and so on – six first prizes, one second and a third. I was pleased and said, 'That's great, Mum.'

Tears of joy welled up into her eyes. She was a modest, refined lady and had no idea her talent would be so appreciated. We spent half an hour looking at the other stalls and eventually made our way out of the tent, towards the sports field. It was three fifteen and my race was due to start at three thirty.

My parents wandered off to speak to some friends and Jane and I walked towards a small tent used as a changing room. 'If you wait here, Jane, I won't be long.' After a few minutes, I emerged in my shorts, vest and plimsolls. I was, and still am, rather slim and wiry.

'You look fit, Tom,' said Jane, and smiled encouragingly.

The announcer's voice boomed out. 'All competitors for the one hundred yards race please assemble at the starting line.'

'See you later, Jane.'

She kissed me. 'Best of luck, Tom.'

I reached the starting line; there were six other competitors. Bending down to the starting position, I glanced to the left and right. There were some big chaps in the race. The starter's whistle blew. We were off. I have always liked sprints, and with all the dancing and swimming was very fit. I ran as fast as I could. A few yards from the tape, there was only one young chap ahead of me. I thrust myself forward and breasted the tape. I had won. Panting, I sat on the grass and heard someone say, 'Well done, Tom.' It was Jane, and her face showed her pleasure. 'I was shouting for you.'

I looked up. 'Come and sit down, Jane,' I said. We sat there for ten minutes or so; it was a marvellous day.

I got dressed, and after another hour Jane and I made our way back to my Cortina. She said, 'Thanks for asking me, Tom.'

'Thanks for coming,' I commented. In the company of some ladies one often feels lucky. Jane, I felt, was such a lady. I hoped that our relationship would last a long time.

I DECIDED TO have a few days off, away from my office. Although I liked my work, I felt it was time to take a short holiday.

My old headmaster, Mr Downing, at the boys' secondary school, had invited me to call to see him and some of the teachers, and I decided to telephone to see which day would be convenient for me to call.

The school secretary said, 'Won't be long, Mr Read.' A short pause, then I heard Mr Downing's low but clear voice.

'I'm pleased you've telephoned, Tom. Tomorrow afternoon at two thirty would be fine. We'll look forward to seeing you.'

The last time I had seen him was when I had visited the school with my parents, after I had obtained a considerable number of GCE O levels. He was extremely pleased, as I had created a record for the school, not only by the number of O levels, but by the very high marks. Leaving the school as head boy had been a tremendous boost to the start of my professional career.

Arriving five minutes before two thirty, I parked my Cortina down a side street and walked briskly towards my old school. I turned a corner and the Victorian building came into view. Memories came flooding back. At eleven years of age I had first seen the school and I thought then what a formidable looking place it seemed. Little did I know that I was to be educated there to a very high standard and the headmaster and teachers were going to provide me with the stepping stone to my professional career.

I wandered across the playground, which was empty. The pupils were in the school. The old outdoor toilets were still there. I remembered some pupils in my first year were subjected to awful teasing and bullying. Vivid pictures came into my mind of children being subjected to 'lavatory flush' treatment by some of the older pupils. This involved the unfortunate victim having his head thrust down the toilet pan, which was then flushed. Another favourite trick of the bullies was the 'greasy pole' torture. I looked across to the flagpole, still in position. In those days, it was somehow greased; I never did find out where the grease came from; the screaming pupil was forced against the pole, his legs were crossed and then he was made to sit. Of course in that position, he had to stay there until the bullies got tired of their game and friendlier children helped the unfortunate boy to his feet. Thankfully many of these rituals gradually disappeared; children can be cruel if they see someone weaker or different from themselves.

There was one poor lad I remember in particular and he was shunned by the other pupils who called him 'stinky' Joe. He ponged all the time but it was not because he was dirty. The problem was caused by a gland disorder. The lad went through hell and was shunned like a leper. Eventually the headmaster held a special assembly to explain the matter to pupils generally. It had little effect. The unfortunate lad still left the school and had to be taught at home until an operation cured the ailment.

Nearly reaching the main entrance to the school, I passed the spot where I had my only fight. I was fourteen and was holding a rope which was used for tug-of-war competitions. This was before the school event had commenced. I was winding the rope and suddenly one of the bullies – his name was Thompson – grabbed me by the scruff of the neck and said, 'You've scorched my hand.'

He started punching me hard. I had no idea that he had been holding the rope.

'Fight, fight!' chanted the milling kids. I reacted by defending myself. I am not a violent person but put in that situation, one has to fight or run. I decided to fight. I found to my surprise that I could punch quite hard also, and all of a sudden Thompson was on the ground beneath me, squealing and bleeding like a stuck pig. After that fight, I was the hero of the day – until the event became history and fights between other pupils occurred.

All these thoughts were flashing through my mind and then I opened the school entrance doors.

Walking up the inner concrete steps, I reached the first floor and came upon the headmaster's office. Pausing, my mind went back to the only occasion I experienced the humiliation and pain of having the cane. I was twelve years of age and had purchased a 'bomb'. This was a shell-like metal object, about an inch long, made up of two halves. A cap containing gunpowder was placed in the 'bomb' which, if dropped from a height, would explode with a loud bang; hence its name.

I did not misbehave on too many occasions, but I had my moments like most children. I had climbed the high staircase and dropped the 'bomb' from the top to the bottom. The noise was tremendous and echoed throughout the building for what seemed, at the time, like eternity. This was the reason for the cane: six of the best on the backside. I couldn't sit down for some time afterwards.

I knocked at the headmaster's door.

'Come in,' said Mr Downing. Entering, I approached him and held out my hand, which he shook warmly. 'Sit down, Tom, and tell me about your career. I hear that you have your own accountancy practice.'

Mr Downing was a very large man. He was perhaps twenty stone and over six feet tall. He towered over me as he drew up a chair for me to sit on. He had a big round face, highly coloured, with a walrus moustache. His dark hair, greying at the sides, was parted down the middle; kind brown eyes looked at me astutely through heavy-rimmed spectacles. A smart cavalry twill brown suit covered his huge frame. He had a habit of rubbing the tip of his nose with his forefinger when he was in a thoughtful mood.

He listened patiently to my experiences since I had left school and said, 'You've done well, Tom. I'm proud of you.'

'Thanks, Mr Downing. Without your help and that of the other teachers, particularly Mr Tower, I would never have become a Chartered Accountant.'

Mr Downing rose from his chair, saying, 'I knew that you would like to meet Mr Tower. He's still with us, although many of the other teachers have either retired or left to go to other schools. Please follow me, Tom.'

I followed his huge bulk through his office door and along a corridor and turned right. As he opened a classroom door, the chattering pupils sitting at rows of desks became quiet. Mr Downing had great presence and one of his looks was enough!

'You remember Tom, John,' he said.

Mr Tower looked up from his desk and his thin, bony face creased into a smile. 'Pleased to see you again, Tom.'

We shook hands warmly. This was the English teacher; without his assistance – he often worked overtime concerning the teaching of pupils who were trying their best – I would not have passed the GCE O level with such a creditable mark.

'I would like to thank you for your persistence, Mr Tower,' I said. 'I remember that you spent many hours teaching me to get to the high standard when I left school.'

He looked first at me and then at Mr Downing. His eyes became moist and the pleasure of the moment was very moving – for him, Mr Downing and myself. I saw one or two pupils look up from their desks with interest.

'I'll leave you, John, to talk to Tom. I'll see you before you go, Tom,' said Mr Downing, who then strode away purposefully.

Eventually, I said my farewells to Mr Tower and Mr Downing and made my way back to my Cortina. I started the engine and drove slowly back home. Some teachers are dedicated and I had been very lucky to have had the experience of that dedication from two very special men.

As I was sorting through my weekly tax magazines which were necessary to keep me up to date with current tax matters, my phone rang. I deposited the pile of journals on a nearby chair and strode over to my desk.

'Hello, Tom Read speaking. How may I help you?'

'My name is Raymond Pope. Mr James has recommended your firm. You act as his accountant.'

'What business are you in, Mr Pope?'

'I used to be a manager for a large food store, but just over a year ago I opened up a small fruit and vegetable shop in the high street – R. & B. Greengrocers.'

'Yes, I know it. It's near Mr James's grocer's shop,' I said.

'Could you pop down to see me one day this week, please?' he asked.

I looked at my diary. 'Wednesday at 2.30 p.m. be all right, Mr Pope?'

'That'll do fine. See you then.' He replaced the receiver.

I made a note in my diary and resumed the sorting of my tax magazines. After about half an hour, I made myself a coffee and was standing looking out of the window at the pedestrians and traffic. My light blue Cortina was parked outside; I was admiring it. I had spent several hours on the Sunday cleaning and polishing it. As I was looking, a black Wolseley 1500 drew up behind my car. It was being driven by an elderly lady whose grey hair and wrinkled face I could just see above her steering wheel. She edged towards my car. Surely she was going to stop in time... I nearly spilt my coffee in my haste to open my office door. There was a splintering sound. I rushed over but I was too late. The old lady had bumped my car.

She got out of her Wolseley and we confronted each other.

'Is that your car?' she asked, pointing to my Cortina – my prized possession – its bumper now dented and mangled. I looked at her car, which had hardly a scratch. 'I am so sorry, I didn't realise I was so close.' She looked flustered and upset. 'I'll pay for the damage,' she said. She was trembling and obviously suffering from shock.

'Don't worry about it,' I said and went to assist her as I thought she might faint. 'You come and have a sit down in my office.'

I helped the old lady towards my office and made sure that she was seated in a comfortable chair.

She was a very small lady, barely five feet tall, with very long grey hair and a thin face which looked downcast. She was wearing a medium length, good quality blue dress with a large silver brooch. She looked towards me with sorrowful eyes.

I carried my cup of coffee and placed it on my desk.

'Won't be a minute. I'll make you a drink. Would you like coffee or tea?'

'Whatever you are having,' she replied gratefully. Soon she was sipping the hot liquid and her wan look soon disappeared.

'I do appreciate you not getting annoyed,' she said. 'My name is Mrs Alice Barnes.' She held her hand out and I shook it.

When I saw my car being bumped, I felt like expressing my annoyance loudly but seeing the frail old lady close to, my rage disappeared. Her name rang a bell. Then I remembered. She was a well-known authoress who had sold many thousands of books.

'What do you do for a living?' she asked. 'No, don't answer. I have just seen your certificates.' She stared at them intently. 'You get your car repaired, Mr Read, and send me the bill. I don't want to worry about insurance companies.'

Generally I am a good judge of character. There have been exceptions, but not many. 'All right, Mrs Barnes. I'll do that,' I agreed.

'Have you been practising long, Mr Read?' she went on.

'A few months. I've recently qualified.' I took my certificate down from the wall and showed her.

'My accountant is moving out of the district. Would you be interested in acting for me, Mr Read?'

Mrs Barnes, a famous authoress as one of my clients! I nearly jumped out of my chair with my eagerness to say yes. Instead, I paused as if considering the matter, and then replied, 'I would be pleased to, subject to corresponding with your present accountant.'

'There won't be any trouble. He's retiring next week,' she said. She was now smiling and, I was pleased to note, relaxed.

'I won't detain you any longer, Mr Read, and thank you for your patience in dealing with an old lady.' Her eyes were now twinkling and she walked briskly to the door. 'May I have one of your business cards before I go?' she asked. I got one quickly from my desk. 'Thank you. My address is 24, Church Lane; goodbye.'

I waved to her as she went off down the high street. That's how I became the accountant of a famous authoress. She did, of course, reimburse me for the expenses incurred in repairing my Cortina. It only needed a new bumper which was fitted within days.

Reflecting on the day's events, I thought, I could have got upset and showed my annoyance, but on seeing the old lady, I didn't. Restraint is sometimes best, although there are occasions when you have to vent your anger; otherwise some people confuse your being considerate with being weak-willed or soft.

My reflections over, I settled back in my armchair and picked up a client's file; I was soon engrossed in writing a comprehensive letter to the Tax Inspector.

WALKING ALONG THE high street during my lunch hour, I passed Mr Gage's office equipment and stationery shop. He had supplied all the essentials prior to me commencing my own practice. He had heard about the end of my close association with Rose but he realised it was all part of life's rich tapestry and these things happened. I was still on friendly terms with Rose, whom I saw occasionally. She had left Davis & Co. to work for a commercial firm. However, her life was now with Ken.

Mr Gage was standing at his shop doorway and called out, 'Hello, Tom. How's your practice?'

'Fine. It's flourishing and the main point is that I'm enjoying the work and being my own boss.'

'I have something that's just come in. I think you may be interested.'

Mr Gage was a good businessman, but there was no need for him to lure me into his shop. He was wealthy and had an established business; I was intrigued. He was a middle-aged man about my height but broader and nearly bald; he had a bushy black moustache, greying in places. Smartly dressed in a dark charcoal grey suit, a brilliant white shirt with a blue tie kept in place with a gold tie tack, he looked the picture of health. I followed him into his shop with anticipation. Never before had he called me in from the pavement to show me any of his stock. It had to be something special.

'What do you think of that?' he asked.

We had both reached the counter and he had picked up a small black rectangular object covered in tiny buttons. I recognised it from my magazines. It was one of the first pocket calculators invented by Clive Sinclair, the British electronics engineer. He was a young man of my age, and absolutely brilliant.

Mr Gage showed me the instruction leaflet which I had difficulty in understanding. Although calculators are very sophisticated now, the first models were not what one calls user-friendly. Eventually, I did manage to work the calculator and I was amazed.

It could add, subtract, multiply and divide in seconds. Pocket calculators now are commonplace, but the first ones were very unusual. I felt that I had to have one; it would, I thought, be a boon to me in my practice.

'How much is the calculator, Mr Gage?'

When he told me the price I asked him to repeat it. I was so impressed with the electronic device that the high price did not deter me. 'I shall have to buy one,' I declared.

'I thought you would be interested,' said Mr Gage, wrapping it up and handing it to me. 'I hope that it helps you in your work.'

When I got back to my office, I immediately endeavoured to do some calculations with my new possession. There was no doubt it was a marvellous invention, but after a couple of hours I was tired of it. I much preferred to use my own brain.

I often think about the first calculator I had ever seen. No doubt it's a collector's item now. I still have it. Modern calculators are part of everyday business and it is hard to imagine being without them. I certainly wouldn't like to work without one.

READING A TAX textbook, I was endeavouring to solve a particularly difficult problem when the phone rang.

'Don Calder here. You used to act for my Dad, Brian Calder, when you were at Davis & Co. Dad's had to retire through ill health. He's had a heart attack and I'm running the business myself. As you will remember, we were in partnership.'

'Yes, I do remember,' I said.

'Could you call to see me?' he asked. 'I'm married now and Dad and Mum have a small bungalow, not far from the house in which they used to live. I live in the detached house with my wife, Jenny.'

'I'll be pleased to call to see you,' I said. 'Would tomorrow at 11 a.m. be all right?' I heard the sound of rustling papers.

'I've got a small job to do in the morning but I'll be back by ten thirty, Mr Read.'

'Fine,' I said. 'I'll bring a new accounts book with me. Do you wish me to draft it for you when I call?'

'Yes, please,' he replied. 'I've never done any bookkeeping before. Dad always did that.'

I rang Davis & Co. to ascertain if it was all right for me to act for Mr Don Calder and I promised to send the usual etiquette letter. There were no objections. They were quite used to me contacting them about clients transferring to my practice. They understood it is the client who makes the decision whether to make the move from one firm of accountants to another.

The next day, I drove my Cortina to the neighbouring town of Southerton. It was only a few miles away. I parked my car outside Mr Calder's house and again I was impressed with the substantiality of the building. I looked at the massive oak door with its huge brass letter box and door knocker and then upwards to the massive roof covered in large peg tiles. That house was built to last.

I knocked at the door, which was soon opened by Mr Calder. Although shorter than his father, he was heavily built – some would say portly. He had a round, clean-shaven smiling face, and a mass of thick, curly red hair.

His brown eyes looked at me astutely. 'Come in, Mr Read,' he said. I wiped my feet on the mat. 'Don't worry about a bit of dirt. We don't stand on ceremony here.' He laughed loudly so as not to offend me. I followed him along a wide hall, turning into a large kitchen and then left into a well-furnished lounge.

A lady of about thirty years of age dressed in a staff nurse's uniform rose quickly from an armchair.

'This is my wife, Jenny,' said Mr Calder. 'Jenny, this is Mr Read.'

'Pleased to meet you, Mr Read,' she said. 'I waited until you came as I was anxious to meet you. I'm going now as I've got to call to see an elderly lady who has arthritis.'

We shook hands and I saw her and her husband glance at each other in a mutually agreeable way. One could see that they were happy. She was very smartly dressed, as one would expect from a nurse. Her small face radiated kindness.

'Goodbye, Mr Read. I hope to see you again soon,' she said. She waved to me, kissed her husband on the cheek and quickly walked away.

Mr Calder asked me to sit at a small table and as I sat down, so did he. I picked up my briefcase and withdrew the accounts book.

'Mr Calder,' I began, 'I'll work on the basis that you do not know anything about bookkeeping. If you do know some of the points that I will mention, then please bear with me.'

'I don't know much,' he said, 'but I'm willing to learn.'

Going through the book, stage by stage, and drafting it as I showed him, I was pleasantly surprised how quickly he took notice of the points I made. 'That's good, Mr Calder,' I told him. I asked him a few questions to make certain he knew what was required. 'Do you wish to ask me any questions, Mr Calder?' A few simple points were quickly clarified. 'I suggest that you maintain the book for a few weeks and then pop in to see me at my office and I will ensure that you are completing it correctly.'

'I'll do that, Mr Read. Thanks for your help. Like a cup of tea or coffee? A bit rough and ready, but it'll be hot.'

'Coffee please,' I replied, looking out of the window at the rear garden. 'Where've all your Dad's chrysanthemums gone?' I asked him. All I could see were vegetables – carrots, parsnips, potatoes, but no flowers.

'I like growing vegetables but I haven't Dad's enthusiasm for flowers. He's taken most of his rose bushes and chrysanthemums with him to the bungalow.' Each to their own, I thought.

We walked through the conservatory, which was attached to the lounge, into the garden.

'Like my new shed, Mr Read?' he asked. He opened the door and I looked inside. All his paint tins and brushes were set out neatly and there were several different sized ladders; in the middle of the shed was a workbench and various tools were placed in racks. He was his own boss and it was clear that his method of working was different from his father's.

His father, although a good worker, was untidy. I noticed a difference in Mr Calder junior. He had a spring in his step, which was missing when he worked with his father. He held the reins, could plan his work and carry it out the way he wanted to. This is a great feeling, as I experienced when I started my own practice.

Drinking our hot coffee in the conservatory, I felt directly that we had mutual respect for one another and I made a mental note to assist him with accountancy and taxation matters to the best of my ability.

'Cheerio, Mr Calder. I'll see you in a few weeks' time,' I said. We shook hands at the front door, and as I drove away I saw him wave and give me an appreciative smile.

I HAD JUST visited a client's business premises in Hayford, after teaching a young female clerk the rudiments of bookkeeping; I decided to take a short cut down a road where my parents and I used to live.

Driving my Cortina slowly past the maisonette where we lived until I was sixteen years of age, the memories came flooding back. I parked my car and sat quietly. A lot had happened since my parents had moved into the small dwelling.

In March, 1939, I was born, and six months later the Second World War commenced. It was a worrying time for my parents, bringing up a baby in those uncertain and devastating years.

My childhood memories of the War were vivid but confined to a child's experiences. I was five years of age in 1944 and attended a primary school which was close to the maisonette. My parents decided to stay in Hayford. My father worked as a precision engineer at a local factory and was responsible for making the propellers for the Fairey Gannet and Swordfish – the 'Stringbag' – both excellent aircraft, but slow. I still have a paperknife which he made, the blade of which resembles a propeller.

A child's memories are often limited. Buzz-bombs came to my mind. Children at my school had to dash to large air raid shelters built in the sports field as soon as the siren sounded, and we remained cowering with our protective teachers trying to keep us calm.

Small bottles of milk were distributed every morning to the children and occasionally tiny tins of vitamins, Ovaltine tablets and chocolate were passed around. Orange juice and cod liver oil and malt were made available at the local Town Hall.

Vegetables were grown by people in their gardens or allotments and therefore there was no shortage; but exotic fruit, that was another matter. I remember queuing for an hour to buy one banana.

The grapevine in Hayford was very effective and as soon as the kids got to know there was a delivery of oranges and suchlike they would rush round to the fruiterer's and stay there until they were allowed to buy one or two, or were turned away with the words, 'sold out!' Americans often visited Hayford. There was a small airport there and chewing gum and chocolate were given to the kids.

Rationing was operative and various goods were in short supply. Sweets were very important to children and often parents would forego their own quota for the benefit of the youngsters. However, the black market was rife. One could get virtually anything, provided the money was available.

Looking across at the maisonette, I remember my father building the Anderson shelter in the back garden. It was made of corrugated iron sheets, which were used to cover a deep hole made in the soil. If a buzz-bomb came over, the family used to rush to this little shelter and huddle inside; it was dank but my mother tried to make it more hospitable with the use of blankets, wooden forms and candles. Many people never bothered to use these shelters, thinking that it was safer to be in their homes. Luckily our shelter was never put to the test, although further down the road a family received a direct hit from a bomb. Their house and the shelter disappeared, together with the unfortunate occupants.

Although there were shortages of certain items, food and clothes in particular, people were generally fitter. Their diets were balanced with plenty of home-grown vegetables and home-made bread, cakes, soups and so on.

At night-time I remember the wardens coming round – and woe betide anyone showing a light during the blackout periods.

All these snippets went through my mind as I stared at the maisonette that had been my home for years until my teens. However, I had moved on. My visions of the past faded; I started the engine of my car and drove away. My mind came back to the present and my next client's tax affairs.

I was still attending Miss Williams's dance classes once a week; Jane was now my dancing partner. Rose had ceased to come to the classes for the time being, although I understood she would be renewing her membership later on. Ken wasn't interested in dancing and could not be persuaded to take up this pastime. He preferred his boxing and judo.

The monthly dance at the chocolate-making factory was to be held the coming Saturday and I arranged to pick Jane up at 7 p.m. We had to get to the ballroom at seven thirty to secure well-positioned seats. The dance was to commence at 8 p.m.

Apart from the dance, Jane and I were going to compete in the jive during the mid-session. This sometimes happened as an interlude to the general dancing. Competitors were to take part in the jive and cha-cha-cha.

Parking my Cortina outside Jane's home, I walked up the narrow pathway. I was wearing a pair of my close-fitting light grey trousers with my dark blue blazer covered in small gold coloured buttons. My gold cuff links and tiepin completed my apparel.

Jane opened the door and said, 'Hello, Tom. Won't be a minute. Come in.'

I stepped into the hallway and very soon Jane reappeared. She shouted to her parents, 'Bye, Mum, Dad.' I had not been introduced to them but I had been invited to tea the next week.

Jane looked a picture. She was wearing a bright orange miniskirt and her favourite small brown topcoat with a fur collar and highly polished dark brown shoes. Her pixie-like face had a small amount of powder and dark red lipstick. This time her dark hair was tied back with an orange ribbon to match her skirt.

She held my arm as we walked towards my Cortina. I could not help making a comparison with the situation when I took Rose to dances. This time everything felt right. There were no doubts creeping into my mind!

I held the passenger door open for Jane.

'Thanks, Tom,' she said. She made herself comfortable and I ensured that the door was closed properly, got into the driver's seat and started the engine. 'I'm really looking forward to this dance, Tom.'

'So am I,' I commented. I was wondering how we would fare in the jive competition.

We soon reached the chocolate factory security gates and parked near the ballroom. Picking up our small dance shoe bags we made our way to the entrance to the ballroom, which was brightly lit. A fat man with a dark moustache took our tickets, saying, 'Hope you enjoy yourselves.' He smiled expansively.

A young lady sitting at a small table said, 'Do you want any raffle tickets?'

'Two please,' I said and gave her two shillings.

Carefully walking over the sprung wooden dance floor, we located an unoccupied table close to the band. I waved to Mr Grange who was sitting at his piano. Close by were the guitarist and drummer. Mr Grange waved back. 'Good luck with your jive competition, Mr Read,' he shouted.

'Would you like a drink, Jane?' I asked.

She looked up as she was putting on her dance shoes. 'Yes please, Tom. A lemonade will be fine.'

I rarely drank anything else at a dance. Making my way to the bar I noticed Colin Brand queuing just ahead of me. 'Colin,' I called.

He looked round and said, 'I hoped you would be here. Dawn is at a table over there.'

I saw her not far from the bar and she gave me one of her cheerful smiles.

'Perhaps we can sit together later in the evening, Tom,' said Colin.

I soon purchased the lemonades and walked carefully back to Jane. Suddenly there was a loud crashing noise, just behind me. Looking round, I found to my dismay a large fat lady lying on her back. Her hair was dishevelled. She had slipped and fallen heavily. Putting my glasses of lemonade on a table, I quickly walked a few paces towards the lady who was looking up ashen-faced and bewildered. Another man and I helped her to her feet.

'Are you all right?' I queried.

'I was just walking along with a tray of drinks and suddenly my feet went from under me,' she said. The colour was coming back into her face and I gave her a sip of my lemonade; perhaps she wished it was something stronger. A young lady came rushing over with a small pail, a cloth and a dustpan and brush. The debris from the smashed glasses and spilt drinks was soon removed.

'Thank you, young man,' said the fat lady, who had recovered. She was joined by her partner, possibly her husband, and I left them chatting away.

'Did you see that woman fall, Jane?' I asked.

'No, I didn't. All I heard was the crashing noise. I saw you helping the lady up.'

Jane looked at me with her deep brown eyes. She didn't say any more but pressed my hand appreciatively.

By this time, Mr Grange and his fellow musicians had begun playing and a number of couples were dancing a waltz.

'Would you like to dance, Jane?' I asked.

She was soon at my side and we walked on to the dance floor. Pulling her gently toward me and listening to the beat of the music, we were soon spinning and turning. Jane had on a lovely perfume and I noticed her sensual warmth. I could have danced and danced. The sensation was relaxing and therapeutic.

Other dances followed: the quickstep, one of Jane's favourites; the foxtrot – we were still learning the rudiments; and then the Latin American dances.

We had reached the time for the competition in the jive and cha-cha-cha. Jane and I were going to concentrate our endeavours on the jive.

Mr Tim Moon walked up the steps to the stage, where Mr Grange and his colleagues were relaxing with a few drinks, clutched the microphone and said, 'Ladies and gentlemen, after the raffle there will be a short competition for our younger couples.'

The raffle was held. Neither Jane nor myself was lucky. Can't win every time, I thought.

We watched the couples competing in the cha-cha-cha. The winners were from Miss Williams's silver medal class and I saw her smile with pride.

It was now our turn to compete. I took Jane by the hand and on to the dance floor. The music commenced; directly I heard the beat most distinctly. We went into our practised routine at a very fast pace. Jane was light to spin and twirl and I was keeping the time steps going. I did not go offbeat at all. I looked at Jane. Her eyes and her whole countenance displayed her pleasure when dancing with me. We were a pair, and seemed to fit like a glove. The music stopped, and perspiring profusely, I led her to the side of the floor.

Mr Moon picked up the microphone. 'I'm sure that you all enjoyed seeing our young couples dancing. They were all very good but there can only be one couple that wins.'

I held my breath. He paused and looked at a piece of paper.

'The winners are – Jane Brown and Tom Read.'

I took Jane by the hand and we walked towards the stage. Mounting the steps, I took the small silver cup and gave it to her. This was one of the proudest moments of my social life. I looked at her. She was radiant.

We made our way back to our table and found Dawn and Colin Brand sitting there. 'Well done,' they chorused. Their praise said it all.

The rest of the dance was like a dream to me.

I took Jane home and we kissed at the garden gate.

'That was the best dance I've been to, Tom,' she said. Our eyes met. No doubts this time, I thought.

I T WAS MONDAY morning and I was sitting at my desk drinking my coffee and reflecting about the Saturday dance. It had been exciting to win a competition, especially with Jane. We appeared to complement each other, and not only with regard to dancing. This time I was not deceiving myself; I felt that the feelings were reciprocated. With Rose there had been doubts – hers and mine. True love has no room for doubts. My thought provoking was interrupted by a telephone call.

I picked up the receiver. Mr Keene, a retailer of men's clothes in the high street, spoke. 'Mr Read, could you call to see me please?'

When I was at Davis & Co. I had helped him to prove that an employee had been taking monies from takings before they were banked. He had not forgotten my investigative accounts work and when I left my old firm, he had followed me and was now my client.

'I'll be pleased to call to see you, Mr Keene. Will three o'clock this afternoon be suitable?'

'Yes, that will be fine,' he replied.

I replaced the receiver, wondering what the problem was. Surely, not another theft? I continued with my work, had my lunch, and just before 3 p.m. took his file out of the cabinet, put it in my briefcase, and strolled towards his shop. The door was wide open and I saw him serving a customer.

He saw me and waved. 'Won't keep you long, Mr Read.'

I looked around the shop. All the stock was set out neatly on quality wooden shelving.

'Mr Read – pleased to see you again.' He shook my hand firmly. 'Come through to the back.'

'Hello, Mrs Keene,' I said.

She looked up from the counter. 'How are you keeping, Mr Read?'

'My practice has taken off well,' I replied.

'That's excellent,' she said. She continued to write in a book as I passed her: a small thin lady with grey hair and a Victorian-looking outfit.

I followed Mr Keene through to the rear of the shop into a small room which contained a desk, two chairs, some cupboards and shelves. This was obviously their office.

'Sit down, Mr Read, please,' said Mr Keene.

I sat down opposite Mr Keene. He was fifty years of age, smartly dressed in a charcoal grey suit, white shirt, blue tie and matching pocket handkerchief which spilled over, with a gold tie tack and cuff links. He was a big man, well over six feet, with good posture, and had a large face with a small pencil moustache and thick curly hair.

'I've had this letter from the Tax Inspector,' he said and gave it to me. I read it thoroughly and started asking him pointed questions. 'Have you employed anyone during the last six months, other than Mr Darking?'

'On occasions I do have two or three ladies in to help part-time when the shop gets very busy. Why do you ask?'

I looked intently at him and said, 'Have you been deducting tax from their pay?'

He opened a drawer in his desk and withdrew a wages book. 'I record and declare all the amounts paid.'

'May I see the book?' I asked and he handed it to me. The total for the tax year regarding each casual worker was below the taxable amount. 'If you let me have the addresses of the workers, I'll send lists to the Inspector and that should clear the matter,' I said.

Mr Keene looked relieved. 'Thanks, Mr Read. That's taken a load off my mind.'

We walked back to the retailing area of the shop. I was just about to shake hands, when there was a tremendous crash. Looking at the front of the shop, we saw that the plate glass window had been shattered. Running to the front door, Mr Keene was the first to peer through. A young lad lay on the pavement with a wine bottle to his lips. Another broken bottle was clearly visible among the debris of splintered glass.

'He's drunk,' said Mr Keene. 'Thrown the bottle through the window.'

By this time Mrs Keene had appeared at the doorway. 'I'll telephone the police,' she said, and walked rapidly away, back to the inside of the shop.

The young lad looked up at us with glazed eyes. 'Have a drink,' he said incoherently. His trousers were stained and his shirt torn; one filthy plimsoll lay in the gutter. He tried to stagger to his feet but failed. Within a few minutes, the sound of a police car was apparent and a black Wolseley screeched to a halt. Two burly policemen got out of the car and listened carefully to Mr Keene's explanations.

One of the policemen said, 'We'll take him to the police station. Do you wish him to be charged?'

'As long as he agrees to pay for the damage, that will be the end of the matter,' replied Mr Keene; although ruffled he was not that concerned. Even if the lad did not pay for the damage, the insurance company would.

'All part of being in business, Mr Read,' he said philosophically. My window's been broken several times before and it will no doubt happen again.'

Situations like this he could handle. When people he trusted broke that trust, that was another matter.

'Cheerio, Mr Keene,' I said. 'I'll deal with the letter to the Inspector.'

'Goodbye, Mr Read. I'll wait to hear from you.'

The two policemen had managed to lift the drunken lad to his feet and pushed him unceremoniously into the police car. They had seen it all before. The driver put his foot down and sped away.

I expected a quiet day but it was not to be. As I walked back to my office, the young lad's look of despair was still in my mind; I hoped that he sorted his life out.

THIS WAS THE day I was to visit Mr Raymond Pope who had commenced trading at a fruit and vegetable shop under the name 'R. & B. Greengrocers'. I had been recommended to him by Mr James, the grocer, whose shop in the high street was nearby.

A few minutes before 2.30 p.m. on Wednesday, I stood outside Mr Pope's shop and looked at the window display, which was neat and attractive. On the pavement there was a stall with fruit and vegetables, all of which seemed to be in prime condition.

The shopkeeper saw me looking in and beckoned to me. 'I assume that you are Mr Read. I'm Ray Pope,' he said and offered his hand, which I shook.

He was a neatly dressed man with a clean striped apron; his face was thin and he wore rimless spectacles. His pupils were large and he observed me closely. I noticed his thinning hair. I followed him to the back of the shop. The sweet scent of peaches, plums, apples and pears permeated the air. I passed two assistants, one a middle-aged lady, with blonde hair and red lipstick, who smiled at me, and a young, short lad with a mass of black curly hair who was serving a customer, an old lady.

Reaching the back of the shop, we entered a small room which had a few boxes piled up and in one corner there was a small table and two chairs.

'Sit down, Mr Read, please,' said Mr Pope, and passed an accounts book to me, together with a file of vouchers and bank statements. 'I'm hoping that you will act for me. I'm used to bookkeeping but I need accounts preparing and advice on taxation matters.'

I looked at his records, which appeared on the surface to be kept well and balanced. 'I shall be pleased to act for you, Mr Pope. I'll need to take away your records for your first year of trading to enable me to prepare your accounts.'

'That's all right,' he said, and pointed to another book and file of vouchers on a shelf. 'I'm using a new book and file for my current transactions.'

I picked up the records, which lay on the table, and put them in my briefcase.

I asked Mr Pope a number of questions in accordance with a standard questionnaire, and after approximately ten minutes I stood up, shook hands with him again and said, 'I'll prepare your accounts and calculate your taxation position, then I'll give you a ring.'

'Thanks, Mr Read. I know from Mr James that you'll do your best for me.'

He began serving a customer and I walked away from the shop towards my office.

Firstly, I called at the confectionery shop that was next to my office, and bought some of my favourite mint humbugs. The jars of sweets always intrigued me: Pontefract-cakes made of liquorice, aniseed balls, jelly babies, dolly mixtures, paradise fruits. The list was endless and brought memories of childhood flooding back.

Then I called at the newsagent's, also next to my office, which was squeezed between the two shops, and bought a local newspaper.

I unlocked my office door, strode over to the kitchenette and made myself a coffee. This was one of the advantages of being my own boss. I could pace myself and if I wanted to have a break I could do so whenever I wanted, subject to certain restrictions imposed on me by clients calling.

Spreading the newspaper out, I saw some headlines which caught my attention directly. The factory where my father worked was mentioned. I read the details with interest. An employee – his name rang a bell and I recognised it – had been caught stealing some metal. He had put a thick rod of copper down his trouser leg, and just as he passed the security gate, he had fallen. The trouble had been that having fallen he could not get up. He was assisted by the security man and the rod of copper had been found. The employee had been heavily fined, but he had to face the stigma, which he would have to contend with from neighbours, friends and his workmates – if he still kept his job.

I put the newspaper to one side and commenced my work.

MR BAINES, THE builder, telephoned me at my office. He sounded concerned. The last time I had seen him was at his home some months ago when I worked at Davis & Co. I had called to see him as he had problems with his bookkeeping. When I had arrived at his house, which was situated down a cul-de-sac, about half a mile from the offices of my old firm, he had been to hospital, having fallen off the roof of an old shed he was repairing for a customer.

'Could you call to see me, Mr Read? I've got a problem with the tax man.'

'What time would be suitable, Mr Baines?' I asked, and noted down an afternoon appointment for three thirty. I then recommenced my letter writing.

I drove back to my parents' home for lunch. My father was at work but my mother greeted me in the kitchen. As she was ladling out the stew and potatoes, she was chatting about what had happened at the chocolate-making factory where she was a chargehand responsible for a group of women who wrapped and boxed the chocolates. She looked flushed and I asked her if there was anything wrong.

'Not now, I hope,' she said, and proceeded to explain. 'I took some sewing needles into the factory as I had bought a dozen cartons cheaply from a friend. I resold the cartons to three or four of my friends on the belt where the chocolates were wrapped and boxed. Suddenly one of the girls came up to me and said, "I've found a needle in one of the chocolate boxes." I immediately stopped the belt and got the girls to unwrap about a thousand boxes to search for any more needles. No more were found and the forewoman had not got to know but I'm still a bit edgy.'

My mother looked at me apprehensively. I knew she was extremely conscientious and an excellent worker.

'Don't worry,' I said. 'I'm sure that there is nothing to be concerned about.'

However, inwardly I was rather uneasy. The factory had a very good reputation and management would not want it tarnished.

'Cheerio, Mum,' I said as I left. 'See you this evening.'

She waved to me and I drove back to my office deep in thought. I hoped my mother would not be reprimanded for the mistake.

Arriving at Mr Baines's house, I opened the large iron gates which squeaked as I pushed them. A black and white cat sidled up to me, mewing and looking up at me. I bent down to stroke it but it quickly ran away; it was timid and uncertain of me.

I approached the massive front door, looking round at the unkempt lawn covered in wood, bricks, sand and other building materials. A few seconds after ringing the bell, the door opened and Mr Baines appeared.

'Glad to see you again, Mr Read,' he said. He was heavily built – about sixteen stone, with a round face and a thick black moustache; he was nearly bald, although a few thin strands of hair were combed across in an endeavour to obscure his baldness.

'Please follow me, Mr Read.'

I went along a wide hall and into a spacious lounge where Mrs Baines greeted me with, 'Hello, Mr Read.' She was nearly always smiling when I saw her, although the smile had been a forced one when she had told me about her husband's accident.

'How are you keeping, Mrs Baines?' I asked her.

A little girl about two years of age was playing with her toys in the corner of the room. She looked up at me and offered me one of her toys. I took it and looked at it, saying, 'That's nice.' I gave the toy back to the little girl and turned towards Mr Baines who had some papers spread out on a table.

'Come on, Katie,' said Mrs Baines and picked up her daughter. 'I'll take her into the kitchen and leave you men to sort out your problems.'

'Can you help me with this letter, Mr Read?'

Mr Baines gave it to me and I looked at it closely. It was from the local tax office and indicated that Mr Baines had received some cash from a customer and not recorded it. Knowing Mr Baines's standards of honesty, I found this hard to believe. Although he was a rough diamond, he called a spade a spade; I had never known him to be dishonest.

The sum involved amounted to about two hundred pounds.

'Could I see your accounts book?' I asked. He quickly produced it and I looked at the entry mentioned in the Inspector's letter.

No similar sum could be traced in Mr Baines's book, so I asked, 'Did you receive this sum, Mr Baines?'

'Yes, I did, but I didn't record it as I used the cash to pay for materials on the same day.'

He produced the invoice and receipt for the cost of the materials. The customer had paid him on account, and rather than bank the money and then withdraw cash to pay for the materials, Mr Baines had omitted the entries in his book. An honest error but on the surface suspicious.

However, things are not always what they seem. One has to dig deeper sometimes.

'I'll give the Inspector a ring and make an appointment to go to see him to explain what has happened,' I said. 'If he wishes to see you he'll tell me when I go round to the tax office. Please let me have your accounts book, your customer's copy invoice and the invoice and receipt for the materials.'

Mr Baines looked relieved. 'Thanks, Mr Read. I'll be grateful if you would tell the Inspector it was not my intention to deceive.'

'I'm sure that it will be all right,' I said. 'In future I do advise you to bank all monies received from customers, including cash. If you want some cash for materials or some other purpose, draw it from the bank.'

'I'll certainly do that, Mr Read,' he said. He was now smiling and shook my hand warmly.

'I'll let you know how I get on with the Inspector,' I said. 'Goodbye, Mrs Baines.'

'Nice to see you, Mr Read.' She continued playing with her daughter.

Mr Baines saw me to the door and waved as I drove away. He was clearly relieved. It had been an honest mistake and I was sure that the Inspector would understand.

As soon as I reached my office, I made an appointment to see the Inspector the following day.

I WAS HAVING lunch at a local restaurant. Not Fletcher's this time, but one that had been opened recently. Enjoying my meal and reading my newspaper, I noticed a young man striding confidently towards me. It was Keith, who used to work as an accounts clerk at Davis & Co. He had worked his probationary period of six months and he had decided he didn't like the work, and indeed Mr Davis was not happy employing him. Keith was a likeable lad of about eighteen years of age; sometimes a bit cheeky, but I liked him for all that. He now worked as an assistant manager at a local supermarket.

'Come and sit down, Keith,' I said. 'Are you going to order now?'

'Yes, I'm going to have the lamb today,' he answered.

A waitress quickly came over – a short, redheaded girl. 'Won't be long.' She looked first at Keith, then at me. She was about his age and she again glanced at him. He gave her a wink and she gave him a broad smile. 'Cheeky boy,' she said. The banter continued for a few minutes. I was beginning to feel like pig in the middle, and then she disappeared with Keith's order.

'How's the new job going?' I asked.

'Loving every minute of it,' he said and meant it. 'You would never believe some of the things that go on.' He was clearly in his element. 'Only last week, a load of goods was stolen from the back of the shop.' I had read about the incident in the local paper.

'Today a shop assistant was caught stealing,' he said. 'She had been taking sausages and wrapping them round her waist.'

He grinned. Clearly he was enjoying his job much more than sitting at a desk at Davis & Co. adding up columns of figures.

The waitress returned with Keith's roast lamb. 'How about the flicks on Saturday?' he asked. She looked at him again. Clearly she was interested.

'All right, I'll see you at 7.45 p.m. outside the Regent.' She turned away and he rubbed his hands together with glee.

'I only said it as a joke – but it worked!'

We were both enjoying our meals and talking about staff at Davis & Co.

'I hear that you and Rose have broken up. Pity really. I thought you were well suited.' That was his way – straight out with it.

'She's going out with Ken now,' I said. 'I'm friendly with Jane from the dancing club. We won a dancing competition recently.'

'Good for you. Plenty of fish in the sea,' he said.

He had yet to learn the seriousness of a deep relationship. Life to him was a bowl of cherries and why not? He was very young and anxious to enjoy himself from day to day.

Our seats were near a window and I looked out. A man had parked a brown Ford Zodiac and had opened his driver's door to get out when a coal lorry which was overtaking screeched to a halt, smashing into the open car door. I rushed out of the restaurant with Keith and looked at the car driver who was sitting in his seat, eyes glazed and in shock. He didn't speak. The remains of his door were mangled and lying on the road.

'I didn't see the door opening,' said the driver of the coal lorry, who climbed shakily down from his cab and looked at the piles of coal scattered over the road.

'As long as you're both uninjured; that's the most important thing,' I said.

The restaurant owner rushed out with some glasses of water. 'I've telephoned the ambulance and the police,' he said.

The thin man in the car looked up from his seat, took a glass of water and sipped gratefully. 'It was my fault. I didn't look in my mirror before opening my door.'

The lorry driver was standing by – a tall man, covered in coal dust. 'These things happen,' he said. 'As long as you make it clear to my boss that I was not to blame.'

By this time, the ambulance had arrived and after both the car driver and lorry driver had been examined, it sped away. No one was injured, only shocked. A few minutes later, a police car drew up. A policeman took a few particulars but seemed totally unconcerned – a minor incident to him, no doubt!

The lorry driver got a shovel and soon deposited the spilt coal back where it belonged, and after exchanging documents and looking at the badly dented nearside front wing of his lorry, slowly drove away.

The car driver remained seated. 'I can't drive my car in this condition,' he said. Looking at the gaping hole and the damaged door, which had been lifted and placed on the pavement, I could quite understand what he meant.

My Cortina was parked a few yards further along. 'I'll give you a lift home,' I said. He looked grateful as he got shakily out of his car and walked towards mine. He was a small man with a pale face and he looked ruefully over his shoulder at his damaged Zodiac, explaining, 'I've only had the car three months. Heaven knows what my wife is going to say.'

I opened the passenger door of my Cortina and made certain he was seated comfortably. 'Where do you live?' I asked.

'Only about five miles away,' he replied. He mentioned the road, which I knew well.

I soon arrived at his home and he shook hands with me at his front door.

'Are you sure you'll be all right? If you need to contact me, there's my card.' I handed him one from my wallet. He looked at the card: 'Chartered Accountant'.

'I'll bear you in mind. I'm a self-employed photographer. My name's Andrew Collins. Thanks for helping me.' He turned away and I noticed his voice was no longer quavering.

I drove slowly back to my office. In the commotion I had forgotten all about Keith. The last I saw of him was when he was speaking to the policemen, perhaps offering to be a witness if required. I would telephone him later.

Reaching my office, I sat in my armchair. It was some time before I could bring my thoughts back to my work, but eventually I settled down and commenced preparing a set of accounts.

I HAD SEEN Mr Brian Crane, who owned a grocery store, several times since he had converted his shop to a self-service system. When I was at Davis & Co. he had experienced pilferage and had installed a two-way mirror to catch the thieves. He had been successful on several occasions but had been so worried through losing goods, he had decided to revert to the old-fashioned counter system.

He was now my client and every three months I called to see him to ensure that his bookkeeping was being done correctly. The records were simple, but he liked to keep them balanced and up to date.

I opened his shop door and he looked up from the counter; he was forty years of age, a chubby man, neatly dressed with a thick crop of fair hair. Recently he had resorted to using spectacles and he looked over the top of them with his dark brown eyes.

'Come through to the office, Mr Read, please.' I followed him to the far end of the shop into a small room. 'They're all there for you to check.'

'Thanks, Mr Crane. No problems I hope?'

'I'll leave you to it, then,' he said. He closed the office door and I watched him through the two-way mirror which had remained in place since he had experienced the pilferage.

He still employed two assistants: a young lady, short, petite and cheerful whom the customers liked; and a thin young man who seemed to me to be a dreamer. His main interest was music and I believe the work in the shop was only a stopgap; he played in a group most evenings. His singing was rated highly by the teenagers.

Working steadily, I soon made the necessary test checks to Mr Crane's records, found the accounts book balanced and was enjoying my cup of tea and a biscuit which Mr Crane had brought in for me when I looked through the two-way mirror.

A small man dressed shabbily with an old torn overcoat and a grubby cap had approached the counter. His piercing grey eyes were focused on Mr Crane. To my horror, he slowly withdrew from his pocket a large double-bladed knife which he held in front of Mr Crane. The office door had been left ajar and I heard him say, 'Put all the cash from the till in this bag.' He handed a shopping bag to Mr Crane who was trembling and seemed dazed.

Slowly I picked up the telephone and dialled 999. A woman at the other end of the line soon spoke. I whispered the address of the shop, explained what was happening and very carefully replaced the receiver.

I continued to look at the scene which seemed unreal and as if it was a film. Mr Crane was taking the money from the till and putting it into the bag and all the time the knife was being held inches from his face. The young lady and lad together with a customer, an elderly lady, were cowering in the corner; they seemed like statues, unable to move.

The little man with the knife was grinning and thumping the counter with impatience. 'Hurry up,' I heard him shout. There was a sound of a car screeching to a halt, and as the man with the knife turned towards the shop door, Mr Crane picked up a tin of biscuits and knocked him on the head; he slumped to the floor and the knife went spinning. Two policemen, broad and aggressive, ran towards the man who was sitting, holding his head in his hands. One policeman picked up the knife; the other one dragged the man to his feet. He was only stunned but his eyes had become glazed.

One of the policemen said to Mr Crane, 'Are you all right?'

'I'm fine now,' replied Mr Crane. 'It was frightening at the time.'

'We know the man. He is not quite all there and has spent time in a lunatic asylum,' said the policeman. He was looking at his colleague, who had handcuffed the man. By now he was chatting away and none the worse for his experience except a lump on the head, and probably an impending spell of confinement.

The employees and the customer had grouped together and were discussing the attempted robbery.

I was standing at the doorway with Mr Crane looking at the Wolseley police car. One policeman sat with the little man who had attempted to steal the takings in the back of the car and the other policeman strode over towards us.

'Are you the young man who telephoned the police station?' he asked, looking intently at me. 'That was quick thinking and I shall be telling my Inspector when I get back to report to him. Well done!'

He held out his hand which I quickly shook.

The episode had seemed unreal but, as they say, 'Life is often stranger than fiction.'

I went back to the shop with Mr Crane to collect my briefcase.

'When you came to check my books I bet you never thought you would have such an exciting day,' he said. Mr Crane was laughing partly from relief and partly I suspect from his vision of banging the chap on the head with the biscuit tin. I began to laugh too, but stopped when I thought of the unstable man. Perhaps I should have felt sorry for him.

'Thanks for your help, Mr Read, and this time I don't mean in connection with checking my books!' We shook hands warmly. There was now a bond and to this day it has not been broken.

M R JIM GRASS was a car mechanic, but in his spare time he was a wrestler. I had seen him once in a tournament and I thought at the time, I would hate to have an argument with him. Standing over six feet three inches and built like a tree trunk, he was very muscular. Most of his aggression was used within the wrestling ring and seldom was he violent away from his sport. However, once I did see him very angry, and that was shortly after he had called to ask me to act as his accountant.

Sitting in my office he was as quiet as a lamb; however, that was about to change.

'I've received a letter from your previous accountants in answer to my usual etiquette letter,' I said. 'They have advised me that you owe them forty-five pounds for outstanding fees and they are going to hold your business records as a lien until the money is paid.'

There were various overlap items I needed to prepare the current accounts and Mr Grass had promised to let me have them; regrettably they were still with his previous accountants.

I looked at Mr Grass sitting opposite me. He was a huge man, dressed in a smart silver grey suit, blue shirt and orange tie. His large face matched his frame; a mass of long red hair rested on his shoulders. A stubbly beard, which he stroked thoughtfully, and bright wide-open blue eyes completed the picture. Like a volcano slowly erupting his face became redder and his voice became louder.

'I've paid the bill to prepare my last accounts.' He forced the words from his pursed lips.

'This forty-five pounds is for work they say they have done for you since then,' I said. I tried to remain calm.

He slowly rose menacingly from his chair. 'Right, I'm going round there to sort them out. I've only received one letter from them since they did my last accounts and that was to ask me for the money,' he announced.

'Did they send you a bill detailing the work covering the fee?'

'Yes, they did and there it is.' His bulk stretched over my desk as he handed me the bill.

Apparently they had written a few letters to the Tax Inspector and as far as I could see the time spent could not have warranted the charge; I wasn't going to say that to Mr Grass, however.

'Do you think this is fair, Mr Read?' he asked, looking down at me. I was not going to offer an opinion and suggested he went round to his previous accountants and discussed the matter with them.

'I want my records,' he thundered. His temper was up – just as I had seen him in the ring. 'I'm going now and it won't be long before I'm back.'

'They have the right to keep your records until they get paid,' I said.

Normally docile out of the wrestling ring but now angry, he strode away, saying, 'I'll be back within half an hour.'

I wondered if he would. My office door banged and he was gone.

A few minutes after he left, my telephone rang. 'This is Mr Whitley from Blecking & Co. Mr Grass is here demanding his records. He is threatening to smash the place up and rather than call the police, I am going to give him his records, but I would ask you to have a word with him when he calms down. He owes us forty-five pounds and we intend to be paid.'

The receiver crashed down. Charming, I thought. Perhaps I had better think again before acting for Mr Grass.

Fifteen minutes later he reappeared. Perspiring and still red-faced, he placed the records on my desk. 'I told you I would get them,' he said. His anger had disappeared.

'I think it would be better if you paid the forty-five pounds,' I said.

He looked at me calmly. 'I have every intention of doing so but I am not going to be held to ransom.' We said our farewells, after I promised to contact him again.

I did decide to act for him and I never again saw evidence of his temper, outside the wrestling ring.

I HAD BEEN helping Ben with his studying. He had attempted to pass his final exams on three occasions, but had failed each time in a couple of subjects. One of these subjects happened to be taxation, my favourite. During the weeks prior to his fourth attempt, the revision had been intensified and in my opinion his knowledge was greatly improved. When we were articled clerks at Davis & Co., we had been great friends. I liked his sense of humour. He was cheeky but never in a way to offend.

Having taken my final exams, I was fully aware of the considerable time required for studying. Ben's leisure time, apart from visiting the swimming baths and the occasional visit to the cinema, was limited. I had persuaded him to have one more try to pass his finals and I had promised to assist him with his studying. The time was fast approaching for Ben's last attempt.

When I took my exams, my friend, Henry, had taken me to London to the exam centre, by his car, dropped me off and then collected me later when I had finished the exams for the day. I was going to drive my Cortina into London and take Ben in the same way.

The first day of Ben's exams had arrived and I was sitting in my car waiting for him. I had deliberately got to his home early as I wanted to have plenty of time to make the journey into London. I turned my radio on; I liked listening to The Beatles. Their first hit, 'Love Me Do', was being played and I closed my eyes. My mind started drifting back to my early schooldays. I had come a long way since then. It didn't seem so long ago since I was at my primary school.

The children often made their own entertainment. Apart from hopscotch and leapfrog, rudimentary metal roller skates were available and the kids made full use of them, travelling at tremendous speeds on the pavements; needless to say there were often collisions, sometimes with adults.

I used to collect cigarette cards, stamps and matchbox tops – probably worth a small fortune now, but lost or mislaid over the years. Children didn't think in terms of value then, but collected various items as hobbies. Visions of the children in the street where I lived playing with multicoloured marbles and fivestones came vividly to mind.

Suddenly there was a knock on the car window. It was Ben saying, 'I'm ready, Tom.' I opened my eyes. Sitting in my car listening to the radio, I had dozed off. My dreams of the past quickly disappeared. I leaned over and opened the passenger door. 'Get in, Ben.'

He came round to the other side of my car and sat beside me. 'Thanks for giving me a lift, Tom.'

'I'm pleased to help you,' I said. I knew what he was going through and I was thankful the trials and tribulations of my exams were over.

We reached the exam centre with half an hour to spare and I said goodbye to Ben. 'Best of luck. I'll pick you up at 6 p.m.'

'Thanks, Tom.' He gave me a forced smile and wandered off to join the groups of other students.

I drove back to Hayford, hoping that Ben would do well in his exams. Having taken a few days off from my practice, which was doing well, I decided to use the time cleaning and polishing my Cortina and also my Capri scooter, which I used occasionally at weekends.

At 4.30 p.m. I began the journey to London and drew up at the exam centre a few minutes before 6 p.m. Ben was waiting for me at the kerbside. He jumped in my car and I knew by his manner he was relieved. I didn't say much to him as I knew all about the stress involved in taking exams. However, he volunteered a comment. 'The first subject was taxation, and some of the questions we had covered in the revision.'

I continued to take Ben into London and collect him until he had completed his exams.

'Well, how do you think you've fared this time?' I asked.

'I felt much more confident than previously. I think your assistance in my revising might have tipped the balance,' he replied. I hoped that he was not being too optimistic. If he failed this time, he had told me that he was not going to try again.

Several weeks passed and I got on with my work at my office. I had seen Ben several times since he had taken his exams. He was still working at Davis & Co. and we had lunch together sometimes.

The phone rang. It was Ben; he was jubilant. 'I've passed, Tom! I'm a Chartered Accountant.'

I was so pleased for him. 'Come round at lunchtime and we'll celebrate,' I said.

At 1.10 p.m. Ben came through my office door. 'Well done, Ben,' I said. I rose quickly from my armchair. We shook hands vigorously.

'I would like to thank you, Tom, for helping me.'

'I might have helped you, but the success is down to your splendid efforts,' I said.

It was not so long ago that we were two articled clerks – then both Chartered Accountants. Ben had persisted and succeeded.

J OHN COOK, A close friend of mine, had a brother who was a Ford Motor Company salesman, and I had bought my Cortina from him.

I had known John since primary school days and although he was now a Chartered Surveyor, we had not lost touch. He lived near Hayford and sometimes we would meet and socialise. We were the same age and were interested in looking at the aeroplanes at London (Heathrow) Airport which was not far from Hayford. When we were youngsters, we used to go bird-nesting, collecting eggs; there was a large fen there and we spent hours picking blackberries, collecting newts and putting them in jam jars. Wildlife was abundant – swans, coots, moorhens and mallard ducks. Unfortunately, from the point of view of children like John and me, this special place was swept aside when the airport was built.

Heathrow Airport covers a vast acreage and it was necessary to compulsorily purchase a number of people's homes along the route. This caused much havoc and distress at the time, but was unavoidable in order to build the new runways and terminal.

I picked John up at his home. He was standing at his garden gate waiting for me. His girlfriend, Ann, had gone to Yorkshire to visit a sick relative for a few days, and he and I decided to spend a few hours at Heathrow Airport where there was a sightseers' platform. He was very keen on aeroplanes, and kept a notebook where he entered details of those he had seen; I was interested merely looking at the planes.

After a time, we made our way back to my Cortina where we sat reminiscing. John had gone to a different secondary school to mine, but our time at the primary school remained vivid in our minds. We were both in the same classes throughout the six years of schooling there and academically were on the same level. In 1945, when we were both six years of age, we celebrated VE and VJ days with parties at school and also in the streets outside our homes. We were young, but the joyful celebrations impressed upon us the importance of the occasions.

Although we didn't understand what was happening regarding the end of the War, we did know that it was a time for children to enjoy themselves. Details of the parties, where tables and chairs were brought out from people's homes, put in the streets and covered with tablecloths of various hues, remain imprinted on my mind to this day.

I remember looking around at the grown-ups and other children with their colourful paper hats, the paper chains and the Union Jacks displayed all over the place.

Our reminiscing over for the time being, I started the engine of my car.

'We'll call at a restaurant on the way back home, John, if that's all right with you?'

'Fine, Tom,' replied John.

Heathrow Airport was about eight miles from Hayford and I knew a good restaurant about halfway. We were soon on the main road and travelling at 50 m.p.h., following a stream of traffic. Just in front of us was a Ford Anglia, being driven by a lady with blonde hair. Suddenly her car started veering to the left.

'I think she must have a puncture,' said John. The Anglia was weaving all over the road and swung abruptly. I was keeping my distance but I could see what was going to happen. She was going to end up in the ditch. I was right. Her car veered off the road, crashed through a low wooden fence, turned over and came to rest in a fast flowing stream. Stopping my car quickly, I leaped out with John and scrambled down towards the Anglia.

The lady, about thirty years of age, was trapped; blood was coming from a head wound, but I was worried about the water lapping around her car. 'Try and get the doors open, John.' I tugged at the driver's door and John at the passenger's.

'Tom, I've got the door open,' said John. He reached across to the lady, who was sprawled across the roof. Although dazed and in shock, she mumbled some words. Both John and I were standing in three feet of water – we had to get her out.

We pulled her, and suddenly she was free and out of the car. Carrying her up the riverbank, we laid her down on the grass verge. By this time a small crowd had gathered.

'I've called for an ambulance,' said a small thin man with glasses. 'Shouldn't be long now.'

'Are you all right?' I said to the lady, who was sitting up and holding her head. Getting my handkerchief out, I covered the wound to stop the flow of blood.

'I don't know what happened,' she replied. 'I was driving along and then my car went out of control.'

'Do you hurt anywhere else?' asked John, putting his arm round her shoulders.

'No – only my head,' she replied.

I ran to my car and pulled out my sports bag. Soon back at her side, I opened the bag and took out my vacuum flask. 'Have a sip of coffee,' I said. She sipped gratefully.

In the distance was the sound of a siren. 'The ambulance will soon be here,' said John, and pressed her hand reassuringly.

All of a sudden, two ambulance men were at our sides with a stretcher.

'We'll take over. Thanks, lads.' They looked at the lady attentively, put her on the stretcher and took her to the ambulance.

'Thank you,' murmured the lady, as she looked towards us.

We stood there dripping wet but relieved. A handclap came from the small crowd. We had saved the lady's life, but at the time we did not think of danger – only that something had to be done about the situation.

A police car drew up and the policemen walked quickly towards us, saying, 'We'll have to take some particulars.' One of them got out his notebook.

After explaining the situation, we made our way slowly back to my car. I got two rugs from the boot and put them on the front seats. We were both slightly shocked, but the exuberance and resilience of youth soon took over and we were in high spirits. While sitting there for ten minutes or so, I said to John, 'That woman could very easily have been drowned.'

He looked towards me and his expression said it all. The close bond of friendship had been reinforced.

I slowly drove back to Hayford. We didn't say much but there was no need for many words.

The incident was followed by a reporter from the local newspaper interviewing us later in the afternoon and an article appearing the following day: 'Two professional men save lady from drowning.' I still have the newspaper cutting and it is one of my treasured possessions.

A few days after the accident, the lady wrote a letter of appreciation to us. She had got my name and address from the police who had interviewed us. Later, we went to see her at the Hayford Hospital and were pleased to see that she had nearly recovered. She had suffered a slight concussion, but the cut was superficial. Trauma affects some people more than others, but it seemed that she had quickly got over the shock of the accident.

Back at my office, later in the week, I was sitting in my armchair. I was glad to be back in my comfortable environment; I began to prepare another set of accounts.

M Y PRACTICE HAVING become really well established, I decided to devote more of my spare time during the evenings and weekends to social activities.

I had arranged to go with Jane to a social dance at Bartwell, a neighbouring town about twenty miles away. Although we could have driven by car, we decided, as a change, to go by public transport.

Social dances are usually more relaxed than ballroom dance functions and I therefore dressed more casually. A pair of my close-fitting beige trousers with a fawn jacket, a cream shirt and a yellow tie completed my attire. I used one of my favourite colognes, given to me by Jane for my last birthday.

Jane was waiting at her garden gate. She was wearing a yellow miniskirt, a light blue top with a brown coat. Her small round face had a touch of powder and her usual dark red lipstick; her hair was neatly tied back with a yellow ribbon.

'Hello, Tom. You look smart this evening,' she said. I saw her glance at my fawn jacket, which was made from mohair.

'You look really nice,' I said, looking at her radiant smile and noticing her lovely perfume – a Max Factor product.

She kissed me fully on the lips. Her lips always reminded me of sweet cherries. We held hands as we walked the few yards to the trolleybus stop. After a few minutes chatting to each other, a bus came along and we jumped on. 'No room downstairs,' shouted the clippie and rang the bell. Climbing the stairs, we found two vacant seats. After five minutes, we reached our destination, Hayford Station, raced down the stairs and jumped off the bus. We made our way to the railway ticket office. A large man with a florid complexion, a dark blue uniform and peaked cap, peered at us.

'Two return tickets to Bartwell, please.' I placed a ten-shilling note on the counter.

He handed me my change and the two tickets. I saw him glance at Jane admiringly. She certainly did look a picture.

We walked down the concrete steps towards the platform, pausing to purchase two bars of Nestle's chocolate from a machine. Strolling along the platform with Jane, I felt content. The contentment was hard to explain, but when I was with Jane she made me feel confident and I felt at ease with her.

After a few minutes, we heard the sound of a steam train and then it came into view, its funnel billowing smoke. A steam locomotive hissing, wheezing and making all sorts of other noises, really does seem to have a life of its own. The driver looked out of his cab, tipped his cap to us and smiled. We climbed into the compartment and slammed the door behind us. A whistle blew and looking out of the window, I saw the guardsman wave his flag; we were off.

We had chosen a non-smoking compartment, as neither of us smoked; sitting down, we looked around us. There were two other occupants: a small middle-aged man with a bowler hat, dozing; and an elderly lady, grey-haired. She smiled at us and continued with her knitting.

After about fifteen minutes, we pulled into Bartwell station.

'Careful about the step, Jane.' I thought she was going to trip and held her hand tightly.

'I'm all right, Tom, thanks,' she said. She did not let go of my hand, however. We walked along the platform and the ticket collector clipped our tickets and returned them to us.

It did not take us long to walk to the community centre where the social dance was being held. The building was well lit and we joined a group of people just outside the large entrance doors which were wide open. We knew in advance that we had to bring our own food and drink.

Jane and I both had bags which we opened as we went into the community centre. A lady, plump and cheerful in a red dress took our tickets and also the food.

'Thank you, dears. You can put your coats over there.' She pointed to a side room. All the food was to be collected and placed on tables which were to be brought into the dance hall, halfway through the dance.

We passed through the inner doors and into the very large room, which was used for all sorts of activities. That evening, it had been hired by the local social dance club. Looking round the room, we saw about a hundred chairs placed against two of the walls; at the end of the room there was a small stage and a tall man with thinning hair was looking at the gramophone and the records. We located two seats not far from the stage. Jane pointed. 'Look, Tom, there's piles of boxes of chocolates and bottles of whisky, gin and rum.'

'They must be for the raffle,' I said.

The seats were beginning to be taken fast and I looked at my watch – 7.45 p.m. The dance was due to start at 8 p.m.

The tall man on the stage selected a record and placed it on the gramophone. A quickstep by Victor Silvester began playing. Although it was not quite eight o'clock, various couples got up straight away and started to dance. There was no proper sprung floor, only a hard asphalt surface, but no one seemed bothered. They were there to enjoy themselves. I looked at the dancers – untrained, but they were determined to make an evening of it.

Proper dance shoes were not needed; the floor was crowded. It didn't matter to some people if they danced properly or not – just as long as they got round the floor without falling over.

'A waltz,' shouted the man on the stage.

'Would you like to dance, Jane?' I asked. Jane, wide-eyed and smiling replied, 'Of course, Tom.'

I held her close and then we were off – one-two-three. There was no room to dance our sequences, so I improvised – one of the best ways of dancing in a crowd. A few bumps, nothing serious. A large man with a pencil moustache knocked into me as he was attempting to turn his partner.

'Sorry,' he said, and smiled apologetically, continuing flat-footed around the room. I thought to myself, That could have been me a year ago.

A woman's high-pitched voice penetrated the room. 'Time for the raffle.'

Everybody sat down and a frantic search began to locate their tickets, which had been bought earlier in the evening. A large metal bucket was placed in the centre of the floor and a little girl began pulling the counterfoils out. Number 81 was called. A young lady with short red hair scampered over with her ticket and chose a large box of chocolates. There were about twenty prizes altogether. Jane looked at her ticket – number 22. She had won. Before I could ask her if she wanted me to get the prize for her, she was strolling across the floor. She brought back a large box of marshmallows. Her pixie-like face was a picture.

The man on the stage had located a microphone. 'Latin American time, ladies and gentleman.'

A few dancers got up and I nudged Jane. 'Shall we do our silver medal routine?'

She nodded. A jive was played – my favourite – then a cha-cha-cha. At the end of the Latin American record, there was a round of applause from the other dancers and we made our way back to our seats, red-faced.

'Are you professionals?' asked one lady, not realising that we had only really begun serious dancing.

'They're just simple routines we're taught at the dance school at Hayford,' I replied.

There was commotion at one end of the room. The tables for the food were being brought in. In a matter of minutes they had been assembled and ladies from all directions were placing plates of sandwiches, cakes, sausages on sticks and other food on to the tables.

'Grub up!' shouted one short, portly man with a brush cut. People walked quickly towards the tables, took small plates and started putting the food on them.

'We'd better be quick, Jane, otherwise there'll be nothing left.' I was joking, of course. There was enough food to feed an army.

A furry object flew across the floor. 'There goes Bob's syrup of fig.' A man scooped up the wig and gave it to his friend who, unperturbed, replaced it.

We made our way back to our seats and were soon chatting to people either side of us, between mouthfuls of food. Dancing at any level is therapeutic and there was a happy atmosphere.

After about half an hour, most of the food had disappeared. We had brought our own drinks in our bags and we resumed the dancing. The end of the dance came too quickly and Jane and I were soon walking out of the community centre. We looked at each other. Neither of us said a word. There was no need. We made our way home in a buoyant mood.

'Thanks for taking me, Tom.' Jane's deep brown eyes looked up at me and we kissed lingeringly; reluctantly, I waved goodbye as she stood at her garden gate.

HAVING JUST BALANCED a comprehensive set of accounts, I sat back in my office armchair with satisfaction. Time for a break; my usual cup of coffee was soon made and I was sipping it and reflecting on the social dance at Bartwell with Jane; it had gone well and our relationship seemed to be developing on a sound basis.

My musing quickly evaporated. There was a ring at my door and in strode David. He had been articled at Davis & Co., and we often went on outside audits together. David was much taller than me and heavily built, and was very interested in sport, including rugger. Once when we had been sent to a client's business premises at an industrial estate, he had skived off to go and watch a rugger match. Mr Davis, the principal, never found out. I had been left pondering over the episode. I came to the conclusion that each person sets his own personal standards and must live by them.

David, despite several attempts at his final exams, did not pass; a pity really, as he was excellent at the practical side of accountancy. He had been called up and had served his two years in the army doing National Service. His wife, a dental nurse, had got very upset when he received his call-up papers but he seemed to accept the situation; in fact he seemed to relish the idea. The two years since had gone quickly and he was shortly returning to civvies.

He held out his hand, saying, 'Pleased to see you again, Tom.'

I responded by offering my hand and we shook hands warmly.

'I'm pleased to see you, David; sit down,' I said, coming round to his side of my desk to sit next to him. He had his army uniform on and I thought how smart be looked: boots and buttons highly polished and short back and sides haircut. This was the last year of National Service so he had been one of the last to be called up.

'What do you intend to do after you come out of the army?' I asked him.

'I've been for an interview during my leave and I've got a job as an accountant in charge of an audit team, in the City,' he replied. He looked pleased and knowing his standards of auditing, I thought that would be ideal for him.

'Have you been to the old firm, David?'

'Yes, I called in just before I came here. Hardly anybody I recognised – only Ben, who's leaving shortly, Mrs Teaming and Mr Andrews,' he replied; the last two were accounts clerks.

'I understand old Johnson can't get a job. I saw him yesterday. Poor old boy is as thin as a rake,' he said. David was never frightened of Mr Johnson and with hindsight I realised this was because he stood his ground. Bullies, if they sense someone is frightened of them, take advantage of the situation.

I looked at David more closely. His nose looked as if it had been broken.

'How did you do that?' I asked.

David grabbed his nose with his finger and thumb. 'Got that injury when I took part in the army semi-finals boxing championship. I also got my jaw broken. I had to have it wired up and could only have liquids for several weeks.' He smiled ruefully. 'You should have seen the other chap. He still won on points, I must add!'

David seemed different, and of course he was; he had matured. Life in the army had been good for him. He was always a bit of a tearaway and discipline had worked.

'I spent most of my time in Germany,' he told me. 'After a few months doing clerical duties, I joined the boxing team and from then life was a bowl of cherries.' He laughed loudly but then winced. 'My jaw still feels tender,' he added. He rubbed his hand against his cheek.

We both stood up, David towering over me.

'Best of luck, Tom.'

'Same to you, David.'

We had mutual respect for one another and have remained good friends over the years. He and his wife ended up with four children: two girls and two boys. I often think of when he left me ticking away at leather-bound ledgers on an outside audit, whilst he skived off. We shook hands, I saw him to my office door and he marched away.

I HAD SEEN Mr Thompson, an upholsterer, when I was at Davis & Co. His tiny shop was very close to my office and we frequently spoke to each other. Recently I had called to see him to have a piano stool reupholstered, and I asked him how his business was progressing. He didn't have any employees; he couldn't afford to pay any, but he had made a reasonable profit in his first year of trading.

As we got on very well together, he had decided to have me as his accountant and it was very convenient for him to call to see me or for me to pop into his shop.

He had asked me to see him about his accounts book, as he had experienced difficulty in balancing it. Everything about him was neat. He was a small man with a short back and sides haircut, highly polished black shoes and a fawn protective apron; his eyes twinkled as he watched me cast the figures.

'I've found the error, Mr Thompson. Ten pounds has been added as if it were one hundred pounds – that's the ninety pounds difference.'

'That's splendid,' he said. 'Good job you're virtually on my doorstep.' He paused and added, 'I've finished your piano stool.'

I looked at it – excellent craftsmanship. 'I'm pleased with your work,' I said. 'You let me have your invoice and I'll settle up with you.'

'I'll put it through your letter box later in the week.' He motioned me to sit down and we were chatting away when he looked out of the window and pointed. A group of Rockers – about twelve of them – had appeared on their motorbikes and were revving up their engines. The din was tremendous.

'I'm not having that outside my shop,' said Mr Thompson, walking towards the door.

'I'd watch your step,' I said. One or two of them I had recognised and I knew them to be mischievous.

He took no notice of my warning and opened the door, shouting, 'Clear off or I'll call the police.'

The Rockers looked towards him. 'He's got an apron on,' one of them shouted. Another made a rude gesture. 'Clear off, back to your rat hole,' said another.

This was too much for Mr Thompson who, although small, was not frightened; he had got his dander up. He had right on his side and he was going to make his point.

'You're nothing but louts,' he said. His face showed his annoyance and he confronted the lads, who were all in their leathers. I was standing by his shop door and I knew from experience that usually it was when the Mods and Rockers got together trouble brewed, not normally with people like Mr Thompson. However, in this case I was wrong. One young lad got off his motorbike and approached the shopkeeper menacingly.

The boy was about nineteen years of age and he was set to show off in front of his mates. Mr Thompson looked at him cool-headedly. The lad lifted the apron. 'Don't touch my clothes,' said Mr Thompson. Taking no notice, the boy, with his mates forming a ring, jeered. 'What are you going to do about it?' said the boy, leering mockingly. Suddenly there was a chain in his hand and he waved it towards Mr Thompson who looked at him impassively.

In a matter of seconds, the young lad was on the ground in an armlock; the chain was kicked to one side and Mr Thompson sat astride him. The boy's mates advanced and I noticed Ken amongst them.

'Come on, that's enough. This was supposed to be a game,' he said. The Rockers, including the young lad who had got up from the pavement pop-eyed and shaking, mounted their motorbikes and sped away. The sound of a police siren was heard and a police car drew up. Someone had obviously phoned for assistance.

'Did you recognise any of them?' they asked Mr Thompson.

'No I didn't. We'll let the matter rest.'

'Are you sure?' they asked.

'Yes, I don't believe they will be back.'

The two policemen got in their car and drove off.

Mr Thompson and I walked back to his shop and he must have noticed my surprised expression.

'I have a black belt in karate,' he said. 'Comes in handy sometimes.' He smiled wryly and said, 'Back to the mundane side of life – making a living.' Again his eyes twinkled.

J ANE HAD PROMISED to let me drive her red Triumph Herald 13/60 and the coming Saturday we were going to Caxton-on-Sea, a small resort on the East Coast. I arrived at her home at 8 a.m. and parked my Cortina on a neighbour's driveway, as arranged. He had sold his car and was pleased to let me park my car safely, rather than leave it on the road.

I walked briskly up the pathway to Jane's front door and rang the bell. Mrs Brown greeted me.

'Come in, Tom. Jane won't be long.'

I followed Jane's mother into the house. She was small and petite like her daughter.

'Hello, Tom,' said Mr Brown. He reminded me somewhat of my father, who also smoked a pipe and had a thick moustache.

'Like a cup of tea, Tom?' asked Mrs Brown. She smiled as she adjusted her apron which had become undone.

'Yes, please – milk and two sugars.'

'Won't be long,' she said and off she went to the kitchen.

I sat on the settee with Mr Brown who had taken his tobacco pouch from his cardigan pocket and was filling his pipe. A packet of Gold Block tobacco was placed on the coffee table.

'You smoke the same brand as my father,' I said and pointed to the name.

'Great minds think alike,' remarked Mr Brown. He chuckled and blew a cloud of smoke in my direction. I coughed. 'Sorry, Tom. I should know by now you're a non-smoker.' He tapped the ash from his pipe into a tray and placed the pipe on a stand with some other ones.

'There you are, Tom,' said Mrs Brown, coming into the lounge with a tray on which was placed the teapot, cups, saucers, milk and sugar. Just behind her mother followed Jane, wearing a pair of cream slacks, a red jumper and a light duffel coat. She had on sensible walking shoes. Her small round face glowed with the radiance of youth.

'Hope I didn't keep you long, Tom,' she said. She kissed me on the cheek and placed a tin of biscuits by my side on a small table.

'You help yourself, Tom.' Jane's parents were, like her, very easy to talk to, and we were all soon chattering away.

After about fifteen minutes, Jane looked at her watch. 'We'd better be going, Tom, if we are going to miss the heavy traffic.' She picked up a bag, which I knew contained the picnic fare, and another small bag, which probably held her swimming costume and towel.

We made our way to Jane's Herald. 'Won't be a minute,' I said. I walked quickly to my Cortina, opened the boot and took out my sports bag containing my swimming trunks, towel and a box of candies. I saw Mr Frame look out of his window at my car, which was parked on his driveway; he waved and smiled.

'You drive, Tom.' Jane sat in the passenger seat of her Herald. The car was pointing towards the road and after waving to her parents, who were standing at their doorway, I opened the driver's door and eased myself into the seat. The steering wheel, as in all Heralds, was slightly offset. This was a bit disconcerting until one realised the position was standard. There was no synchromesh on first gear so one had to be careful not to damage the gearbox. I started the engine, which purred agreeably, and slowly drove on to the road. The steering was light and the all-round vision very good. I soon felt confident driving the little car. 'Jane, this is an excellent motor,' I commented. I glanced sideways.

'I'm pleased with it. I wouldn't wish to change it,' she said.

We were soon on the open road and Jane asked, 'Do you want the radio on, Tom?'

'It would be nice to listen to some music. You select the channel,' I said, concentrating on overtaking a slow-moving lorry. Jane soon located a wavelength and big band music filled the car. What a dream to drive, I thought. I liked my Cortina but this little car was in a class of its own.

Halfway to Caxton-on-Sea, we stopped at a lay-by and I turned towards Jane. 'Shall we have a coffee, Jane?' Her deep brown eyes looked at mine.

'You get the flask and I'll hold the cups,' she said.

I poured the hot liquid out and we sat there munching our chocolate biscuits and drinking our coffee. Jane reached up and opened the sunroof. The sunlight streamed in and I looked at the azure, cloud-free sky. Some sparrows appeared and looked towards us expectantly. We threw them a few pieces of biscuit and they flew down, eagerly pecking away.

We had finished our coffee and biscuits and I'd put the flask away. 'Shall we go, Jane?'

She nodded, leaned over and kissed me on the lips, saying, 'That's for luck.' Her eyes sparkled. She made me feel content; it was difficult to explain, but being with her made me feel confident and right with the world.

The engine fired first time and we continued with our journey. We soon arrived at the resort and pulled up alongside the seafront. I got the bags out of the car and Jane opened the boot and showed me two small deckchairs. 'I thought these would be useful in case we couldn't hire any.'

'That's fine, Jane,' I said, and picked them up. After locking the car, we walked across a grass area, on to the promenade and the sandy beach. We found a good spot about ten yards from the sea, spread our rugs out and placed the deckchairs and bags down. The air was bracing and I licked my lips and tasted the salt. Seagulls circled and as we looked out to sea, a ship moved slowly on the horizon. There were others like us, sitting and looking at the sea. There were children paddling and a few adults were swimming.

We wriggled into our swimming costumes. Jane, although small, was perfectly proportioned and I glanced at her bright red outfit admiringly.

I had been swimming with Jane on several occasions at the indoor pool at Hayford and I knew that she was an excellent swimmer, especially at the front crawl, a stroke I had not perfected; I tended to swallow too much water. 'Shall we go for a swim after we've had our sandwiches, Jane?'

'Love to, Tom,' she replied.

We had eaten our sandwiches, drunk our coffee and were just about to get up and go for our swim when we heard a crowd of people coming towards us. We looked around and were surrounded by hippies. They had long hair, jeans and beads: they were dancing and singing loudly. Each one had a garland of flowers and some had glazed eyes. One came over and gave Jane and me flowers. 'Peace and love go with you,' he said, and joined his friends who had passed us and were walking towards the promenade. These were the 'Flower People'. I had been reading about their beliefs. They believed in Flower Power. They regarded it as an instrument in changing the world. Sadly, they were proved wrong.

Jane and I looked at the group disappearing in the distance. She looked at her flower thoughtfully and carefully put it to one side, and said, 'Let's have our swim, Tom.'

We raced each other to the sea and shallow-dived in. The sea water was cold but stimulating. After ten minutes or so, we had had enough, scampered back to our deckchairs, dried ourselves and got dressed.

We sat there for about an hour talking about our lives and our aspirations, which seemed to coincide. Contentment is a quality difficult to define, but when it is there you definitely know.

Our journey home was pleasant; Jane drove and I was happy to be in her company.

We said our farewells at her home. She kissed me and this time the relationship appeared secure. I had some serious thinking to do about the future.

M Y OFFICE WAS not far from Hayford Station and sometimes at lunchtimes if I was not meeting Jane or Ben, I would meander to the bridge which overlooked the railway line. I have always been a dreamer, but I believe one can achieve one's dreams by persistence. When I was articled at Davis & Co., and studying hard for my intermediate and final exams, I would stand on the bridge waiting for sight of a steam train – *The Flying Scotsman* if I was lucky – and allow myself the luxury of thinking of a goal and then filing it away in my subconscious mind. I had used this method of reflection, since I was a young boy, without fully realising its significance. My dream of becoming a Chartered Accountant had materialised, but it hadn't been achieved without considerable hard work.

I had experienced a hectic morning with clients calling to see me and I had been rushing to finish an urgent tax case. I decided to wander down to the railway bridge. Locking my office door, I made my way to the station and after a few minutes, I arrived. I bought a platform ticket, got a bar of Nestle's chocolate from a machine and walked along the platform to the bridge. A station, especially one where steam trains stop, has a very special atmosphere. Passing the waiting room, I peered in; three middle-aged women were sitting, chatting. They looked up and smiled at me.

Two young boys, train-spotters, with notebooks in their hands, were eagerly awaiting the next train to add the number to their collection. I climbed the steps to the bridge and reaching the top, looked down on the railway lines and the two platforms. Suddenly I heard the sound of a train moving fast. I could see it was an express; it was not going to stop. I was in luck. It was *The Flying Scotsman*, which had recently created a record for speed. In a matter of seconds, the sleek, shiny engine had passed, leaving a cloud of steam in its wake. I looked down at the two boys on the platform who were pointing excitedly and waving their notebooks.

The noise had been deafening – it was a very powerful engine indeed, pulling several heavy coaches. Silence again enveloped me and my thoughts began to drift. I was looking forward to the coming Saturday when Jane and I would be competing in another dance competition, this time the cha-cha-cha. We had been successful in the jive and hoped that we would again win a prize.

Having finished my studying for my final exams, my social life was improving fast and I had time to develop my favourite pastimes which, as well as dancing, included swimming.

My dreaming was momentarily interrupted. A slow train was approaching, one that probably stopped at every station to London. Clouds of steam covered the station, and passengers alighted, hurrying towards the ticket collector who either took or clipped their tickets. Other passengers climbed on to the train, slamming the heavy doors behind them. A shrill whistle from the guardsman, a wave of his flag, and the train slowly chugged away: different from the express, its racing cousin, but charming in its own way.

I finished eating my chocolate bar, looked around at my special place of dreamland and slowly walked down the steps to the platform. I showed my ticket to the collector, a short, smartly-uniformed man wearing a peaked cap, and made my way back to my office. Everyone has the right to dream and to endeavour to make dreams come true. I realise this is not always possible, of course; there are limitations.

My deliberations over, I returned to my office with my mind refreshed and settled down to prepare some complicated tax computations.

MOST LUNCHTIMES I either went to a restaurant with Jane or to the workmen's café with Ben, but one particular day I decided to go home. I had been suffering from a heavy cold for several days and I wanted a hot drink with lemon juice and honey – an old-fashioned remedy which sometimes gave relief.

Parking my Cortina outside my home, I was surprised to see my mother standing at the doorway. She had a responsible job as chargehand at the chocolate-making factory and usually her shift did not finish until 4 p.m.

I followed her indoors. She looked pensive as she shut the front door.

'What's up, Mum?' I asked.

'I'm afraid Maud Smith, the forewoman, has been caught stealing chocolates and as she held a position of trust, it was decided by the manager that a number of workers should momentarily cease work. They would be paid for a full shift,' she told me.

The security staff at the gates made spot checks to ensure that chocolates were not taken from the factory. Over the past year, several workers had been caught and instantly dismissed. Forewomen were in positions of trust and were rarely searched. I sat opposite my mother in the kitchen, sipping the hot lemon and honey drink, and listened to her.

'Maud had taken in her large vacuum flask,' continued my mother, 'but someone had informed on her. When she got to the security gate, she was asked if she had any chocolates and she vehemently refused to answer the question. As a result, the manager was called and again Maud was asked the same question. She said she hadn't any chocolates, but was apparently trembling and her possessions were examined. The vacuum flask was opened and chocolates were found.'

After a heated discussion, management had decided to sack Maud Smith and contact the police. She lived just round the corner from us and I had noticed a police car parked outside her house.

My heavy cold had been momentarily forgotten when I was listening intently to my mother. I decided to have a light snack with her and then return to my office.

'Cheerio, Mum. See you later,' I said.

'I'll tell you what happens as soon as I hear anything,' she said. She later phoned me. Maud's house had been searched and numerous boxes of chocolates had been found. She had been arrested!

I settled down to writing a few routine letters when the doorbell rang. It was Ben.

'Hello, Tom,' he said cheerfully. 'I've had several interviews and I'm awaiting the outcome.' As he had recently qualified, he thought it was going to be very easy to obtain a good position, but this had not proved to be the case.

'Would you like to do some subcontracting work for me whilst you're waiting for employment?' I asked.

He had left Davis & Co. as soon as he had qualified, expecting to find exactly what he wanted very quickly. His eyes lit up. 'I would be pleased to. I've got a large study at my parents' home.'

That was the beginning of an excellent professional relationship which was to last many years. We had been close friends during our articleships and continued our friendship after we both qualified.

I went to my cupboard where I kept clients' records and took out a box and said, 'You can do that one for me.'

He looked at the name. 'Jack Potter! I remember him – a plasterer who excelled at long-distance running.' Ben's freckled face gave me a broad grin and he ran his hands through his tousled hair. He picked up the heavy box. 'The first of many, I hope,' he said.

Ben had bought a second-hand Riley 1.5 car some months previous and I walked to the vehicle with him. He put the box in the boot. 'Nice looking car,' I remarked. I thought that he would purchase a more sporty motor, but he was content with luxury motoring for a modest price.

We shook hands and our professional association was sealed. He drove away. My thoughts turned to the expansion of my practice.

CRANFIELD PARK WAS a favourite haunt of mine. My parents used to take me there when I was a toddler. At that time during the War, there was a huge mansion there which was still owned by the Cranfields. Approximately two thousand acres of beautiful parkland surrounded the house and one had to pass a gate lodge, which was occupied by an elderly couple. They had an orchard and the local kids used to go scrumping. If children could scrump a few sour apples it was considered by them an act of bravery. Unfortunately some kids got caught and their parents were contacted to collect them. A telling off was all that was needed to momentarily stop the petty thieving. It was not long before the pranks recommenced, however.

There were secret tunnels leading to the mansion and rumour had it that these were used by eighteenth century occupants to escape their foes. Of course, the local kids got to know about these tunnels and I remember when I was fourteen years of age going into one at the dead of night with two friends. The entrance was above the waterline of the moat, which had been dry for many years. We were looking for treasure but were disappointed to find only some empty wine bottles. When the park was opened to the public, the great house was demolished.

My childhood memories lingered and I considered the park as one of my special places; I took Rose there and also Jane.

My accountancy practice was expanding fast and with the assistance of Ben, I was able to take on more clients. My dream of running my own business had crystallised, but I was anxious to have a full social life as well.

I telephoned Jane. 'Would you like to go to Cranfield Park on Saturday?' I asked.

'I'd love to,' she replied. 'What time?'

'Two o'clock be okay?'

'Fine. See you then.'

She sounded cheerful. She was still assisting me with typing, evenings and weekends, but eventually I would have to get a full-time secretary. For the moment my practice was coping.

I picked Jane up at 2 p.m. on the Saturday, as arranged. We were taking part in another Latin American dance competition in the evening, so we would have plenty to talk about. She was, as usual, smartly dressed. This time in a pale lemon miniskirt and a cream top. Her dark brown eyes held mine as she sat in the passenger's seat. Since our first meeting I had always felt at ease with her.

On reaching the park, I drew up by the old church. I often pictured Dick Turpin many years ago hiding in one of the outbuildings. We got out of my car. 'Look, Jane,' I said. I pointed to some old bricks that had been formed as part of a wall, to enable riders to mount their horses. The riders walked up the few steps and were then at the right height to get on their steeds.

'I see them,' Jane said, and passed her small hands over the brickwork, perhaps visualising the same scene as me – the highwayman getting on his horse to ride at speed to try to escape his pursuers.

Leaving my car alongside the church, we walked leisurely along a narrow lane to a humpback bridge. We both looked down at the murky water lazily flowing under the bridge. There were bulrushes with their brown poker-like flower spikes.

'Let's go down and walk by the river, Jane.' I held her hand as we slid down the steep dirt incline. There was a small well-worn pathway and we followed it by the river's edge. There were a few flat stones lying nearby and I picked one up and threw it, skimming across the water. Three times the stone reappeared and then sank. 'You have a go, Jane,' I suggested. She picked one up and threw it. 'That's four,' I said. 'Well done.'

We held hands and continued our walk, noticing the weeping willows, their branches trailing in the sluggish river.

'I know a short cut,' I said. Jane followed me down another narrow pathway, bordered by blackberry bushes. We picked a few berries.

'These are sweet, Tom.' She licked her lips.

'Your lips are black,' I said.

'So are yours,' she said, and smiled, her pixie-like face pink with the warm sunshine. Following the pathway, we were surrounded by sycamores and oaks. The fallen leaves were moist beneath our feet. Jumping across a ditch, we were suddenly in the park, its vast greenery spread out before us, with a copse a few hundred yards away.

The tranquillity of the moment was shattered by shouts. I had noticed when I parked my car a number of motorbikes and scooters. My foreboding, which I had not conveyed to Jane, had materialised. We watched as our dreams vanished. On one side of the copse appeared a group of Rockers and on the other side several Mods. They were soon fighting and rolling in the grass.

I had seen it all before but could never understand the animosity between the gangs. They often went to places like the seaside resorts to meet their 'enemies'.

The magic of the park had been lost for the moment and I said, 'Let's go, Jane.' We made our way back to my car and changed the subject to a lighter one – the forthcoming dance. We talked enthusiastically when I pulled in at a lay-by.

I took Jane home. Her peach-like face pressed against mine. I soon forgot about Mods and Rockers and looked forward to the jive competition.

'Pick you up at seven thirty, Jane.'

'Okay, Tom.' She waved and her dark brown eyes told me all I wanted to know.

M Y CORTINA WAS being serviced and therefore I had to resort to public transport. The trolleybuses went by my office and there was a bus stop about a hundred yards away.

My appointment to see Mr Don Jordan, a singer and entertainer, was at 3.30 p.m. and he lived three miles from my office. I had untangled his tax affairs, prior to my leaving Davis & Co., and he had asked me to act for him within my own practice. He was scared stiff of the Inland Revenue, although I had assured him that his fears were unfounded. An estimated assessment had been raised regarding his trading profit when he was at Davis & Co. The amount of tax was two thousand pounds and he had got so het up, he had gone to the collector's office and pushed an envelope containing that sum in notes through the letter box. Luckily he had put his surname on the envelope, but that was all. The collector was bemused, but eventually the majority of the money had been repaid to Mr Jordan.

Although he was highly strung, I had been to a local nightclub to see him, and once on stage he was transformed. Gone were his nerves, and as soon as the spotlight was on him he sang and entertained as if he did not have a care in the world. If only he had this same confidence when dealing with his financial affairs! Sadly this was not the case, and he was continually getting himself in a mess. At one stage he was nearly made bankrupt. He earned considerable monies from the nightclub, but just did not understand his financial affairs at all. Despite this shortcoming, he refused to employ a bookkeeper or financial adviser on a weekly or monthly basis.

I was standing at the bus stop with a group of people and the trolleybus appeared. Two passengers alighted and I followed two middle-aged women and a small boy on to the bus. 'Room for four downstairs,' said the clippie, a young redheaded woman with a smart dark blue uniform, and rang the bell. The little boy took no notice and raced upstairs; the two middle-aged ladies sat down on one of the two platform seats, just inside the bus. I made my way along the gangway and sat next to an elderly man with a grey beard; he had rimless spectacles perched on the end of his nose and a trilby.

I put my briefcase on my lap. The short journey would not take long. Just in front of me was a lady with blonde hair and a youth with lank greasy hair and a holey cardigan.

The bus slowed. This was my stop. I got up and was going to walk along the gangway when there was a shrill female's voice, 'Come back!'

I looked up. The youth had grabbed the blonde lady's necklace and was about to rush off with it. I stuck my foot out and he sprawled on the floor. A stocky man grabbed the youth by the arm. 'I've got him,' he said. The clippie squeezed past and rapped on the window, attracting the attention of the driver who quickly got out his of cab and joined us.

The necklace had been retrieved and given to the lady.

'Go and call a policeman, George,' said the clippie. The driver quickly stepped off the bus and I saw him call at a nearby newsagent's. In a matter of minutes a tall, broad policeman appeared in answer to the telephone call from the shop and looked down at the youth who was sitting next to the stocky man. The boy, probably not older than seventeen, was ashen-faced and was trembling as he was led away by the policeman. Sticking my foot out and tripping the youth was a reflex action, but with hindsight a dangerous one. He could have had a knife or a gun!

Other policemen appeared on the scene, and my name and address were taken in case I had to appear as a witness. The bus driver came over and spoke to me, 'We get all sorts of things happening on the bus but we're instructed not to get involved by direct action.' He patted the clippie's shoulder reassuringly, saying, 'Don't worry, Gale. All in a day's work.'

She gave him a weak smile. 'I could do with a cup of char, George.' Just inside the bus was a cubby hole; she withdrew a bag and opened it. She poured some tea into a cup from a flask and sipped the hot liquid.

I stepped off the bus's platform and tried to compose myself. I had to go to see Mr Jordan, who no doubt would be nervous as usual.

As it turned out, he was quite relaxed. He had in fact obtained the services of a local bookkeeper who was keeping his business records up to date and error free.

I collected Mr Jordan's records from him and decided I would walk back to my office. The incident had been unsettling for me, but I wondered how the youth was feeling. He had frightened the blonde lady and attempted to steal her necklace, so he deserved to be punished. His cowering appearance was vivid in my mind.

Reaching my office, I made myself a coffee and thought about the day's events, which had turned out completely different from my expectations.

I relaxed in my office armchair and I closed my eyes for a few minutes, endeavouring to focus on my next task.

M R HARDING, WHO was speaking to me by telephone, was one of the first clients to follow me from Davis & Co. His business had prospered, but his health had deteriorated, and at one time I thought he would have to discontinue trading. However, he had taken on a young man to assist in the making of the ornamental iron and steel gates. Mr Harding's health had improved; he was still running his business but his expertise was being passed on to someone with the vibrant health of youth.

'Mr Read, would you like to come over? We can discuss my records and I'll introduce you to Jimmy, my assistant,' he said.

I picked up my desk diary. 'When would you like me to call, Mr Harding?'

'I'm free any time to suit you, except Friday,' he replied. 'I've got to visit my sister who has bronchitis.' I made an entry in my diary.

'I'll see you on Wednesday at 11 a.m., if you're sure that's all right?'

'That'll be fine.' He put the receiver down.

He lived with his wife in an old thatched cottage about forty miles from Hayford, and the last time I had visited them, I had hired a Ford Anglia. I recollected how I had dreamed of owning a new car; my dream had materialised and I had my Cortina.

It was my coffee break and I picked up the local newspaper. Flicking through the pages, I noticed an article mentioning the chocolate-making company where my mother worked. A young boy had been caught stealing waste chocolate from behind the factory, which backed on to a canal. I remembered as a child going over a small bridge to reach the rear of the factory stores. Often waste chocolate was thrown into large bins, and at night-time rarely was anyone caught. Unfortunately, this lad had been greedy. He had found a lump of chocolate the size of a boulder, and had been seen carrying it along a main road by a policeman. The boy's mates had fled. He was reprimanded by the police and no doubt that was enough to act as a deterrent. It was just as well the boy did not eat any of the boulder of chocolate. It was later found to contain bristles from a broom, wrappings and other rubbish. Sometimes there would be chocolate spillage, swept up and put to one side for disposal.

I finished my coffee break and concentrated on locating a difference in a set of accounts I had prepared.

Wednesday morning, I collected Mr Harding's file from my office and walked towards my Cortina. The journey took me about one and half hours and parking my car in the leafy lane, I again looked across at the lath and plaster cottage. Memories flooded back. The last time I had come I was an articled clerk. I had returned as a Chartered Accountant. The small, white wooden gate opened easily and I strode along the narrow winding cinder path bordered by fuchsias, marigolds and pansies – a riot of colour. Reaching the front door, I noticed again the two white urns brim-full with multicoloured busy Lizzies. The hanging basket contained a huge fuchsia – a beautiful mauve. A chaffinch flew down and perched at an angle on the rim of the basket, searching for insects.

The door opened and Mr and Mrs Harding greeted me. Mrs Harding, a small thin woman of sixty years of age, her face weather-beaten and wrinkled, looked at me kindly. Mr Harding was still thin but his face was no longer sallow. 'Come through,' they chorused. I followed them along the narrow hall and into a large kitchen. The black cat I remembered from the last visit shyly approached me and sidled up to me, mewing and looking up at me with its bright eyes.

'Like a coffee, Mr Read?' asked Mrs Harding.

'Yes, please,' I replied. We all sat down at the kitchen table and looked on to a large lawn edged with colourful flowers and shrubs. It started to rain and I listened to the patter of raindrops on the small conservatory adjoining the cottage. At the bottom of the garden, a young man opened the door of the workshop, looked up and lumbered towards us. Shaking off the rain from his mac which he hung on a hook, he looked at me astutely.

'This is Jimmy, Mr Read,' said Mr Harding. The young lad was bright-eyed, very broad, with freckles and ginger hair. He held out his hand and said, 'Pleased to meet you.'

I shook hands with him and noticed his firm grip. I felt he could have squeezed my hand to pulp if he had wished to. 'I'm pleased you're assisting Mr Harding,' I said.

The old man looked at the boy with affection, saying, 'I'm teaching him all I know and he's a fast learner.' We sat round the table and the atmosphere was relaxed.

'I live about fifty yards down the road so I don't have far to come to work,' said the boy, who looked fit. I noticed his well-muscled physique. Mr Harding was able to continue running a business because he now had the strength and vigour supplied by Jimmy, who in turn would profit from the advice and experience of an older man. The benefits were reciprocated.

I went quickly through Mr Harding's records. The rain stopped and I made my way to my car. He looked at it and then at me. 'This time, it's your car,' he said, his eyes twinkling.

I got into my Cortina and waved to Mr and Mrs Harding and Jimmy. Their cheerful goodbyes echoed as I drove away. They worked together harmoniously, each helping the other.

My journey back to my office was a pleasurable one. I was so pleased that Mr Harding's health had improved. I sat in my office armchair and put his file to one side, shut my eyes for a few minutes and pictured the contentment on his face.

MR DOME, THE artist, sat in my office. I had prepared his first year's accounts since he had returned to Hayford and bought his detached house. He now had an international reputation.

'Before you discuss my accounts with me,' he said, 'I would like you to accept this as a gift.' He stood up and handed me an oil painting about two feet six inches by one foot six inches.

'Thanks, Mr Dome.' I took it from him and rested it on a chair. 'That's splendid,' I said, looking at a beautifully painted landscape; the details had been painstakingly executed. The painting had been framed ornately in gold leaf. 'I shall hang it there,' I said, pointing to the wall just behind my desk.

Mr Dome's smiling face expressed his pleasure. 'I hoped that you would like it. The scene is from a place in Devon.'

I began to ask Mr Dome questions to enable me to finalise his accounts, and after about fifteen minutes the queries had been cleared. It would not take me long to complete the trading and profit and loss account together with the balance sheet. 'Your net profit is exceptional,' I remarked. He was commanding high prices for his paintings and there was great demand for his work. As soon as he had finished another work of art, it was snapped up. I could not help thinking back to when he was destitute and scraping a living. Talent had won through and eventually he had been financially rewarded.

'I'll work out your exact taxation position, as soon as your accounts have been finished,' I said. His balance sheet disclosed ample funds at his bank to meet the tax liability I had estimated.

Mr Dome stood up again and I noticed how smartly dressed he was. His fawn trousers were pressed and he had on a cream shirt and a brown tweed jacket. He had gained weight and his rosy face sported a trim beard and a small moustache. 'I hope that you are not going to trip over my false leg this time?' he said. He gave me a sideways glance and a broad smile.

He would not let me forget the time when I tripped over him in the old dilapidated shed whilst he was struggling to survive. He limped towards the office door and we shook hands. It was not just the money that had changed him. He had regained his self-respect.

'Thanks for the painting,' I said.

He looked over his shoulder. 'I hope that it gives you as much pleasure as I received when painting it.' Limping away, but completely self-assured, he made his way to his new silver Rover car – no doubt adapted with hand controls because of his disablement. Success can be sweet, I thought.

I shut the office door and decided to have a break. I turned the radio on, as I knew that Cassius Clay was boxing Sonny Liston for the heavyweight championship of the world. Liston was a giant, and not many people thought Cassius Clay would stand a chance. The twenty-two year old had bragged that he would 'Float like a butterfly and sting like a bee.'

The commentator was talking fast and I turned the radio up. It was round six and Liston had been taking a beating. Surely the young man was not going to take the title from the giant? There was uproar. Round six had ended and

Liston just about got back to his stool. Pandemonium continued. Liston was not coming out to fight in round seven. He had surrendered his title. Clay was champion of the world! I switched the radio off. The young man had persisted and he had succeeded.

I sipped my coffee, musing over the fight. Soon I had to clear my mind and concentrate again on my work.

SOMETIMES, SITTING IN my office armchair, after solving a particularly difficult tax or accountancy problem, I would endeavour to relax and reflect on what I had achieved so far and whether I wished to progress in my business, by perhaps moving to larger premises and employing a large number of staff. I had come to the conclusion that I was happy running a small office, and dealing with clients who had small or medium-sized businesses or required specialised tax services.

I looked round my office and I was content. My clientele since I had left Davis & Co. had grown considerably and soon I would reach saturation point. Ben, who worked on a subcontract basis from his home, was proving to be a great asset. We had always got on well together when we were articled clerks and worked harmoniously as two Chartered Accountants. Eventually, no doubt, he would like his own practice; but he seemed content for the time being assisting me in mine.

My interest in people has always been profound; qualifying and having my own practice had enabled me to meet many people from all walks of life; my future professional life looked rosy. There would be problems, as life is not always plain sailing. I would experience life's rich tapestry. Thinking back to my schooldays, I was thankful that my headmaster and my teachers had taught me to a high standard, thus enabling me to commence my professional career.

I continually looked back, as I believed one can learn from events of the past.

Persistence is a great asset in achieving success, but of course success varies with people. The essential point I believe is to be happy in life, and this does not necessarily entail accumulating money or possessions. I have often seen a small businessman happy and enjoying life with just sufficient funds to keep him and his family above water.

There are people who are quite content to enjoy simple things such as laughter, the respect of intelligent people, the appreciation of honest critics. To appreciate beauty and to find the best in others is to have succeeded.

As one gets older, one finds that to achieve a goal such as getting a professional qualification is important, but if one can make another person's life better in some way, that is success too. It all depends on one's interpretation of the word.

It was my intention to maintain the success of my personal tax accountancy practice, but also to develop my social life. My thoughts of the Saturday dance came to the fore and the picture of Jane flashed through my mind.

The door opened and Jane stood there looking at me with her deep brown eyes. Neither of us said anything. There was no need. My eyes met hers and we embraced. The passionate kiss said it all. My thoughts of success were embodied in that simple act of affection.

I HAD JUST returned to my office after calling to see Mr Rawling, the butcher. After the modernisation of his shop, his takings had increased dramatically. New customers had been attracted and his business was booming.

Looking in the mirror on the wall near my desk, I could see that I needed a haircut. I put Mr Rawling's file in the cabinet and my briefcase in a cupboard, locked the office door and joined the busy thoroughfare. Walking slowly along the high street, I came across a busker. He was a young man playing a guitar, very professionally. I stopped to listen. The tune was often played by The Shadows and I wondered why this young chap was on the street, busking for a few pounds. I played the piano and had reached grade five with The Associated Board in London; I could tell the young man had real musical talent. He was sitting on the concrete steps of a shop that had been closed for several months. I estimated his age to be about the same as mine; he had holey jeans, a threadbare denim shirt and scuffed boots. His face showed three or four days' stubble and his blond hair was tied at the back in a ponytail. He concentrated on his playing, occasionally looking up at the passers-by. Some dropped a few coins on a chipped plate at his feet.

He must have sensed me looking at him and met my gaze with his bright blue eyes. Smiling, he nodded and continued playing. I walked over and put a shilling and a sixpence on to the plate. 'Thanks mate,' he said. He stopped playing, picked up a mug and poured some beer from a bottle.

'I hope you don't mind me asking, but why do you busk?' I asked him. I sat on the steps by his side, expecting a facetious remark, but was surprised by his reply.

'I do play in theatres in London and I get well paid. I like to come on to the streets and meet people to get their reaction to my music,' he said. He was intelligent and after an in-depth discussion with him, I could see that he knew exactly in what direction his life was going.

His pleasure was in the playing. Money was not that important to him, as long as he had enough to live reasonably comfortably.

'I'd better be going. I wish you all the best,' I said. He reciprocated my good wishes, gave me a broad smile and continued with his playing.

I continued with my leisurely walk to Mr Dart's barber's shop and after a few minutes I looked through the window. There were two people sitting waiting to have their hair cut. I looked at my watch. My next client was not for another half an hour, and so I decided to join the queue.

On my opening the door, the old-fashioned bell clanged and Mr Dart looked up.

'Take a seat, Mr Read. There's some newspapers and magazines over there,' he said, pointing to a vacant chair. He continued to cut the customer's hair and I picked up a newspaper and sat down. Mr Dart's nickname was 'Curly'. This was because he was as bald as a coot. I looked at the expert at work. There were various styles of haircut and the young man in the barber's chair was having a DA – often preferred by the Rockers. Mr Dart was polite to all customers, unless they were disrespectful to him; then he quickly showed his authority. I knew that he kept a baseball bat handy for the odd customer who turned nasty.

Mr Dart was a small man but stocky. His interests included boxing and judo and rarely did he experience any trouble in his shop. His white overall was spotless and his bald head shone. He wore half-moon spectacles and often glanced at customers by looking at their reflections in the mirror.

The other two customers sitting waiting were also reading. One of them, an old man with hardly any hair, except at the sides and a few strands on top, stood up as the young man with the DA rose from the barber's chair.

'Thanks, Curly,' said the young man. 'Keep the change.'

He dropped half a crown in Mr Dart's outstretched hand and looked at himself again in the mirror, straightening his tie and smoothing the sides of his hair to accentuate the DA. I recognised him as one of Ken's mates. We nodded to each other. He was a Rocker, whilst I was at one time close to being a Mod. We were on different sides of the fence.

The old man sat in the barber's chair and I looked at him. I believe I could have cut his hair in a matter of a few seconds. Perhaps it was the company he was seeking. The other customer sitting next to me was a few years older than me and he had a 'Tony Curtis' hairstyle – swept forward at the front. He repeatedly pulled his hair; habit, I suppose.

I remember that once I had a brush cut when I was fifteen years of age and my parents had gone up the wall. Not much hair was left, and I got a telling off from my headmaster. From then until I left school, I continued to have short back and side haircuts, and seldom varied the style. It was neat and I suppose it suited the way I dressed.

Eventually it was my turn, and I lowered myself into the barber's chair. I believe barbers are some of the most informative of people. They are constantly hearing snippets of gossip and news, and Mr Dart was no exception.

'Have you heard that President Kennedy was shot in Dallas?'

'Surely not?' I asked.

'Yes, it was on the radio about an hour ago.'

My heart sank. I was an admirer of the man. Mr Dart finished cutting my hair, I paid him and I walked back to my office. I turned the radio on. Yes, it was true. All the details were made known to the whole world. I did know that he was respected and admired by many, many people.

I resumed my work, thinking what a strange and tragic world it was at times.

I HAD EATEN my sandwiches and drunk my coffee – a makeshift lunch – and locked my office door. There was a craft fair being held at a deconsecrated church not far from the high street and I strolled along, joining the milling crowds. The hustle and bustle of the weekly market held in an open area near the disused church was infectious and I gazed around. The market traders were shouting, advertising their wares: fruit and vegetables, fish, poultry, confectionery. 'How about a hand of bananas? Two bob – you can't do better than that!' The trader held up the fruit, trying his best to attract the attention of the shoppers.

'I'll give you one and sixpence,' said an old lady with grey hair.

'Sold to the lady over there. Any other takers?' The stallholder wrapped the bananas and, smiling, gave them to the old lady, who put them in her shopping bag and hobbled away. The sweet smell of the fruit pervaded the air and a strong odour of fish competed with it.

As I reached the disused church, I passed two bench seats and four women with children sitting there eating fish and chips. I made a mental note to call at Mr White's shop and buy some of his – the best in the town – later in the day. A little boy held up a chip and offered it to me. I looked at the lady next to him.

'You take it, love. He likes to share his food.' She gave me a friendly smile and I took the chip from the little boy who delved into his newspaper-bound bag and munched away.

'Thank you,' I said. The little boy turned away shyly and held the lady's hand.

A flower seller proffered her bunch of chrysanthemums but I slipped by into the building. The pews and the altar had been removed and the cavernous space was filled with stalls displaying many handicrafts and other items. Walking slowly, I passed a stall with jars of honey and jam. 'Tastes lovely,' said a young lady with red hair and a wide smile, pointing to the jars.

'I'll think about it,' I said and went on to the next stall. Every item was made from wood – bowls, stools and chairs – all works of art. I looked at them, intently, thinking of the hours of skilful work necessary to produce them.

The next stall displayed miniature water colour and oil paintings. I picked one up and studied it closely. Every detail was perfect. The stallholder, a middle-aged lady with a mop of dark hair, round face and glasses, came over.

'Do you like it?' she asked. She picked up another picture with an oval frame. 'This is the same price – two shillings.'

'Do you use a magnifying glass to paint them?' I asked.

'No, only my spectacles. I'm nearly blind in one eye.'

What tremendous talent, I thought. 'I'll have this one, please.' It was of a scene in Cranfield Park and I recognised it immediately. I handed over half a crown and the lady gave me sixpence change and the gift-wrapped miniature.

'I hope you get a lot of pleasure from it,' she said.

'I'm sure I will. I'm going to put it on my office desk. Thanks.'

I moved on to the next stall. The swarthy man, balding with a thick moustache, glanced at me. I looked at his wares, all made from leather: bags, purses, wallets and key fobs.

'How much is this one, please?' I asked, picking up a pigskin tray purse.

'One and sixpence,' he replied. The stitching was neat and the leather was top quality.

'I'll have it,' I said and handed it to the stallholder, who wrapped it up and returned it to me. The smell of leather is very evocative and that particular purse seemed just right.

I walked past stalls with ornaments, artificial flowers, books and jewellery. Remembering the stall with wooden objects, I made my way back. I picked up a stool, which had been covered in a top-quality cloth; the work was excellent. I had done woodwork at school and I knew the precision necessary to achieve the mortise and tenon joins.

'What do you think of it?' asked the stallholder, a man about thirty-five years of age, sallow and with thinning hair.

'Did you make it?' I asked.

'Yes, I made all these.' His arm swept across the stall.

'I think your work is of top quality. I've done woodwork at school so I know the standard of your work,' I said.

He looked at me with pride, and explained, 'This is only a hobby. I'm a toolmaker by trade.'

As my father was a precision engineer working to tolerances of 1/10th of 1/1000th of an inch, I then understood why the man's work was so accurate.

'I'll have this stool, please,' I said. I picked it up and the man put it in a large carrier bag.

'Hold the bottom of the bag as it may split.' He carefully gave me the stool.

'Thanks very much. Cheerio,' I said, and made my way out of the building.

When I reached the large doorway where I had entered, the young lady with the honey and jam was sipping a mug of hot liquid. The steam was apparent and she was gently blowing the drink to cool it. As I approached she put the mug down and looked at me.

'I thought you would be back.' She gave me another wide smile. 'A jar of honey – right?' She was right. How, I don't know. 'A bob, please.'

I searched through my coins and came across a sixpence and two threepenny bits and gave them to her.

'You're loaded down,' she said. 'Take this.' She gave me a strong paper bag and I put the jar of honey, the miniature painting and the leather purse into the bag.

'Thanks, that's nice of you,' I said. Before I turned away she gave me a meaningful glance which set me thinking.

Walking back to my office with my purchases, I was pleased. I looked at my watch – one and a half hour's lunch break. Still, I wouldn't get the sack! However, being my own boss, I would have to make the time up. Every hour lost meant fee time down the drain!

I opened my office door, put my bags down by the side of my desk, made myself a cup of coffee and quickly took a client's file out of the cabinet. I had some catching up to do.

SOME LUNCHTIMES I used to go to an open-air swimming pool which was about four miles away from my office. After the exercise I felt refreshed and found that my office work improved. Having a sedentary occupation, I found it was very easy to neglect essential exercise, but swimming and dancing enabled me to keep very fit.

I decided to travel to the pool by trolleybus and locked my office door. My light blue Cortina was parked just in front of my office. It had proved to be extremely comfortable and reliable; my dream as an articled clerk of owning such a vehicle had materialised and I looked at its sleek lines with pride.

Trolleybuses often passed by my office every fifteen minutes or so and I stood at the stop, which was within a few yards. After a few minutes a bus pulled up and I jumped on, grabbing the static pole tightly. I sat on one of the bench seats just inside; the young clippie, a dark-haired girl, rang the bell and I commenced my short journey.

'Fairbridge swimming pool,' I said, handing the clippie a two shilling piece. She gave me my change – sixpence or some would say a tanner, together with my ticket from a machine which she turned with a handle. The machine registered the tickets sold and the money received. Later she would be able to check the monies held in her leather bag.

Holding my towel and swimming costume on my lap, I looked around me. I was sitting between a fat lady, who was holding an overflowing shopping bag, and an old man, shabbily dressed in stained trousers and a torn grey shirt. I edged away from him. He smelt somewhat and I was glad my journey would be short. Opposite, sitting on the other bench seat, were two schoolboys from the local grammar school. One snatched the other's cap and threw it up the aisle.

'Stop mucking about! You should know better,' said the clippie. She picked the cap up and gave it to the smaller of the boys. They both sat back, duly admonished, and were quiet. Then they giggled.

The bus stopped just past my old principal's offices. He had to give up his practice because of poor health; I had recently heard that he was seriously ill in hospital. He had not treated me properly when I was an articled clerk, but I could not help feeling sorry about his predicament. I looked up at the offices above the bank and saw a young man sitting where I used to sit. He glanced down at the bus and I wondered if he had similar dreams of success to mine.

The clippie rang the bell and as the bus moved off I looked at the people passing to get to their seats. 'Tickets please.' I looked at a moustached man in a dark mac and peaked cap with a clipboard. It was the Inspector. I pulled my ticket out of my pocket.

'That's all right. Thank you.' He moved on to the old man next to me, who was frantically searching for his ticket.

'I know I bought one,' he pleaded.

The clippie stood just behind the Inspector. 'Yes, I do remember giving him a ticket,' she said.

'No ticket no ride, I'm afraid,' said the Inspector. 'I shall have to ask you to leave the bus and I will require your name and address.' He looked down on the old man who was wiping his moist eyes with his grubby handkerchief.

The old man rose ponderously from his seat, holding on to the rail. 'I bought my ticket,' he repeated. 'How do you sleep at nights? I wouldn't have your job for all the tea in China.'

He pulled a face at the Inspector, who said, 'I'm only doing my job. Rules are rules.'

The old man stepped off the bus; he looked over his shoulders and gave me a despairing look. No doubt he had bought his ticket. The indecisiveness associated with some old people is pitiful to see and I felt sorry for him.

I reached my destination, had my swim and decided to walk back to my office. The exercise had done me good but I couldn't help thinking of that old man on the bus; I wondered if he belatedly found his mislaid ticket.

I WAS SITTING at my office desk having completed a set of accounts and the relevant tax computations; I was in one of my reflective moods. It was time for my morning break and I made myself my usual coffee; I picked out one of my favourite biscuits and several chocolates from a packet of 'staff sales', given to me by my mother, and contemplated.

When I was six years old in 1945, and at my primary school, the War ended. I remember I was a dreamer then. Towards the end of my primary school education I used to dream of becoming a top scholar and eventually ended up head boy at my secondary school.

On leaving my secondary school I dreamed of becoming a Chartered Accountant and after six years of studying I achieved my aim. The next step was to have my own successful personal tax accountancy practice, and that materialised. Dreams never end: they move on.

Everybody has the right to dream and if possible to make those dreams become reality.

My practice had very quickly become established; I enjoyed the work and I enjoyed dealing with my clients.

However, it was important to have a full social life as well as a good working life, and I intended to try to get the right balance. My relationship with Jane was progressing well.

As I looked up from my desk, my reflective thoughts put to one side, Jane opened my office door and walked towards me.

'Surprise visit, Tom,' she said.

'So I see.' I rose to greet her. We embraced and kissed passionately. Her scented warmth enveloped me.